*from Modey
Dec '07*

*In Subordination:*
*Professional Women, 1870–1970*

D0221693

From 1870 to 1970 between ten and twenty per cent of women in paid work held jobs described by the Canadian census as "professional." In this important study Mary Kinnear examines the experience of the first generations of professional women in Canada.

Kinnear presents case studies of women in five professions – university teachers, physicians, lawyers, nurses, and schoolteachers – in Manitoba. She shows that all five professions had three characteristics in common: unequal pay, lack of control by women, and the belief that marriage and the professions were not compatible. Most women, whether in male- or female-dominated professions, were forced to accept subordinate positions, to which they responded with acquiescence, indifference, resentment, or resistance. Kinnear considers the reasons for and the cost of these various strategies.

In addition to quantitative data from census and other records, Kinnear has collected the testimony of more than two hundred professional women. A significant contribution to the growing literature on women and the professions, *In Subordination* helps explain why professional women continue to fight for equality today.

MARY KINNEAR is professor of history, St John's College, University of Manitoba.

# In Subordination

## Professional Women, 1870–1970

### MARY KINNEAR

McGill-Queen's University Press
Montreal & Kingston • London • Buffalo

*For my daughters, Sara and Lucy*

© McGill-Queen's University Press 1995
ISBN 0-7735-1278-0 (cloth)
ISBN 0-7735-1279-9 (paper)

Legal deposit second quarter 1995
Bibliothèque nationale du Québec

Printed in Canada on acid-free paper

This book has been published with the help of a grant from the Social Science Federation of Canada, using funds provided by the Social Sciences and Humanities Research Council of Canada.

McGill-Queen's University Press is grateful to the Canada Council for support of its publishing program.

**Canadian Cataloguing in Publication Data**

Kinnear, Mary, 1942–
    In subordination: professional women, 1870–1970
    Includes bibliographical references and index.
    ISBN 0-7735-1278-0 (bound)
    ISBN 0-7735-1279-9 (pbk.)
    1. Women in the professions – Canada – History.
    2. Sex discrimination in employment – Canada – History.
    I. Title.
    HD6054.2.C3K46 1995    331.4'133'0971    C94-900806-0

This book was typeset by Typo Litho Composition Inc. in 10/12 Baskerville.

# Contents

Acknowledgments   vii

1 Professions, Evidence, and Gender in General   3

2 Discourse by Default: Women University Teachers   30

3 Medicine: "Tough Old Birds"   53

4 Law: "That There Woman Lawyer"   78

5 Nursing: "One of the Truest and Noblest Callings"   98

6 Teachers: A Majority in the Margins   123

7 In Retrospect: "Delighted to Be Accepted"   152

APPENDICES

1 Tables   171
2 Survey Respondents   187

Notes   191

Bibliography   223

Index   243

# Acknowledgments

Women worked in professional occupations in large numbers. Over the century 1870–1970, between 10 and 20 per cent of women in paid work were occupied in jobs described by the Canadian census as "professional." Women were found in male-dominated occupations as well as in the female-dominated professions of teaching and nursing. Their very presence was a witness to the success of the nineteenth-century feminists, whose major objectives included women's access to higher education and the professions. By World War I, this had been achieved. But were the women on equal terms with men? What did the professions look like from the inside? Was it possible to be a normal woman and, say, a normal lawyer? What was normal? This book sets out to discover the dimensions of professional experience for the first generations of female university teachers, physicians, lawyers, nurses, and teachers.

So few women professionals had entrusted their life stories to print that I had to search for sources beyond the confines of traditional archival collections. This proved to be an unexpected pleasure, for the most comprehensive resource was in the memories of living professionals who worked before 1970. Surveys conducted by interview and questionnaire with more than two hundred willing subjects enlivened the research and provided a rich and complicated mine of information. My first acknowledgment is to the women who took the time, energy, and sometimes great effort to recover for me their experiences of many years ago. Inevitably, the transformation of their testimony into history must result in some distortion, but I hope the academics, doctors, lawyers, nurses, and teachers who generously gave me their time will nevertheless recognize themselves.

The work of many colleagues gave me inspiration and encouragement, and I particularly want to pay tribute to Alison Prentice, Connie

Backhouse, Judith Fingard, Cameron Harvey, Alison Mackinnon, Kathryn McPherson, and Veronica Strong-Boag. I am grateful to those who helped in the identification and selection of material. For the chapter on university teachers, I thank Ms Barbara Henchard and Ms Barbara Rothy in Staff Benefits, Ms Madeleine Mayar in the Alumni Association, Mr Richard Bennet, Mr Michael Mooseberger, and Ms Debbie Prokopchuk in the Archives, Mr Bob Raeburn and Ms Mary Birt in the Board of Governors office, and Ms Thelma Lussier in Information Systems of the University of Manitoba. For the chapter on doctors, I thank Dr Morison, Dr Walker, and Dr Brown of the Manitoba College of Physicians and Surgeons, and Dr Storrie and Dr Roe of the Manitoba branch of the Federation of Medical Women of Canada. In the Faculty of Medicine Library, Professor Audrey Kerr and Ms Natalia Pohoruk were enthusiastic and efficient collaborators. For the chapter on lawyers, I thank Ms Deborah McCawley of the Law Society of Manitoba and Professor Cameron Harvey, Professor Karen Busby, and Professor Wesley Pue in the Faculty of Law. For the section on nursing, I am most grateful above all to Ms Elaine Tresoor, archivist of the Alumnae Association of the Winnipeg General Hospital School of Nursing, and I also thank Ms Dorothy Froman of the Manitoba Association of Registered Nurses and Dr Ina Bramadat of the University of Manitoba Faculty of Nursing. For the chapter on schoolteachers, I am grateful to Mr Murray McPherson and Ms Margaret McPherson for their help with retired teachers' associations, Ms Linda Guise of the Winnipeg Teachers Association, Mr Aubrey Asper of the Manitoba Teachers Society, and Ms Denise Tellier, archivist of the Winnipeg School Division, and I thank Ms Monique Hébert and Dr Rosa Bruno-Joffre for their advice.

I thank Cathy Chatterley, Daphne Gilbert, and Barbara Chatterley for research assistance, and I am grateful to June Dutka of Government Records, Barbara Bemmell of Interlibrary Loan, and Patrick Wright, librarian of St John's College for their help in tracking down material. I thank the many friends and colleagues who have contributed to the formation of my ideas and have criticized previous drafts, especially Connie Backhouse, Angela Davis, Barry Ferguson, John Kendle, Michael Kinnear, Debra Lindsay, Karen Ogden, Alison Prentice, Veronica Strong-Boag, Anthony Waterman, and Kathryn Young.

I am happy to thank the Social Sciences and Research Council of Canada for financial assistance, and I particularly want to thank the council for a release time stipend, which allowed me to concentrate my energy and spend one academic year on the book without distraction. I was glad of the opportunity to present papers based on the research at a conference on Marriage and the Family at Carleton University in

1992 and at the conference Suffrage and Beyond, commemorating the centenary of women's suffrage in New Zealand, at Victoria University in Wellington, 1993. I am grateful to the Research School of Social Sciences at the Australian National University, Canberra, which gave me a visiting fellowship for three months in 1993. I am especially grateful to Paul Bourke and Bev Gallina, and to Kenneth Inglis, Alison Mackinnon, Sue Rickard, Barry Smith, and Jay Winter, who commented on a paper I presented on the subject of professional women. I thank President Anthony Low and the Fellows of Clare Hall in the University of Cambridge for awarding me a visiting fellowship for the academic year 1993–94. Their generosity allowed me to complete the writing and editing in pleasant and calm surroundings.

I thank the editors at McGill-Queen's University Press for their help and encouragement, especially Don Akenson, Joan Harcourt, and Joan McGilvray. I am most grateful to my copy editor, Carlotta Lemieux, for her eagle-eyed efficiency accompanied by patience and tact.

I thank the following for permission to reproduce material previously published in another form: the editors of *Historical Studies in Education*, who published previous versions of chapters 2 and 4, in "Disappointed in Discourse: Women Professors at the University of Manitoba before 1970," vol. 4, no. 2 (1992): 269–87, and in "'Mostly for the Male Members': Winnipeg Teachers 1933–66," vol. 6, no. 1 (1994): 1–20; the co-editors of the *Canadian Journal of Women and the Law* for a previous version of chapter 4, in "'That There Woman Lawyer': Women Lawyers in Manitoba, 1915–70," vol. 5, no. 2 (1992): 411–41; the editor of *Manitoba Medicine* for part of chapter 3, in "How Difference Made a Difference: Women Medical Students at the University of Manitoba in the 1940s," vol. 63, no. 4 (1993): 135–6; and the editor of the *Canadian Medical Association Journal* for permission to reprint an extract from "Thinking Back" by Elinor Black, vol. 105, 24 July 1971, 143–4.

Finally, I thank my family for never letting me forget that professional women, like other people, are human beings.

Mary Kinnear
St John's College, University of Manitoba

*In Subordination*

### CHAPTER ONE

# Professions, Evidence, and Gender in General

"What have women to do in society?" asked Mary Wollstonecraft in 1792. Chiding her eighteenth-century readers with a Shakespearean reference, she continued, "Surely you would not condemn them all to suckle fools and chronicle small beer! No. Women might certainly study the art of healing, and be physicians ... Business of various kinds they might likewise pursue if they were educated in a more orderly manner."[1]

Nineteenth-century feminists wanted women to have access to public life, which they interpreted as politics, property, and the professions. Women should be able to participate in politics through the vote; women should enjoy protection for their property through legislation, including married women's property acts; and they should have access to professional work. In the twentieth century many specific goals were met, but they were unaccompanied by the hoped-for equality. In 1967 the Canadian government established a royal commission to discover why. Its report, published in 1970, found that almost all working women were "handicapped by discrimination in policy and practice."[2] Professional women were among the most favoured women in the paid labour force, yet individually they were almost all in subordination to men. This book contributes to an understanding of the dimensions of discrimination.

Since the first decades of the twentieth century, there have been many studies of women as paid and unpaid workers, and with respect to Canada, there is a considerable body of scholarship on women's paid work in the industrial sector, in domestic service, and in office work, augmented by analyses of women's unpaid work in the home and on farms.[3] Women in the professions have attracted less attention.[4] This has partly been because of the general paucity of conventional records about women's work. For this study, I have tapped the memories of professional women who worked in Manitoba before 1970. The difficulties and delights of working in the professions are seen through the remembered consciousness of the women themselves. Their insights help to explain why the hopes of early feminists are still unrealized.

This book studies the experience of women in five professional occupations in one Canadian province during the century before 1970. The population of Manitoba grew by leaps and bounds through massive immigration at the end of the nineteenth century. Its economy was based on agriculture and trade, and was diversified in resource extraction and manufacturing. Its capital city of Winnipeg was the third-largest city in Canada in the early twentieth century. A population sustained by agriculture, industry, trade, and government generated a demand for professional services on the same sort of scale experienced throughout modern Western society.[5] At the turn of the twentieth century, Winnipeg provided a stimulating setting for proposals of social and economic reform, and Manitoba was the first province in Canada to introduce women's suffrage, in 1916.[6] Neither very rich nor very poor, the province of Manitoba, geographically in the middle of Canada, generally scored in the middle of various indices of prosperity and progress. The experience of its professional women, therefore, can be seen as a manifestation in miniature of women's participation in professional work throughout modern Western society.

In this introductory chapter, I outline the vision of some of the most widely read feminist prophets and define the term "profession." In the context of the segregated labour force found in all Western industrialized countries, I identify the particular proportions of professional work in Manitoba and consider when female pioneers breached the ramparts of five occupations: university teaching, medicine, law, nursing, and schoolteaching. Finally, I review the nature of the evidence available for a study of subordination in professional work.

## PROFESSIONS AND
## FEMINIST PROPHETS

Nineteenth-century feminists considered women's access to professional work a priority. John Stuart Mill and George Eliot in England, and August Bebel in Germany, emphasized that women should be free to choose from among all occupations, including the best paid. Similar ideas were expressed in North America and elsewhere. Charlotte Perkins Gilman in the United States and Olive Schreiner in South Africa were just a few of the early feminists who expressed yearnings for equality. They focused reform campaigns on secondary and higher education for women and on access to the professions.[7] A woman's freedom to earn her own living was seen as an essential aspect of the woman of the future, who, in Bebel's words was to be "socially and economically independent ... no longer subject to even a vestige of dominion and exploitation ... free, the peer of man, mistress of her lot."[8]

In 1869 John Stuart Mill appealed to justice. He explained the continuing subordination of women by reference to men's current inability to tolerate "the idea of living with an equal." Otherwise, "almost every one ... would admit the injustice of excluding half the human race from the greater number of lucrative occupations [which were] interdicted to them, in order to be preserved for the exclusive benefit of males."[9] Mill considered that women should have "the free choice of their employments and ... the same field of occupation and the same prizes and encouragements as to other human beings." All human beings had an "equal moral right" to such choice, and society would reap the benefit of "doubling the mass of mental faculties available for the higher service of humanity."[10]

In the same year, George Eliot – while admitting that "there is no subject on which I am more inclined to hold my peace and learn, than on the 'Women Question'" – declared her conviction that the lives of men and women should be based on a common moral and educational experience: "Women ought to have the same fund of truth placed within their reach as men have ... the lives of [both] ought to be passed together under the hallowing influence of a common faith as to their duty and its basis. And this unity in their faith can only be produced by their having each the same store of fundamental knowledge."[11]

Ten years later, August Bebel, in *Woman under Socialism*, predicted the woman of future society:

Her education is the same as that of man ... she is able to unfold and exercise her mental powers and faculties. She chooses her occupation in such a way as corresponds with her wishes, inclinations and natural abilities, and she works under conditions identical with man's. Even if engaged as a practical working-woman on some field or other, at other times of the day she may be educator, teacher, or nurse, at yet others she may exercise herself in art, or cultivate some branch of science, and at yet others may be filling some administrative function. She joins in studies, enjoyments or social intercourse with either her sisters or with men, as she may please or occasion may serve.[12]

Translated into English in 1904, Bebel provided a more explicit vision of the hopes of Wollstonecraft, Eliot, and Mill.

Bebel's vision was echoed in the writings of Charlotte Perkins Gilman, whose *Women and Economics*, published in 1898, was translated into half a dozen foreign languages and was widely influential.[13] Her plea was for women and men to share modern life with all its pleasures and responsibilities. Modern life included a specialized industrialized workforce, in which women ought to participate fully, she maintained. Although by the end of the nineteenth century, "woman's progress in the arts and sciences, the trades and professions, [was] steady," women had been "tied to the starting post" and had to be given complete freedom in "free productive expression": "A civilised state was one in which the citizens live in organic industrial relation. The more full, free, subtle and easy that relation, the more perfect the differentiation of labour and exchange of product, with their correlative institutions – the more perfect is that civilisation." The foundation of Gilman's vision of a civilized society was women's economic independence, earned among the same choice of occupations as men had.[14]

Olive Schreiner enjoyed a reputation as the voice of the New Woman after the publication in 1883 of her novel *The Story of an African Farm*. This, together with her *Woman and Labour* (1911), was "a trumpet-call summoning the faithful to a vital crusade."[15] Schreiner was down to earth in her condemnation of the "parasitism" in which women had been held, and she praised the "Woman's Movement" as "a great movement of the sexes towards each other ... towards common occupations, common interests, common ideals, and towards an emotional sympathy between the sexes more deeply founded and more indestructible than any the world has yet seen."[16]

In Canada, as in the United States and other Western industrial societies, a connection between feminism and the professions was forged by the end of the nineteenth century. Manitoba was the first of Canada's western provinces to join Confederation, in 1870, and by the 1880s there were signs that women in Manitoba were reaping some benefits from the modern age. During that decade women entered the colleges of the University of Manitoba as students, and in the following decade one woman was appointed a college instructor. In 1890 a woman was admitted as a student to the medical college. Schools of nursing were established in the province. In 1912 the provincial law society allowed women to be admitted to the Bar. By World War I, women were securely employed in nursing and teaching, and had been permitted access to the learned professions of medicine, law, and scholarship.

## DEFINITION OF PROFESSION

The term "profession" is a "taxonomic quagmire."[17] Much of the content of this study revolves around the degree to which certain work and workplace behaviour was considered professional. Part of the problem is semantic: different people used different meanings at different times. To justify the inclusion of these particular five occupations, I rely upon a widespread understanding of the term as an occupation with at least four requirements. The first three are postsecondary education and training in a subject requiring scientific or esoteric skill and knowledge; a certification test; and a degree of self-regulation by practitioners. The fourth criterion involves the provision of service to the public.

All five occupations accommodated these loose criteria, even though standards were vague and perfunctory at times. Over the years the criteria fluctuated in intensity, mostly becoming stronger, and by the end of the nineteenth century these characteristics were widely understood to constitute a profession. Occupational categories in the Canadian census regularly classified the five occupations under the rubric "professional service."

The 1886 census of Manitoba counted lawyers, physicians, teachers (female and male separated) in "professional class," along with architects, artists, engineers, clergymen, government employees, musicians, nuns, and stenographers. Other occupations were distributed among four other classes – agricultural, commercial, domestic, and industrial – and a fifth "not classified" group. In 1886 midwives and nurses, of whom there were only thirty-one noted in the province, were included within the domestic class. By the time of the 1911 census, nurses had been reclassified. More discrete categories had evolved, and although there was a nurse counted under domestic and personal service, this referred to a children's nursemaid. Health-care nurses, along with dentists, physicians, and veterinarians, were now under the "medical" subdivision within the "professional" rubric, which had seven subheadings: art, music, and drama; educational; engineers; legal; medical; religious; and various. For the first time, schoolteachers were distinguished from university teachers. All five occupations – university teaching, medicine, law, nursing, and schoolteaching – were designated professional service.

Although statisticians counted these occupations as professional, public opinion was more ambivalent. Physicians and lawyers assumed the status, but collectively they were not so confident that they could afford to relax their efforts to secure and consolidate their position. In both occupations, organizations were established to protect and promote their interests. University teachers in Manitoba were at first hybrid creatures. Their main claim to professional status was by virtue of the scholar's control of the creation, arrangement, and transmission of knowledge. The earliest university teachers were clergymen and could be considered professional through their ordination. Lay teachers of higher education were slow to organize into associations, and they offered little evidence of a self-conscious profession in Manitoba until the 1930s. The more numerous schoolteachers organized sooner than the university instructors and, for much of the time before 1970, repeatedly insisted on their professionalism. Nursing, from the beginning, identified itself as a woman's profession. Certainly, it was a female occupation: only tiny numbers of men were counted as male nurses by the successive censuses. Inside the occupation, there were at times activists who urged tactics that were considered to be less professional and more associated with trade unions – but the other occupations had militants too. From within and without, nursing's claim to professional status was disputed.

Beyond the commonsense acceptance of the description "professional" in government statistics and in a widespread cultural understanding, there was a serious debate about the precise nature of the term, both within the relevant occupations and among academics. Lacking the obvious strength endowed by the ownership of capital, a professional person's assets lay in his or her training. People in these occupations cared what others thought and whether they were in a profession rather than a trade or a mere job. Their concern was linked to status and power in modern society. Professionals wished to differentiate themselves from wielders of financial power on the one hand and, on the other, from factory workers and agricultural labourers, whose manual labour was their only bargaining power and who tended to resort to confrontational tactics. However, a scrutiny of the claims made by professionals for their privileged position, bolstered as it often was by legislation, suggests that the differences were magnified by the claimants, and it leads to the conclusion that they suffered myopically from their own self-regard; that is, other groups in society shared many of the features that professionals claimed as their own. Their proprietary interest in these features arose not so much from the inherent nature of their work as from their ability to persuade numbers of people of their credibility.

Women activists of the nineteenth and early twentieth centuries were anxious to enter the professions for a variety of reasons. They wanted to earn a living comparable to that of their brothers. They wanted to share in the status attached to professions. Professional work seemed by its nature amenable to many of the civilizing qualities that women thought they had in abundance. Also, they regarded the professions as less inaccessible than work in the higher levels of government and business. During the twentieth century "the professions themselves, expanded and reformed by the credo of science, bulked larger as sources of power and prestige ... the professions embodied the notion that organized knowledge is power ... the 'career open to talent' was epitomized in professional ideology. Theoretically, brains and commitment were the only prerequisites for the training that would lead to expertise ... the hallmarks of the professions were training and service ... [Professions] became a magnet among the potential areas of paid employment for women."[18] To aspiring women, the professions offered rewards based on apparently gender-blind standards. Women who succeeded in entering professional occupations were glad to accept any advantage bestowed on them by membership. As time went on, however, they found that the rewards they had expected failed to materialize.

In retrospect, this is readily understood by reference to the sexually segregated workforce, in which the gendered nature of the professions was so completely taken for granted that there was no need even to justify the exclusion of women. Indeed, even in the late twentieth century, scholarly analyses continue to ignore gender as a dimension.[19] Gender was – we can now understand, if we have eyes to see – a central organizing principle of the professions. A professional person at the beginning of the nineteenth century could naturally assume that the practice of the professional occupations of theology, law, medicine, higher education, and "arms" (the armed forces) would be undertaken by men only. He could also count on a wife to manage his household economy. Literally unthinkable was either the presence of women in the professions or the absence of women from the prerequisite support systems. It was difficult to have any other outlook before there were alternative views of what a woman was or could be. If women were to be recognized and understood as full human beings who could share certain capacities with men and simultaneously experience differences without detracting from their human nature, then the world would be a different place. Such an acceptance of women's identity is still, at the end of the twentieth century, contentious. This present analysis helps to make inroads into the territory of fossilized assumptions about women that date back to a pre-industrial economy.

When, more than a hundred years ago, a few women sought to enter this territory, which was at least indifferent and at worst hostile, they, like their brothers, were inclined to take the rhetoric of talent, objectivity, and service at its face value. The women soon learned that both the rewards and the nature of the professions were not what they initially seemed.

So much depended on what you were looking for. As the American sociologist Eliot Freidson remarked in 1983, "the concrete, historical character of the concept [of professionalism] and the many perspectives from which it can legitimately be viewed and from which sense can be made of it, preclude the hope of any widely-accepted definition of general analytic value."[20] A recognition of the changing content of definition over time is helpful, however, for past usage of the term can "shed light on its current ambiguities."[21]

One of the most sympathetic expressions of the nature and functions of professions is to be found in the work of the American sociologist Talcott Parsons. He came to consider that "the professional complex, though obviously still incomplete in its development," had already (in 1968) "become the most important single component in the structure of modern societies." Parsons noted that at the centre of the system was the university, which both created and transmitted knowledge. The first criterion of a profession was its requirement of formal training, providing technical skills but with prominence accorded to an intellectual component. Training subsequently had to be validated by a test. A second core criterion demanded an institutional means for putting professional competence to socially responsible uses, the "service to the public" concept. Parsons acknowledged that the boundaries of professions were sometimes "fluid and indistinct," and he could give an unequivocal nod only to law and medicine besides scholarship in the university. He acknowledged the right of clergymen and engineers to be considered professional, but when he debated the validity of an artist's claim, he showed how amorphous his criteria were. He was inclined to dismiss as nonprofessional someone who exploited "opportunities to live from the sale of his product on some kind of market," and he derogated an occupation whose "skill component predominates ... over that of intellectual mastery." He showed no sign of recognizing the problematic definition of "socially responsible uses" or of acknowledging the difficulty of discriminating between skill and intellect, nor did he seem aware that he was assuming that the sale of a service had superior merit to the sale of a finished product.[22]

An English social historian, Harold Perkins, shared Parsons's assessment of the twentieth-century importance of professions and the place within professional society of the university and its professors. Perkins showed that late-nineteenth-century academic circles, influenced by the civic idealism of T.H. Green, considered professional work superior to both the money-grabbing of capitalists and the endowed idleness of the landed aristocracy. Professional work embodied selfless public service for the common good. In contrast with pre-industrial society, in which power was based on property in land, and industrial society, in which power was derived from the management of capital, modern twentieth-century society was composed of career hierarchies of specialized occupations – professions. A professional was selected by merit, his authority was based on expertise, and he was judged by his peers.

This system accorded privilege to human capital created by education and enhanced by strategies of closure; that is, by the exclusion of the unqualified.[23] Perkins's gloss allowed the term "professional" to be applied more widely than under Parsons's definition of it, but both men emphasized the inevitability and desirability of a meritocratic society whose main supports were the career ladders of professional occupations. Perkins was readier than Parsons to discern arrogance and condescension as a concomitant of professionals' privileges, and Perkins also acknowledged difficulties in identifying any society's notion of the common good.

While Parsons and Perkins analysed professionalism in terms of the large canvas of modern society, other scholars have taken a more detailed approach.[24] Margali Larson examined the most common claims of modern professions and concluded that most professions experienced a progression over time. At first, an association that represented practitioners claimed professional status because of the body of knowledge and skills at the core of the practioners' work – knowledge that demanded training to master. The skills were seen as useful to society, and the profession enforced high standards of skill and service to the public through self-regulation and codes of ethics. This autonomy, according to Larson, at a subsequent stage was parlayed into a market monopoly. Through control of the market, the profession regulated its own numbers, remuneration, and privileges to the advantage of its members. When generalized in these terms, the altruistic edge to a profession's pronouncements could be interpreted as decoration to more self-interested tactics.[25] Unfortunately, by not considering medieval guilds (which simultaneously rather than sequentially pursued the goals of apprenticeship, certification, self-regulation, closure, and monopoly), Larson lost an opportunity to differentiate a modern profession from its medieval counterpart.

Professional attributes would normally involve a combination of the following: focused postsecondary education to acquire specialized information and skills; vigorous achievement tests and licensing; a special code of ethics or conduct; an occupational career pattern or ladder; self-regulation; an acceptance of a direct relationship with the consumer of professional services, usually described as "service to the public"; high economic rewards; high social prestige; and the monopolization of the market in particular services.[26] Freidson studied the American medical profession and distilled professional attributes into three common demoninators: expertise, credentialism, and autonomy.[27] In the American context, a self-respecting profession would interpret autonomy in terms of collective freedom from state control in the internal management of the profession. However, as recent work on professions in Europe has emphasized, autonomy is a relative concept.[28] Moreover, even in the United States, common usage would not deny the term "professional" to a minister of religion or an army officer. People in the church and in the armed services could not expect high economic rewards; nor, with their requirements to obey higher masters, could they lay claim to autonomy.

Nursing and schoolteaching as occupations lacked the self-possession enjoyed by physicians and lawyers. This has led some sociologists to label them "semi-professions": "Their training is shorter, their status is less legitimated ... there is less of a specialized body of knowledge, and they have less autonomy from supervision or societal control than 'the' professions."[29] Yet the older professions, too, at different points in their history only incompletely satisfied the criteria that twentieth-century American sociologists have demanded for the definition of profession. Components of professional work such as theoretical training, self-regulation in the application of credentials and conduct, monopoly control, and a highly developed sense of service to the public were not always present *in combination* at all times. One feature may be stressed or de-emphasized in certain circumstances. The criteria of professionalism upheld by sociologists are open to criticism on the grounds that they do not take into account changing circumstances of time and culture. In a blithe assumption that the professional worker is male, sociologists have been slow to recognize that work performed by some women could meet professional criteria.[30]

In the development of each of the five professions considered here, the state played a highly significant role. With legislative power and with increasing involvement in the provision and delivery of social programs, different levels of government were harnessed advantageously by professions. In Manitoba, local municipalities and the provincial government furnished secondary education, thereby qualifying high school graduates for admission to the further training necessary for a profession. Eventually, the government came to direct and finance the specific vocational training for all five occupations. In response to lobbying pressure, the provincial legislature established professional bodies with some degree of control over admission to the professions, in the form of certifying or validating the training, and some degree of subsequent self-regulation, in the provision and enforcement of codes of ethics for practitioners and expected standards of service to the public. Legislation in some instances conferred monopolies in the provision of certain services.

In other highly important ways, there was an umbilical connection between a profession and the state. As government became more involved in providing education and health care, more and more professionals were in receipt, directly or indirectly, of government-funded salaries.[31] College-level education was funded less by religious institutions and the fees of students and more by the federal and provincial governments. Schoolteachers were paid by local school boards, whose funds were furnished from public taxes that were levied at local, provincial, and federal levels. Physicians – most of whom were paid directly by patients until after World War II – increasingly received more of their income from private insurance companies; and by the end of the period, they were paid almost exclusively with public money provided by the provincial government, using both provincial and federal funds. Nurses were paid in a variety of ways. Before World War II, private patients paid the private-duty nurse either from their own pockets or through private insurance. Nurses working in public health, community health, or a hospital, were paid through a salary furnished primarily from municipal or provincial taxation. With the rapid demise of private-duty nursing after 1945, nurses were paid almost totally from public funds. Of the five professions we are considering, only the lawyers retained a business independence, still billing clients, who had to pay out of their own pockets.

The professions in Manitoba viewed government more often as a beneficent partner rather than an adversary in their attempts to strengthen their own positions. Yet this was not invariably the case. Nurses were frequently not satisfied with the incomplete response of government to their demands for greater self-regulation. In the 1960s there were individual doctors who saw the introduction of medicare as an intrusion into their own field of expertise. On the whole, however, the dependence of professions on authority conferred by legislation, on the educational services provided by tax-funded schools, universities, and training institutions, and on income paid by employers funded by public money, was neither resisted nor resented.

This acceptance of a close relationship with the state was a marked feature of Canadian professions, and it suggests that the sociological literature defining professions must be used with care. Most theoretical analysis of what constitutes a profession has been American and has emphasized self-regulation to the point of autonomy as a necessary component of a profession. Professions have often used the authority of the state in order to consolidate their power and have resisted claims by the state to monitor or discipline the service they offer.[32] Such behaviour can only be maintained in a social context in which incomes originate principally in the private sector. In the United States, where much health care is provided by religious societies and private corporations and where many schools and universities are privately funded, a profession's independence from state control can readily be seen as significant. The situation is different in Canada.

Autonomy may still be considered important, but not so much in terms of the relations between the state (in the form of government departments of heath and education) and the profession (in the form of institutional associations). Rather, autonomy within a profession can be seen as an individual practitioner's control of her (or his) own daily work. A professional should be able to carry out her profession in way that, as a trained professor (or physician, lawyer, schoolteacher, or nurse), she sees fit, in the light of her professional training and in the context of her professional ethics. In this study, the focus is less on the profession as an institution and more on the individual worker. The structures of the profession are important insofar as they require, or permit, the individual professional to experience a considerable degree of autonomy over her own working day.

Autonomy in this sense can never be complete. There is always room for dispute – or, at any rate, manoeuvre – on the boundaries of a professional's freedom to act according to private judgment. A professional must work with colleagues, partners, supervisors, and subordinates. Among professionals, some have more room for individual initiative, and more demands for individual responsibility, than others.

### WOMEN IN LABOUR

Professions exist within a social context. Industrialization created a society in which the professions could flourish. When nineteenth- and twentieth-century feminists wished to be able to enter the public sphere of extradomestic work and service, they naturally turned towards the occupations which they envisaged as epitomizing the modern world. The "scientific" rules and standards claimed by the professions – in contrast to the worlds of high politics and business, where wealth and connection mattered enormously – were appealing to novices who had to make their own way without benefit of reliable and sympathetic mentors. Modern society contained more than a collection of professions, however, and at least two other components were important in setting the context for women's entry into this area.

First was the existence of a sexually segregated economy, reinforced at many different levels. In most modern Western economies, women were concentrated in certain areas of work and were clustered in the lower levels of pay and responsibility. Over time, the specific dimensions of segregation have shifted, but a sexually segregated economy existed just as noticeably in 1970 as a century earlier.[33] In the nineteenth century, women who worked for pay tended to be young and single; they were concentrated in manufacturing, domestic service, and hospitality occupations, and they were at the lower levels of pay and responsibility. A hundred years later, women in the labour force were no longer only the young and single but included the middle-aged and married; domestic service had all but disappeared, but other female-dominated occupations had appeared instead, in sales and office work; and women were still clustered at the lower levels of pay and responsibility. By 1970, the professional service group of occupations was accounting for between 10 and 20 per cent of all working women's occupations. Within that group, women were not completely sexually segregated, in that women and men were more equally represented overall, even though men had more of the higher salaries and responsibilities.[34]

The sexually segregated workforce was culturally reinforced in the nineteenth century by the ideology of separate spheres. Man's sphere was the public world of work and government; woman's was the home and family. Insofar as a woman entered the public sphere at all, it was only when she was in transit between the original family of her parents and the new family she was to create with her husband. In the brief time she participated in the public sphere, the greater responsibilities would be exercised by a man, whose longer-term work interests gave him the experience and outlook valuable for supervisory or managerial tasks. A woman's low pay would be insufficient for self-support, still less for the support of dependants; but she lived in the parental home anyway and did not need a man's wage (if she conformed to expectations).[35]

These expectations were as much a product of ideology as of the material circumstances which the ideology attempted to justify. In the twentieth century, the imposition of the separate spheres ideology on actual circumstances became blurred. The very distinctions "public" and "private" were no longer exclusive – if they ever had been.[36] On the one hand, concerns of state had an impact on family life. On the other, women participated in paid work and government structures. There were moves towards the merging of public and private, but they could not begin to be complete until the workforce became more sexually integrated.

Notions about woman's proper place in the early-twentieth-century economy were predicated on another important aspect of women's work. Women were expected to be economically dependent. As Victor Gollancz, a progressive British publisher wrote in 1917, "the girl knows that she will be in dependence on her father until she substitutes for it dependence on a husband."[37] The normal smallest unit of society was the family, where ideally the man earned a family wage, sufficient to support himself and his wife and children, and the family's domestic life was serviced by the unpaid labour of the wife in the home. If a woman were to become economically independent she could not be expected to conform to this model, which required dependence as the foundation for her social and political subordination in society.

The presence of women in professions both challenged and reinforced this ideology. The self-sufficiency of a respectable woman who could decently support herself with her own trained and tested labour was itself an affront to the notion of gendered dependence. Yet when a professional woman remained single, her supposed celibacy reinforced her image as an honorary man, whose sexuality was effectively neutered. Professional women's gender could be overlooked, so long as their numbers were small. The commonplace thinking about women's work could accommodate a few exceptional circumstances.

During the twentieth century, various aspects of the model were gradually undermined. Equal pay for equal work, equal pay for work of equal value, and then the greater participation rate of women in the labour force all served to erode the concept of a family wage, which had always been more of an ideal than a reality: "When over half of even married women are in employment, 'the myth of the male breadwinner' seems insubstantial."[38] But ideals could continue despite their practical inefficacy. In 1970, although the economic dependency of women may no longer have been acknowledged as desirable, it was still a powerful relic of common law ideology, and it continued to "exercise seductive power over women's everyday existence."[39]

Ideas about the proper place of women in public life, in the workplace, in the family, and in society generally were as much a part of the culture breathed by the women who wanted to enter the professions as were shiny modern notions of self-support, a career open to talents, and meritocratic efficiency. Few institutions or conventions of any sort were unaffected by gender. The occupations with any pretension to professionalism had already been structured by men on the assumption of a split between public and private life, with the women normally confined to the latter. Nursing, from the beginning, was an exception that tested the rule. Among its models were the professions initiated by men: religious orders, the military, the emerging profession of physicians. From the start, nursing encountered contradictions that rose to the surface when women behaved like men. Teaching, too, experienced tensions. From a very early time, women who entered professions learned that claims to impartial assessment could not bear critical scrutiny. Such standards were used as screens behind which those in power perpetuated their notion of a gendered profession.

## THE MODEL PROFESSIONAL
## PERSON

The gendered nature of a profession was shown particularly in common assumptions, outlined in sociological treatises, regarding a career ladder. A professional was supposed to be ambitious and single-minded, committed to service and to his work, even, if necessary, at the expense of normal working behaviour. When a doctor had a sick patient, he visited him in a place and at hours that were determined by the disease, not by the doctor's office hours or by personal convenience. The professional recognized that his patients or clients or parishioners had the legitimate prior claim on his time and energy. Devoted service would be rewarded by promotion and success. A man would enter the profession on the ground floor after an intensive and extensive training, a period also of considerable expense not only in terms of fees paid for his education but also in terms of forgone earnings. After building up his experience and responsibility, uninterrupted by diversion, he would rise up the ladder. Nor would he dabble in other occupations. As a normal breadwinner, he would earn enough to make a respectable, even superior, living for his family, and he could expect his wife to manage the household and children and to provide him with emotional support.

Only with difficulty, and often not at all, could such ideas be modified to encompass the professional who was a woman. An adult woman was not supposed to be ambitious beyond the bounds of her family – certainly not for herself. A woman was committed to her husband and children, to their interests, their comfort, their future. If a woman had a sick child, she was supposed to attend to it regardless of other calls on her time and energy. The first claim on her was neither herself nor potential clients, but her own domestic life. A married woman could not demand or expect unreserved emotional support from her husband, for he would have his own career to think of.

Not surprisingly, a married woman who was also a professional was considered a contradiction in terms. As late as the 1990s, an able, aware, and ambitious woman could remark on her own youthful "inability to understand that 'woman' and 'professional' were compatible."[40] The idea of a profession dominated by women – married or single – was an oxymoron, and this was particularly evident in the literature regarding nursing.[41] A single woman was not immune to the dominant notions of gender. Until she was old enough not to have children, there was the perpetual expectation that she might lean towards the primary obligation of a woman rather than exhibit unanswering commitment to her profession. There was therefore less incentive for mentors or sympathetic employers to invest her with training and opportunity, for such career investment was a risk. Having achieved the menopause, the single professional woman was less well equipped to assume the responsibilites associated with men of comparable age; and, of course, she could not count on a spouse for the domestic and emotional support desired by professionals in stressful situations.

Women understood these conventions as well as men. The history of women in the professions is partly the story of how the conventions were challenged, reinforced, and subverted. The conventions were in some instances maintained and in others reformed. Different professions responded in a variety of ways, and individual women developed a myriad of strategies to cope. Most of the five professions considered here experienced only one major internal change before 1970 – that concerning marriage. After World War II, marriage no longer disqualified a professional woman from paid work. With few exceptions, however, maternity remained a barrier, although not permanently. A woman might return to professional work after an interruption for the care of infants.[42]

The Manitoba situation mirrored both the larger Canadian experience and, in a more refracted way, two other English-speaking cultures, those in the United States and the United Kingdom. In some ways, there were clear contrasts with the United States and the United Kingdom (training systems, for example, were not always parallel with those in Manitoba). With little variation, the women in professions in Manitoba fairly faithfully duplicated trends of women in the professions in other Canadian provinces.[43] The examination of their experience in this keystone Canadian province can be seen as a paradigm of women in the professions in Canada and as a microcosm of the broader international context.

PROFESSIONS AND THE
MANITOBA ECONOMY:
THE PROPORTIONS

Tables 1 to 3 in appendix 1 show the position of professional women in the Manitoba economy relative to other female workers in 1881, and compared with men and women in selected occupational groups in the prairie provinces 1891–1931 and, in Manitoba 1931–71. In table 4, the category of professional Manitoba women is analysed, and the occupations of university teacher, physician, lawyer, nurse, and schoolteacher are seen in relation to one another, 1911–71.

Men were working in the four occupations of university teacher, physician, lawyer, and schoolteacher at the time of Manitoba's entry into

Confederation. By 1881, women too were counted as schoolteachers, and as nurses. Females were then noted in the following categories: dressmakers and milliners; farmers, female; laundresses; midwives and nurses; nuns; seamstresses; servants, female; and teachers, female. It is likely that this census, like subsequent ones, missed some working women altogether. Women taking work into their homes, for instance, and farmers' wives were not recorded as being gainfully occupied.

The numbers in table 1 reflect the agrarian economy of the province, which was beginning to be transformed early in the twentieth century. As can be seen, professional occupations in 1881 constituted 13 per cent of the total female labour force if one includes nuns, who were mainly nurses and teachers, among the categories of midwives and nurses, and teachers. For the total working population, the census placed all occupations in six "recapitulations" without specifying what was included. The professional class in this aggregation was 636 out of a total working population, male and female, of 23,261, or 2.7 per cent. Women workers in 1881 and for a long time subsequently were more likely to be employed in professional occupations than men were. With the development of industry, trade, and commerce across the three prairie provinces, more opportunities became available for women in factories, stores, and offices, as tables 2 and 3 illustrate.

Until the beginning of the Great Depression, the number of women working in professional service represented about one-fifth of the total female labour force: 13 per cent in 1891 in the prairie provinces, rising to 21 per cent in 1921 and 1931. During the 1930s, both the numbers and the proportion of women professionals dropped slightly in Manitoba. After World War II, there was an increase in the numbers, but as the economy expanded and more women entered the labour force, more jobs were available in other sectors, notably office work. Professional service diminished in proportion to other categories of employment for women, even though the overall numbers continued to rise. By 1971, the proportion of the female labour force in professional service was 10 per cent.

Tables 2 and 3 show the story of women's work within the context of a dominantly agrarian but modernizing economy. Professional work was not as important an option for men as for women. Before 1931, only a steady 3 per cent of the male labour force was occupied in professional service, but this increased after World War II to just under 10 per cent. By 1971, the proportion of women in professional service was nearly the same as the proportion of men.

Table 4 shows the relative position of university teachers, physicians, lawyers, schoolteachers, and nurses within the census category of professional service. Other occupations included under this rubric were artists and entertainers, engineers, religious workers, accountants, and journalists. All except engineers counted women in their ranks. The university, medicine, and the law each employed a miniscule proportion of working professional women – 1 per cent or less until after 1961, and only 2 per cent in 1971. At every census year, schoolteachers furnished the largest single group of women who were considered professional, and in the period 1911–71 they represented about one-half of the total. Graduate nurses ranged from about one-fifth to almost one-third of professional women. These statistics show dramatically that women's access to a profession did not necessarily result in more than meagre participation. The explanation is to be found in the wider social expectations concerning women, as well as in the structure of the professions themselves.

### PROFESSIONS AND THE MANITOBA ECONOMY: THE PIONEERS

In Manitoba women had entered the five occupations of university teacher, physician, lawyer, schoolteacher, and nurse by the time World War I began, and in the latter two occupations well before then. The year 1877 was an important one for the three "learned" professions. In that year the University of Manitoba was established to be the examining body for instruction, which continued to be provided only in denominational church colleges.

Four women applied for admission to higher education in 1886. "Opposition to the request at once showed itself," recalled one of them, "the late Archbishop Machray of St. John's College and Archbishop Taché of St. Boniface College being the chief objectors ... Public opinion as far as it was aware of the issue inclined ... largely to the liberal view." She added: "I enrolled as a student of Manitoba College at the Fall term of 1886."[44] By 1890, the Anglican St John's had joined the Presbyterian and Methodist colleges in admitting women, and the first woman instructor at the university level was a lecturer in French at St John's, 1893–1900.[45] Before World War I, one woman taught languages at Manitoba College and another at Wesley.[46] In 1910 women were appointed by the Manitoba Agricultural College to teach Home Economics.[47]

In 1877 the Manitoba College of Physicians and Surgeons had been incorporated to serve as a licensing body to oversee practising physicians. Six years later, in 1883, the Manitoba Medical College was established to offer instruction leading to a degree at the University of Manitoba. Although the college was "in theory, co-educational from the beginning," no woman was admitted until 1890.[48] However, women trained elsewhere were accorded licences to practise in the province. The first women licensed by the College of Physicians and Surgeons were both graduates of the University of Michigan. Lillian Yeomans was licensed in 1882 and her mother Amelia in 1885, and in a joint practice they specialized in "Midwifery and Diseases of Women and Children" before moving west to Calgary in 1905 and 1906.[49]

The Law Society of Manitoba was by statute in 1877 accorded the authority to control legal education and admission to the profession. The first application from a woman for admission as a student-at-law came in 1911 and was unsuccessful. However, following precedents set in Ontario in 1897 and New Brunswick in 1906, legislation in 1912 changed the Law Society Act to enable women to practise as barristers on the same terms as men, and two women – Melrose Sissons and Winnifred Wilton – began their study and apprenticeship of law. In 1915 they were both admitted to the Manitoba Bar.[50]

Women had been schoolteachers in Rupert's Land before the province of Manitoba existed. On both sides of the Red River, they organized schools and taught in them. In St Boniface on the east side, Angélique and Marguerite Nolin opened the first school for girls in western Canada in 1829, and they worked as teachers in different locations over the next twenty years.[51] After the Grey Nuns arrived in St Boniface in 1844, they too taught children at the elementary level, and one of their number, Sister Thérèse, founded a secondary academy for girls.[52] In the English-speaking settlements on the left bank of the Red River, girls could attend schools run by women who emphasized "social graces" as well as elementary skills.[53] Teacher training at Manitoba Normal School was established by the provincial government in 1882.[54] A professional society, the Manitoba Teachers Federation, was incorporated in 1920.[55]

Nurses began their transformation into a profession only after regulated training programs were instituted in the newly expanded hospitals towards the end of the nineteenth century. A training school for nurses was opened at the Winnipeg General Hospital in 1887, the fifth to be opened in Canada and the first outside the Toronto-Montreal nexus.[56] Gaining professional status was a long struggle for nurses. The professional criteria suggested earlier included some self-regulation by practitioners, and this proved to be the most difficult for nurses to achieve. A measure towards it came as a result of the provincial legislation in 1913 that required the state registration of nurses, the first such legislation in Canada; this reduced the authoritarian control over nurses exercised by hospital boards of trustees.[57] Nursing remained subordinate not only to hospital administrators but also to physicians.

A continuing problem for the profession was to identify and defend its own territory within a health-care system. However, in widespread parlance, from the early days of the province, nursing was considered "a woman's profession." As Archibshop Matheson, addressing the graduating class of nurses of the Winnipeg General Hospital in 1904 observed, "I am one of the conservative school who believe that the true place for a woman is in the home, but I say that if women are to follow professions then nursing is one of the truest and noblest callings for her."[58]

One hundred years ago, the term profession was commonly understood to include the five occupations considered here, and one of the legacies of the nineteenth-century women's movement was to provide access to the professions for women. The figures indicate that women did not find these occupations particularly appealing in comparison with a career of marriage and unpaid work or with the occupations that traditionally employed women for pay, namely, domestic service, hospitality industries, and manufacturing. Women in the twentieth century tended towards the occupations which, on a large scale, were new to the modern industrial economy: sales and office work.[59] The occupations to which women flocked in numbers were those requiring little specialist training and little theoretical knowledge. They were jobs that demanded low levels of initiative, originality, and responsibility, and ones that levied few penalties for work interruptions during a life cycle. In contrast to these low-paying, low-status jobs, professional work demanded that a person invest time and forgo earnings while undergoing training. Then it seemed to require celibacy on the part of female practitioners. These were serious deterrents to adult women who might calculate that their economic interests woud be better served by marrying a man with money in either assets or income. Nevertheless, between 10 and 20 per cent of the women who worked for pay worked in professional occupations. Their inside experience helps us understand more completely the gendered nature of the professions.

## EVIDENCE

Evidence is available and even plentiful for the women "who did first things," in the words of Manitoba journalist Lillian Beynon Thomas.[60] It is less obvious for the women who followed. Yet it is important "to talk about the group photograph rather than the single portrait," to place the first generations of professionals among their peers.[61] Few women, whether their work was paid or unpaid, left written records of the sense they made of their lives. Those who wrote letters rarely preserved their statements, and still fewer left memoirs or autobiographies. Yet evidence of women's doings is all around: it is in the material history of their house furnishings and decoration, in their recipes, and in the persons of the children they raised and the parents they cared for. With respect to women who worked for pay, evidence is in the institutional records of their schools and colleges, their employers and professional associations, and in the local press and magazines when their activities reached the level of newsworthiness. Newspapers also are a valuable guide to public opinion generally. Quantitative data derived mainly from the decennial and quinquennial censuses establish broad outlines of proportions: how many worked in what occupation at what dates. This is essential to establishing a framework of relationships; but statistics by themselves can say little "about the nature and conditions of work."[62]

A complete reconstruction of the worlds of working professional women, which would include their mentalities, is elusive. One resource is to be found in the memories of women who are still alive to tell their tales. Here is a living archive of evidence – awkward to handle and complicated to interpret, but an authentic testimony to what they now think their life and work were really like.

Of course, there are pitfalls for a historian who goes to living subjects. Individuals misremember, and they sometimes deliberately reconstrue in order to satisfy a personal agenda that is quite independent of the inquiry of a historian. People respond to the same question in different ways, depending on a host of variables, including the persistence of the researcher, the wording of the question, the tone in which it is asked in an oral interview, and the space expected for the reply in a written questionnaire. A student must always be alert for the sort of response that she has not thought of herself. An interview must be structured, in order to compare one person's experience with another's, but not unduly. There must be space for the subject to suggest something new, and the student must be ready to recognize something she has not seen before. A theoretical framework must be capable of being "altered or transformed both by the research and by the women's descriptions and analyses of their daily lives."[63] Unavoidably, the researcher's own personality as well as the list of questions will influence the responses, and it is difficult to measure how much or in what direction. Above all, there is the vexed question of "poor representation and overgeneralization," of judging how typical or representative the respondents are.[64] Surveys of groups of women who worked before 1970, conducted by interview or mail questionnaire in the early 1990s, cannot match contemporary social science research with its disciplined and carefully random selection of the population to be surveyed. The historian cannot deny these very real difficulties. In order to present the evidence elicited from women whose testimony would otherwise be lost, the historian may not invest too much or too little significance in what the women have to say.[65]

Awareness of the difficulties of assessing the witness of women now alive who worked in professions before 1970 should permit us an insight into the historian's sometimes less critical use of more traditional forms of evidence. So often a published or manuscript memoir of experience of one sort or another, carefully preserved in an archive, has been seized on as a spectacular illustration of not just one person's experience but of a typical expression of the time. Reminded by late-twentieth-century social historians that we must pay more careful attention to the varieties of human experience and locate a voice within class, region, religion, race, and gender, it is important to be mindful of the difficulties of generalizing from any small data base, archival or oral, written or spoken. Statistics, too, do not exercise "a monopoly of utility and knowledge."[66] Census categories, although they often contain the finest numerical historical data that exist, fall short of complete accuracy. Female lawyers, for instance, were in some years too few in number even to be noted in the occupational censuses.[67]

In this book, I have tried to avoid underestimating these difficulties, but I have also resisted paralysis. Evidence is not as full or as internally consistent or as nicely comparable as one would wish – but historical evidence never is.[68] In these studies of women in five professions, I have used a variety of sources. Statistics, primarily from census data, have provided a numerical outline of how many women were in an occupation at various times, and these have permitted generalizations to be made about changes in women's access and participation over time. These data have also shown relationships between women and men in an occupation, and the relative position of women in one occupation vis-à-vis other occupations. In order to understand what these figures and relationships meant to the women involved, I have used such few secondary sources as exist, but I am especially interested in using primary source material, accounts created by the women themselves. For this, I depend heavily – although not exclusively – on survey material. By way of illustrating general remarks about the difficulties of assessing evidence, let me describe the "living archive."

University teachers in Manitoba could be employed by colleges founded by the Roman Catholic, Anglican, Presbyterian, and Methodist churches or, after 1904, when the university departed from simply examining students and expanded into teaching science, by the University of Manitoba. The Roman Catholic French-speaking Collège St-Boniface was directed by Jesuits, and no woman taught there on a permanent basis before 1970. The Anglican St John's College was also

a founding college of the University of Manitoba but was jurisdictionally distinct, with its own governing board and revenue sources, until
its fiscal integration with the university in 1970. The Presbyterian
Manitoba College and the Methodist Wesley College joined together as
United College in 1928, and they functioned in a way similar to
St John's, as a jurisdictionally distinct member college of the University
of Manitoba, before becoming a separate university, the University of
Winnipeg, in 1968. Until the late 1960s, each college offered instruction in theology as well as in arts and the lower levels of science. After
World War I, by far the majority of all teaching was performed by the
University of Manitoba, which employed instructors in the Faculties
of Arts and Science as well as in the new "professional" faculties and
schools, such as engineering.

Women university teachers who participated in this study were selected in the following way. The calendars of all the colleges and of the
University of Manitoba for all years up to and including the academic
year 1970–71 were examined in order to identify the numbers and
gender of all academic staff and the names of female staff. A composite
list was developed, and the addresses of women who had worked before
1970 at the University of Manitoba and were alive in 1991 were found.
All who were still living in or near Winnipeg were contacted and asked
if they would participate in the survey. Altogether, fifty-three agreed to
participate, and each was interviewed. An additional six, who lived elsewhere, agreed to participate by mail questionnaire. Both the interview
and the questionnaire covered the same questions.

The group of university teacher respondents was thus a population
of women who had worked at the university before 1970 and in 1991
were alive and willing, and, for the most part, living in Winnipeg. Few
women who had retired elsewhere were included. A handful, when
contacted, refused outright to be involved and declined to say why.
Those who did participate were varied in their views. I do not know
whether information contained in their responses would have been
augmented or altered in substance if more women had been included.
There can be no way of knowing for sure. I found that very few insights
or observations were unique to just one woman. The accumulated testimony provided internal corroboration of the women's perceptions.

For the women physicians, a composite list was developed of all
women licensed to practise medicine in the province up to and including the calendar year 1970; the list was drawn up from the registration
records of the Manitoba College of Physicians and Surgeons. Using this
list, I established the identity of surviving doctors and their addresses.
At each of these two stages, it was difficult to be sure of having complete
lists. The names of survivors with known addresses were then divided

into those who lived in Winnipeg in 1991 and those who lived elsewhere. The Winnipeg residents were invited to participate in the study by an interview. Several refused (a higher proportion than of Winnipeg university teachers). Most of them gave no reason, but since many were still in practice, it may have been because they were very busy. Thirty-nine agreed to participate and were interviewed.

This group represented a smaller proportion of the population of surviving members of the profession than was the case with the university teachers, and for this reason there is more likelihood that information from additional people who were not respondents might have contributed new information. Also, it is possible that those who declined to participate did so because they did not care for the gender-focused questions under discussion. This was true of some of those interviewed, however, and in the report of their opinions I noted the views both of those who recognized gender bias and those who claimed that it was either nonexistent or, if present, insignificant. Another reason why it is difficult to claim that the survey group was indeed typical is that among the group were some intensely individual personalities, people who were highly articulate, well travelled, and sophisticated – and it is not easy to reduce such a group to any notion of homogeneity. On the whole, among the participants there was a remarkably acute awareness of the consequences of being a woman; but a few denied the significance of difference. One cannot be sure whether those who did not participate would have divided similarly into a majority who were gender-conscious and a minority who claimed to be more gender-blind, or whether the two points of view would have been more evenly separated – or even whether additional points of view might have been expressed.

The lawyers in the survey, like the university teachers, represented practically all those who were alive, well, and willing. As with the physicians, the composite list was drawn from the records of the licensing association, which in the lawyers' case was the Law Society of Manitoba. Without a call to the Manitoba Bar, no person could legally practise law in the province after 1877. However, a person could work as a lawyer outside the courts, so there was another category of women qualified to work as lawyers (for example, in business or government) if they had a law degree. In addition to those called to the Manitoba Bar, names were added of law graduates from the University of Manitoba who were not called to the Bar. Addresses for survivors were then sought, and all were asked to participate. This group was the smallest of all five and had the highest degree of cooperation. There were twenty-four respondents.

Both the nurses and the teachers were much more numerous. In 1951, for instance, thirty-five women were working in the province as university teachers, fifty as physicians, and five as lawyers. In the same year, 1,681 were working as nurses and 3,688 as schoolteachers. Although the records of the licensing body for registered nurses exist, they are held by the licensing association and were unavailable to me. There was no single central licensing body for schoolteachers. So it was not feasible to contemplate developing composite lists of all nurses and schoolteachers who worked in the province before 1970 in the same way as the lists for female university teachers, physicians, and lawyers had been drawn up.

The individual identities of the entire nursing population were not known, but one attractive and comprehensive source was generously made available to me. Before 1970, nurses were trained in hospitals, and the largest training institution in the province was the School of Nursing at the Winnipeg General Hospital. Not only was it large, but it had the benefit of an efficient and lively alumnae association, which kept extensive records on all the women who graduated as registered nurses from the school. For most years before 1970, there were twice-yearly intakes of new students, who then normally trained for three years. Each intake had a class representative. I asked each class representative for all the years up to 1967 to participate in the study or to suggest a delegate. Forty-five participated directly. In this way, nurses whose beginning training year ranged from 1926 to 1967 agreed to participate in a survey by mail questionnaire.

Without full demographic and cultural information on the entire population of nurses (or teachers), it is impossible to say how "typical" this nurse survey group was in terms of background or opinions. One substantial section of nurse experience was almost excluded – the hospitals run by religious orders. In Manitoba the largest institution of this sort (never as large as the Winnipeg General) was the St Boniface Hospital, whose alumnae records as a matter of policy were unavailable. In response to an appeal for participants in their alumnae magazine, three St Boniface nurses completed questionnaires. Thus a total of forty-eight nurses were involved in the survey. Without fuller information, it is impossible to know whether the regime of obedience, discipline, and relative poverty was intensified at the Roman Catholic St Boniface Hospital or whether the regime at a secular institution was in fact no different. A further point is relevant. The vitality of the Winnipeg General Hospital Alumnae Association and its officers (who include the class representatives) may possibly be unusual and may bespeak a higher level of commitment to the profession than is widespread among nurses at large. Consequently, there may be less hostility or indifference elicited from the survey group than might have emanated from a wider group. Certainly, there was some criticism of the profession, but there might have been more from a group constructed differently.

Teaching is the largest professional occupation of women and one of the largest categories within the entire female labour force. There is much yet to be learned about teaching. I have concentrated here on gender issues in employment. Without fuller statistics on the demographical and cultural characteristics of teachers, and without more studies of the opinions of teachers, the present state of scholarship does not permit claims of typicality to be made. This study is a pioneer in the area, to be confirmed or modified by later study.

Some published material can flesh out basic data revealed in statistics; and the statistics, though full, are not as gender-specific as one would wish. Nevertheless, the very large numbers of teachers, coupled with their early organization into a professional association, meant that teachers were articulating their awareness of employment conditions in publications that are very useful for the historian. The Manitoba Teachers Federation (Society, after 1942) and its organ, the *Manitoba Teacher*, did not always voice the views of its female members, however, and it was important to seek women's views of teaching in other primary sources too. Women teachers themselves, being talkers by trade and by implication respecters of education and literacy, are marvellous primary sources. But how does one select a survey group that will range over the years, will reflect the variety of subjects taught, and will see if there are differences in the consciousness between teachers in urban and rural locations? (And these are only a few of the variables.) Benefiting from the advice of retired teachers' associations, I asked seventy teachers if they would participate in a survey by mail questionnaire or interview. Forty-six agreed.

The nature of evidence always presents interesting problems for the historian. In this study, I have used a variety of sources in order to avoid the snares associated with excessive reliance on only one type. With respect to oral or survey history, each of the five case studies is based on a wide range of voices, differentiated by age and by the nature of work experience. Altogether, I surveyed over two hundred women professionals, some of whom started to work in the 1920s. Their wisdom, maturity, and judgment provide important insights to complement the explanations of oppression offered by academic theorists.[69] In the following chapters, I suggest both the convergence and divergence of opinion among the several groups of women whose common experiences never served to obliterate their individuality. A careful appreciation of the complexities of their lives is crucial to an understanding of the tensions of women who in some ways accepted and in others resisted the male models of working life.

Chronicling Olive Schreiner's "movement of the sexes towards common occupations" began with women's historians who, even as Schreiner wrote, were examining the topic of women and work.[70] *In Subordination* is another step towards a fuller appreciation of why women want but do not yet have equality with men.

### CHAPTER TWO

# Discourse by Default:
# Women University Teachers

Central to the concept of a profession was the construction of knowledge. People whose work it was to create and transmit knowledge were pivotal to any professional endeavour. In recognizing the importance of the university in this project, Talcott Parsons was a twentieth-century pupil of a tradition with a lengthy pedigree. For centuries, university instructors were clerics who pursued truth while professing a creed.

In a practical way, the university was becoming the major organizer of knowledge for would-be professionals during the nineteenth century. Learning by doing – by apprenticeship – had an honourable provenance, but it gave way before academic claims. The story of the professions during the last hundred years shows how university learning became the prerequisite for professional status. Academic study edged out apprenticeship as a parallel way of learning the ropes, and while practical learning remained important, by the end of the twentieth century in all five occupations considered here, theoretical instruction at a university was a necessary first stage for entry into professional work.

University learning was therefore both a profession and a means of access to other professions. Feminist thinkers since the fourteenth-century scholar Christine de Pisan had asserted the intellectual equality of women, and one of the first aims of the nineteenth-century women's movement was to achieve access to university education for women. [1] Soon after the first women undergraduates entered universities, the first women instructors were appointed. But their numbers were never as great as the numbers of women students.

The proportion of women university teachers in Canada changed little between the 1920s and 1970, when the Royal Commission on the Status of Women found that the number of men was "roughly six times greater than the number of women" and that the women were concentrated in the lower ranks.[2] This chapter analyses the number and distribution of women instructors at one provincial university and uses the testimony and perspective of women academics to help explain their small number and low position relative to men. It argues that informal barriers, the hiring and promotion criteria maintained by the university, and a consensus on the part of both women and men about the appropriate behaviour for women served to keep women's participation in the profession at a low level.

## MANITOBA COLLEGES AND THE UNIVERSITY

Until 1904, all university-level instruction in Manitoba was offered by church colleges: St Boniface, Roman Catholic, founded in 1854; St John's College, Anglican, founded in 1849 and re-established in 1866; and Manitoba College, Presbyterian, founded in 1871. All three had come together in 1877 to found the University of Manitoba, whose function was to examine candidates and award degrees. Instruction was provided by the colleges, whose number was augmented by a fourth, Wesley College, Methodist, founded in 1873 and after 1888 affiliated with the university. In 1904 the university started to provide instruction directly, and the Faculty of Science was established. In 1910, three more chairs, in English, history, and political economy were set up. Over the next ten years, the university established itself as the major instructor as well as examiner. By an act of the legislature in 1917, "the colleges, the mother institutions of the university, were to swing out into more remote orbits ... no longer the constituent colleges of a university republic." Manitoba and Wesley colleges came together in 1928 as United College, and with St John's College they continued to offer courses to students and employment to staff until the late 1960s.[3]

As well as this nucleus of instruction in arts, science, and engineering offered by the university and the colleges (which also taught theology), there were other institutions that gravitated towards the university and were there incorporated. The Manitoba Medical College was founded in 1883, and the Manitoba Agricultural College in 1906. Each eventually became a faculty of the university – medicine in 1920, and agriculture in 1924. The Manitoba Law School was established by the university in partnership with the Law Society of Manitoba in 1914, but although a bachelor of laws degree was awarded by the university, the Faculty of Law was not absorbed into the university until 1966. Most other faculties and schools grew from within the university: education in 1935, social work in 1943, music in 1944, architecture in 1948, commerce in 1949, art in 1950, pharmacy in 1951, dentistry in 1959, and nursing in 1963.[4]

Piecemeal pedagogical growth was reflected in the buildings. The colleges had their own buildings. St John's was near the Anglican cathedral in the North End until 1945, when it moved into a large house, previously a private residence, on Broadway near the Legislature Building. United College was more than a kilometre to the west on Portage Avenue. The university buildings, confined at first to science instruction, were on Broadway. Lillian Allen, later a university teacher, was in 1921 a student registering "in the old red brick law courts building on Kennedy Street called the arts building, ... a low strung-out temporary building with class rooms ... flanked to the north and west by the provincial jail and their exercise yard." She recalled: "We saw a lot of the prisoners since little groups of them with a trustee did a lot of the cleaning and snow removal. Then, like us, they attended the twenty minute chapel held in the Assembly room between the day's first two lectures."[5] The temporary buildings were still there in 1938, "a huddle of shabby structures with a distressingly temporary air like old warehouses pressed into service."[6]

The Faculty of Medicine remained at the old Medical College, three kilometres northwest from the Broadway buildings. The Faculty of Agriculture was situated in distant splendour some fifteen kilometres south, on a bend in the Red River, at Fort Garry, where additional university structures were subsequently built. For over thirty years most third- and fourth-year instruction for undergraduates was offered at Fort Garry or at the colleges, while junior years were taught downtown on Broadway. Only after 1950 was the Broadway campus abandoned and most instruction offered at Fort Garry.[7]

WOMEN'S PLACE

The first women university teachers in the province taught French and modern languages, but little more than names and dates distinguish Madame Moreau de Beauvrière, a lecturer in French at St John's 1893–1900, Lorraine Duval, who taught languages at Manitoba College 1901–11, Marion Rowell, who taught French and German at Wesley 1910–18, and Helen Ross, who taught languages at Manitoba, College 1911–14.[8] The first woman to teach at the University of Manitoba was Maude Bissett, in classics. She had a BA from the University of Manitoba and had won a travelling scholarship to the University of Chicago in 1909.[9] Bissett was first on staff in 1914, having taught for two years at Wesley College, and she remained until 1920.

In 1919 she was joined by three other full-time women: Celine Ballu, "a charming woman ... an excellent teacher," Mlle Haynaud in French, and in English, Emma Pope.[10]

For each of the years 1920, 1921, and 1922 there were three full-time women in arts departments on staff: Ballu and Haynaud in French, and Flora Ross Amos in English. At the same time, a woman was appointed to a science department: Eileen Bulman, in zoology, where she worked 1920–25 before retiring to marry a medical doctor. For the rest of the period until World War II, except for 1927 when Haynaud left, there were two women in the Faculty of Arts. In 1928 the new appointment was Doris Saunders, who had the distinction of teaching English at the University of Manitoba until her retirement in 1967. Saunders and Ballu remained the only women on the university staff, except in 1932 and 1933, when they were joined by a scientist, Jessie Roberts (in chemistry), but she left after failing to get an increase in her salary.[11]

For most of the interwar period there were, in addition to the couple or so full-time employees, several sessional appointments. The first woman described as a sessional appointment was Lucy Chaplin, listed for one year in 1917 in the English department. The designation "sessional" referred to men and women appointed for one session only, not on a continuing basis, and it included lecturers as well as laboratory assistants and demonstrators, who were generally senior undergraduate students. There were anomalies: one sessional was continually reappointed, and one demonstrator was highly qualified, with a doctorate. Both were women. Anna Jones was listed as a sessional assistant in German for a total of sixteen years: 1923–33, 1938–41, and 1943–6.[12] Margaret Dudley, first listed as a student demonstrator in botany in 1927, remained a demonstrator even after earning a Minnesota PHD. Among the general run of sessionals in the Faculty of Arts and Science in the interwar years, the proportion of women ranged between 17 per cent in 1925–26 and 35 per cent in 1930. During the late 1930s, when fewer sessionals were employed by all faculties, the proportion of women was generally higher, about one-third of the total. There were thus more women among the casual academic employees of the university than among the full-time, even though they were still in a small minority there.

Of a different calibre was the administrative appointment of dean of women. Dr Ursilla Macdonnell, dean of women 1920–44, had sound academic credentials. At a time when the doctorate was by no means normal for teaching in the Faculty of Arts and Science, she had a PHD from Queen's University. She was listed in the calendar as an administrator, yet for some years she also taught in the English department.[13]

A Board of Governors report on university residence in 1933 recommended clearly that the dean of women "should be a member of the teaching staff."[14] Academic instruction was in addition to her decanal duties, which carried wide-ranging responsibilities for the welfare of the female students. From the first, her salary was superior to that of the other women. Her starting salary was $2,800 in 1920, at a time when Bissett was paid $2,500, Ballu $2,200, and Haynaud, $2,000. In 1921 Macdonnell's salary was raised to $3,100, while Ballu received $2,500 and Haynaud $2,200. By 1926, she had improved her relative position; that year she received $4,000, while Ballu and Haynaud were getting $2,800 and $2,500, respectively.[15]

Until the end of World War II, most women university teachers were located not in arts or science departments but in the home economics department of the Faculty of Agriculture. Geographically, they were separated from the downtown campus and located at Fort Garry. There, theoretical instruction was augmented by practical training in home and family management, for the students were taught and supervised in housekeeping and child rearing; this training was provided in purpose-built houses on the university site.[16] In 1946 women university teachers in home economics constituted half of all the women on the university faculty. Indeed, from 1924 (when the faculty was incorporated into the university) until 1946, the women in home economics provided more than half the female complement: 80 per cent in 1925, 80 per cent in 1935, and 56 per cent in 1945. This proportion steadily declined. By 1955 it was 29 per cent, and by 1965, 26 per cent, but it was always a substantial enough phalanx of women seriously to affect any profile of the woman university teacher in Manitoba before 1970.

Beginning in 1938, and again during the 1940s, new programs were established that provided opportunities for more women instructors. In 1938 a program in interior design had been started, and from the outset women were appointed as instructors – at first as sessionals, and after 1942 as full-time. The program in social work began in 1943, with two full-time teachers, one of them a woman. By 1951, women had taken over all the full-time positions, a supremacy retained for five years, but by 1960 there were still 76 per cent women in the social work faculty. That percentage declined, for reasons suggested below. Nursing began in 1947, and its faculty was always entirely female. Another opportunity for a few women was inaugurated in 1951, when physical education was made compulsory for all students. The proportion of women instructors never equalled that of women students, but it was relatively high, ranging from 33 per cent to an occasional 50 per cent at some time during the decade of compulsory physical education.

As tables 6 and 7 (appendix 1) show, the highest overall proportions of women university teachers, spread over all faculties (except medicine) were found between 1945 and 1955, when the numbers ranged between 16 and 17 per cent.[17] The 1940s recruitment can readily be explained by the war and then by the temporary postwar accommodation of the veterans in special multi-shift utilization of university resources both of physical plant and of personnel. The post-1950 addition, however, is to be explained not by an increased participation of women in the existing departments but by the creation of the new programs in which more women than men were hired: interior design, social work, and nursing. The Faculty of Arts had 8 per cent women on the eve of the war. This rose to 17 per cent in 1945, and even to 25 per cent in 1947. But in 1952 it was back to its prewar level of 8 per cent, and it went down further over the next dozen years. At the end of our period, in 1970, when the total university full-time staff numbers (excluding medicine) had expanded to 919 (from 319 in 1960, and 197 in 1950), the percentage of women in arts was 8 per cent. Science was lower. In the 1920s and 1930s there had been two full-time women, Bulman for five years and Roberts for two. Science appointed no more women until 1950. From then until 1970, the percentage of women in science ranged from 3 to 9 per cent. In 1970 there were eleven women in science, or 6 per cent.

WOMEN'S WITNESS

Numbers do not communicate the women's work experience. Other sources must be consulted to learn of their perceptions, ambitions, and observations. Written material was sparse. One woman who kept a diary made it available, and another wrote a brief account of her career. Most information came from the memories of the fifty-three women who agreed to be surveyed, either by interview or questionnaire.[18]

A best estimate of the total number of women who taught full-time between 1914 (when the first woman was appointed) and 1970 is 376.[19] The fifty-three respondents were concentrated among the more recent appointments before 1970, but nevertheless they spanned forty years. They were drawn from all faculties that employed women and were found mostly in agriculture and home economics, education, physical education, social work, and arts.[20] The survey was designed to elicit comments on the women's entry into the profession, the changing gender balance within faculties, the shifting emphases between teaching and research, the problems of working mothers, and, throughout, how they understood the profession of university teaching.

The survey also tested hypotheses informed by recent literature describing the behaviour of women university teachers in the past, a literature that can be characterized as having three approaches: celebratory, mythic, and consciously strategic.[21] The first celebrates the achievements of women scholars.[22] The second attempts to explain the women's intellectual persistence in the face of a continuing low status by reference to "a continuum of outsiderness" for women in the university. Life in the university, claim the authors of a book subtitled *Outsiders in the Sacred Grove*, "cast" women in subordinate, supportive roles. Swept up in an intellectual quest of mythic proportions, women were to be seen as minor characters ineluctably confined to the margins.[23] The third approach derives from *Unequal Colleagues*, an account of nine pioneer women professionals who survived through a set of strategies identified as superperformance, innovation, separatism, and subordination.[24] This Manitoba study, however, shows a more complex relationship between the university and its women teachers, who display more of the features shown in the work of historians Alison Prentice, in Canada, and Marjorie Theobald, in Australia.[25]

Women university instructors were not a numerous group. A woman of ninety started her interview with the comment that it was not so unusual for a woman to be a university teacher in the 1930s. She elaborated: "Now they're in the minority, aren't they? I don't think it was much different in my day."[26] She was right. In 1933, when she started teaching, 12 per cent of the full-time university teachers at the University of Manitoba (excluding the Faculty of Medicine, which did not appoint a full-time woman until 1949) were women. In 1970, the terminal year for this study, the proportion was 15 per cent.

## ENTRY AND TRAINING

The first question considered in an interview was "How did you choose your work?" The most common explanation for choice of career was "I fell into it" or "It was circumstances more than anything else."[27] The choice was rarely deliberate. One of the few who had set her sights on university teaching said, "It chose me." However, having qualified herself with a doctorate, she found that the late 1940s were not a good time for a woman to enter the profession. "All the male professors who had been off in the war were returning," she explained, and she therefore worked in a nonacademic job for a year before becoming a university teacher.[28]

Another, at the age of fourteen, intended to become a professor but was mistaken about the particular subject she ended up teaching, although her choices were both in the same Faculty of Arts.[29] One of the few scientists knew from an early age that she wanted to be a university teacher. She casually related how she financed her own grade 12 education in high school before winning scholarships to see her through university. Her family could give her no financial support, but her mother, she said, thought "I could do anything I wanted."[30] All the others described circuitous routes to their final niche of university teaching. There were not too many different routes. Some started off by choosing schoolteaching and working in the public schools. This was very common in the Faculty of Education. Others worked as practitioners in the field. This was true for home economics, social work, and the health professions, including nursing, medical rehabilitation, and dental hygiene. As late as the 1960s, the horizons of many women were limited by the prospect of teaching, nursing, office work, and marriage as appropriate careers for women.[31] If a person had a definite distaste for one or more of these, her options were even more circumscribed.

Few women exhibited wider ambitions. Curiously, two who had arrived at university age apparently innocent of workplace gender stereotyping were both born and trained in England and both had been to single-sex secondary schools. Neither acknowledged traditional women's expectations. At university, one went into science and the other into law, and both decided on a career in university teaching only later. Another graduate of a single-sex secondary school, a convent, had an unusually ambitious scope: "I wanted to know why people behaved the way they did and how varied that could be." She began in medicine and changed to anthropology.[32]

Others began the training for another profession and along the way, before completing their credentials, shifted their focus and started work as a university teacher, even though that had not initially been in their sights.[33] Some were diverted from their original hopes by the financial problems of the Depression; for instance, a woman who worked as a nurse before teaching at university had originally wanted to be a librarian; but, in the circumstances, she considered nursing to be a surer bet for a job.[34] Another was side-tracked by service in the armed forces. She had trained as a physiotherapist, and after World War II she decided to train further in order to be able to teach future physiotherapists.[35] Several went into graduate training as a way to maintain or improve a variety of future options while deferring a decision on a career. [36] Then there were a few who said that nothing better, either in the way of marriage or in an idea for a career, had turned up.[37]

This was an unusual answer; few women explained their entry into university teaching by reference to the presence or absence of opportunities for marriage. Only one recollected explicitly that her early career strategy had been formed on the premise of being single.[38] Others were determined to earn their own living.[39] Most said that they went into graduate work because they liked it and were good at it. This proficiency was usually discovered and fostered in high school – often, though not exclusively, through the direct encouragement of an enthusiastic or perceptive teacher.[40]

Almost all had parents who gave emotional support – and, in many cases, material support as well. Those who mentioned parents were most apt to mention fathers, but mothers also were important. One woman who was raised by her breadwinner widowed mother noted the considerable sacrifices her mother had made; but her mother's support was counterbalanced by the reiterated scepticism of her paternal grandmother. The grandmother had no instinctive respect for a woman or man remaining outside the labour force in order to pursue advanced training: "The typical thing to do was to quit school in grade 10 or grade 11 and get a job and continue to live at home and help out. So my father's family was very critical ... it was a waste to educate a woman ... But when I graduated from university, [my grandmother] was the proudest person you've ever seen."[41]

These assumptions were not widespread among the families rearing the first generations of women academics. Even when the parental education level was low (one woman's father had only three years of formal schooling, in Europe), the family nevertheless revered education.[42] More usual were accounts of families in which at least one parent, usually the father, had studied at university. The mother, too, often had further education, most often teacher training. Although most mothers with a job had retired from the labour force at marriage, the occasional woman continued to work for pay, one or two continuing to do so even after parenthood. No circumstance was reported of parental opposition to the burgeoning scholar.

While a woman's initial predisposition towards higher education may have been regarded benignly, she was less likely to find external support thereafter. In a few cases, a professor's suggestion that a good student continue into graduate studies was indeed critical.[43] Many, however, noted that they had to contend with indifference and even hostility. In disciplines such as mathematics and English, women students came up against the ingrained conservative assumption that the scholar was recognizable only as a man.[44] Doubtless, this widespread perception served to keep out many – perhaps several hundred – potential challengers altogether. Only the determined, persistent, and possibly naive remained to fight the battle in the more male-dominated subject areas.

## SHIFTING EXPECTATIONS
## OVER TIME

In arts and science, a successful male undergraduate would be targeted by his professors and invited to consider graduate work. A master's degree in the first half of the twentieth century was a necessary training for the university teacher, and even though the doctorate was not the almost universal prerequisite it became after 1970, it was still a useful degree to have. Academic qualifications were not so significant in the faculties that offered more of a vocational training. Engineering, for instance, regularly recruited from practising engineers. Medicine at Manitoba until after World War II was geared much more towards clinical training than research, and it mobilized the resources of large numbers of doctors, many of whom worked on a part-time basis, giving an occasional lecture and supervising the clinical training of medical students.[45] Law displayed similar tendencies.[46] This practical model – of the trade school oriented less towards research and more towards the preparation of practitioners in the field – tended to set more store in the teacher who had contacts in the community for students' placement opportunities and who could give the practical instruction valued by a new recruit, who wanted to know how rather than why to practise his trade.

The faculties and schools that employed most women university teachers followed this latter model. Recruiters in home economics welcomed as teachers people who had been working in institutions (for example, as dieticians in hospitals). The Faculty of Education recruited senior practitioners from the schools, including inspectors, officers of the Manitoba Teachers Society, and school principals, as well as schoolteachers who had made a reputation as curriculum innovators. The School of Nursing recruited from nursing supervisors as well as from instructors in the hospitals. Similarly, the Faculty of Social Work hired practising social workers into its ranks.

Not surprisingly, with this emphasis on practical experience, there was a marked tendency on the part of the women university teachers to marginalize, indeed to disparage, the value of a research degree. Lack of respect, bordering on contempt, for the doctorate was understandable when the mission of these schools was to reproduce the existing body of knowledge and apply it in the practical setting of the telephone and power companies, in doctors' clinics, law offices, hospitals, schools, and welfare agencies. After World War II, at different paces in different disciplines, each of these areas shifted the emphasis of its mission to include more analysis of alternative strategies to the status quo. Programs and curricula were reformulated to include more consideration of criticism and a wider education for students, even though the practical training continued to be paramount. In some schools and faculties, the incorporation of a wider context and theoretical and research component was achieved before 1970. In others, the shift was only just beginning. And at the same time, the older mind-set persisted.

The trend in many instances was accompanied by a clear gender implication. In home economics, education, and social work, a high proportion of the old guard was female. Under the new regimes, possession of a graduate degree counted for more than service in the field. For a variety of reasons, women were slower to prepare themselves with this qualification, and they suffered for it most obviously in terms of a declining presence.[47] Home economics in 1965 had its first man appointed as director. This was explicitly to cope with problems perceived to be basically gender-related, not only with respect to qualifications and research-orientation, but also to networking. The dean of agriculture "went out looking for a male dean ... Women were not being heard in the upper echelons" of the university, one survey respondent explained. "Only men could talk to men in washrooms and corridors." It was thought that "we could compete better in that milieu with a male dean," said another.[48] The school saw a reduction in the proportion of its female staff from 100 per cent in 1964 to 87 per cent in 1968, a trend that continued while the overall numbers on staff rose by a one-third, from twenty-one to twenty-eight.

The shift towards a greater emphasis on research, accompanied by a higher proportion of male appointees, was repeated in the Faculties of Education and Social Work. Education in 1959 had six full-time staff, one-third of whom were women. By 1969, there were more than ten times as many full-time staff, sixty-eight, and the proportion of women was beginning to decline: they stood at 30 per cent. Social work in its full-time complement of staff after World War II had more than 70 per cent women, a figure that excluded the part-time field supervisors and instructors, the vast majority of whom were female. During the 1960s the full-time staff increased by a factor of five, yet the proportion of women was reduced from 85 to 51 per cent. In each of these schools or faculties, the trend persisted during the next generation. By 1989, home economics was down to 64 per cent female; education was 22 per cent, and social work was 41 per cent.

Once on the faculty, there was a job to be done and there were expectations to meet. Concerning the work, most women had a good idea of what teaching would be like, although the actual mixture of teaching, research, and administration took some by surprise. Juggling the mixture remained problematic for many.

The demands of teaching were usually straightforward. "I wanted to teach particular things ... theory courses. I had that opportunity. I was good, so I got more and more," commented one woman.[49] Another, who was habituated to the stress and long hours of schoolteaching, was agreeably surprised: "Here you could take a *break* after class. You could *have coffee*. And then there was less preparation."[50] "I discovered I loved teaching," said one. This woman was "fairly successful" and valued "the ego satisfaction."[51] Some tried very hard to live up to their own high standards for the presentation of material and for giving attention to individual students. One, in medicine, had previously worked in a state-of-the-art research institute in the United States and was dismayed at the ill-equipped laboratories and lack of technicians, but she set to work willingly. She found teaching to be an intellectual challenge – "a way to organize yourself well and to get your thoughts in the right perspective. If nothing's clear in your own head, you can't project it to the students." At first she went to the length of practising every lecture: "I would rehearse it."[52] She was unusual in that her department head often attended lectures delivered in his department. Most felt they were on their own: "I had my own expectations, to try very hard." This woman was a good teacher, "although I didn't know it then." She found out only in 1972, when the students' union published a course-by-course review of individual teachers.[53] Another found lecture preparation time-consuming. She always had a heavy teaching load and was aware that she taught more hours than her male colleagues, some of whom were "very bad at it."[54] Only a few women expressed a less than enthusiastic preference for teaching. One discovered at the outset of her career that she was not "cut out to be a teacher" but nevertheless stayed with the job.[55]

Most women were content with the courses they taught. One who was less so was "manoeuvred into doing the drudgery work" while a male colleague in her specialty "built up a publishing record ... and then took over the graduate course." "I wasn't ambitious, I didn't care if I published or not," she said, but she was crestfallen to see a course in which she took pleasure assigned to another, especially as it was one that she knew she did well (the department head had told her he would rather have his own child taught by her than by the member of his department with the greater claim by virtue of publishing).[56]

There was more ambivalence over research expectations. Among the early women teachers, scholarship was viewed as a rather leisurely pleasure to be indulged in almost as a hobby. They felt no pressure to publish. One woman had published several books before her appointment to the university staff but made no bones about describing them as simply school texts "spoonfeeding the teachers." Not that she despised this work: the royalties from the books bought her house.[57] But this was not research. One who taught at St John's College had a heavy teaching load and was bringing up two children on her own: "I did no research."[58] Another took ten years to complete an Oxford research degree, the B LITT, and acknowledged other priorities before research.[59] As dean of junior women in the 1930s, Doris Saunders echoed the ethos of a British rather than American university model in 1944. She quoted the remarks of Sidney Smith, president of the University of Manitoba, 1934–44, at which time he left to become president of the University of Toronto: " 'Intellectualism alone is not enough. In stock-taking and in formulating plans, universities should seek to cultivate, also, the emotional, the aesthetic, and the spiritual life of the individual.' This worthy aim," she said, "requires a staff sufficiently large to guarantee that the individual student will become known to at least one member of the staff capable of guiding him or her in the desired direction. If more time could be devoted to personnel work with students, I believe the whole University and the community would be benefited thereby."[60]

Later generations of university women teachers were mixed in their views on research. One entering the Faculty of Law in the late 1960s had expected that research and scholarship would be stressed more than they were.[61] Another, in arts, similarly thought research would be emphasized more than teaching, and in her first years she tried to give it priority. She found great satisfaction in the anthropological field-work she did. It "provided meaning, and fun, and intellectual inquiry." Her commitment remained strong, though it turned a little sour over a gender-related dispute. When she arranged to take a male assistant with her on a field trip, her department head ordered her to include the assistant's wife, despite the fact that the plans had been approved by all concerned. Since she had the necessary funds from a granting agency, the professor disregarded the head, who left the department soon afterwards. She later discovered that her salary had been severely held back in comparison with other members of the department, an abuse of power she attributed to her defiance.[62]

A woman member of the Faculty of Medicine identified a gender-related problem of a different sort. There were fewer than half a dozen women academics in the faculty and about the same number in part-time clinical positions. At an early research seminar, the female professor made a comment on the previous professional work of a colleague's wife, who was by then not on staff. Afterwards, another colleague took her aside and said such forwardness was unwise. In another instance, a wife who had trained as a nurse criticized the professor's manner as "too abrupt." These episodes "taught me to be very careful of wives."[63]

Administrative chores evoked a variety of comment. One woman, with quiet calculation, avoided committees: "I hated meetings ... I determined to walk a tightrope course, not be so stupid I would be fired, but at a crucial point if my name was up, to ask some rather stupid question, so the voters would think twice before putting me on the committee."[64] Some used to get incensed at the grandstanding that went on in committees and tried to avoid them.[65] One woman found herself always expected to perform administrative functions of a social nature, to arrange for receptions, daily coffee, and retirement parties, and she did so. She was disappointed to receive a negative recognition from her colleagues, in comments such as "I'm so glad you've got the time to do this."[66] One took her administrative responsibilities so seriously that as a department head with a limited budget she did her own typing and managed the departmental office.[67] Another, who for many years administered an off-campus program in addition to a full teaching and research load, was chagrined by the ingratitude of the university when she was not awarded administrative leave on stepping down from the position. Yet she would do it again: "Someone has to do it."[68]

The expectations about teaching, research, and administration shifted over time. Particularly in the newer faculties that had a mission to train practitioners, staff recruited with initial expectations of contributing to that purpose sometimes felt betrayed when their work went unrewarded under a regime with different demands. This change was initiated mainly in the 1960s, although earlier intimations were felt by at least one woman, who identified this as an alien influence. In 1945 a female department head encouraged her staff to have research degrees: "She wouldn't suggest to the dean I get a raise in rank until I had this damn degree. Is that Americanism, or a modern way of thinking about education?"[69]

Most of the women in the social work faculty were hired from the field; they had worked for a social work agency, in many cases as supervisors of students in their clinical setting. During this period, very few had a research background, and they did not see themselves as "academic." Yet new academic administrators (men) introduced a new demand for research into the expectations put on the staff, and this often caused considerable anxiety.[70] The situation was paralleled at a later date in the dental hygiene department. Some teachers were inspired by the prospect: "The research was exciting." But even when the instructors were willing and eager to respond to the new demands in these intensely practical training schools, there was the problem of providing time: "There was no change in the teaching workload."[71] Social workers, nurses, teachers, dental hygienists (and others, including lawyers, engineers, and medical doctors) still had to be shown how to practise their profession. Yet the staff who gained the career rewards were those who produced evidence of research.[72]

In retrospect, a member of the Faculty of Education, who in the late 1960s was just encountering this new orientation, thought the university administration could have done much more to expedite its acceptance through the provision of research assistance. At the time, she preferred not "to play the university game."[73] This to a large extent was perceived as men enforcing new rules to keep women out. In social work, there were very few men in the beginning: "I guess there were some but they didn't stay. Either they went on for further education or they moved into executive positions." Having acquired graduate degrees, men soon came to dominate the administration in social work, education, and even home economics. Women were outmanoeuvred. The new men moved to privilege the new research component. "Men became part of the [social work] profession and that really set a whole different tone ... the subtle kind of discrimination ... the boys' club ... There were things got decided not at meetings," explained a former member of the department. "I just stayed out of it. I thought, 'What the heck,' I didn't really want to move. You know, I just begin to realize how unambitious I really was."[74]

## REWARDS

As late as 1969–70, considerable executive authority was vested in department heads and deans. The era of "due process," committees, unionization, and accountability was still in the future. Paternalism could occasionally benefit individual women. One member of the small pre-expansion Faculty of Education knew that she had a heavier teaching load than the men but never questioned this publicly. Out of the blue, she received an additional cheque for $1,000 from the university president in recognition, she presumed, of an inadequate salary. But she made no fuss: "I was too busy to politick."[75] In another department, a woman who knew some of her colleagues' salaries prepared for a meeting with her department head by taking with her a list of staff: "You could draw a line across the list: women were below the line, and men were above." In an attempt to explain the men's larger salaries, the head coyly referred to the fact that men had dependants. The woman retorted that she understood: there was a baby bonus. The head acknowledged the inequity, and "salaries got bumped up substantially. They were still out of whack but not so badly out of whack."[76]

All the women interviewed were asked whether, as far as they knew, their employment conditions relating to salary, security, and promotion were the same as those of their male colleagues. Some were appointed at a time when they had no male colleagues within their faculty or school, so were unable to compare. A few were confident that the conditions were the same, as far as they could tell. Most had known that their salaries were lower and that their progress through the ranks was slower. This knowledge affected them in different ways.

Doris Saunders, appointed in 1928, was "perfectly sure" the men were getting more. "It never bothered me," she said, adding that she never inquired about such things: "I was not outwardly ambitious. I felt privileged to be there." A woman in arts was similarly unconcerned about equity: "I was simply maintaining what I was interested in – teaching."[77] Another, also in arts, distinguished her own attitude to career progress from that of the men: "They look after themselves. I try to help others."[78] One had a decidedly less sanguine view. In a memorandum, "For the Record. A Condemnation: Why I have no real love for the U of M. My Lament," she noted anger at her perpetually low salary: "I only went up when the floor went up ... I never got a merit raise. I devoted my time to teaching ... U authorities rarely give a damn about ability to teach, it's the letters after your name on the calendar that count."[79]

For those still on staff in the mid–1970s, confirmation that their salaries were indeed lower than those of their male colleagues' came with the first University of Manitoba Faculty Association contract, which included an inequities fund to which an aggrieved member could apply.[80] Several women noted that they had received what appeared to be substantial ($1,500–$2,000) adjustments. One, in social work, was already aware that she had been hired at a salary of $2,000 less than a male peer, but she was awarded an inequities payment and thought the problem was dealt with.[81] Another, in the Faculty of Medicine, was paid the "minimum" and explained this by reference to "the feeling that if your husband was working at the university, you don't really need much money." She was awarded two large increases from inequities funds.[82] Others were aware of inequities and ascribed their low salaries to their initial appointment at a low salary, a situation that was difficult to remedy subsequently in a satisfactory way. One, in science, accepted that as she had not had a PHD when she was first appointed, this accounted for her subsequent lack of parity, even though she gained the degree shortly after her appointment.[83] Another, in arts, felt that her slow career progress, in comparison with a man who completed his graduate degree after her, was due to her being married. "There was an expectation that [my husband] would be moved." She felt resentful but thought it unwise to make too much fuss. "I didn't complain very much ... Having a job was a fluke."[84] With irony, one woman ruefully remarked, "We were much too ladylike to discuss salaries."[85]

Like her, several women disliked the suspicion or knowledge that their salaries were not on a par with equally qualified men, but took no individual initiative to attempt to remedy the problem. Perhaps, like Saunders, a woman might feel it was a privilege merely to be allowed to teach; or perhaps she sensed the general atmosphere of "subtle discrimination" in the university and feared to rock the boat. One woman, in the Faculty of Education, did not sit tight. She had been recruited from the school system at a time when "men and women were paid equal" and "did not know that you negotiate when you join the faculty." She had earned an annual salary of $8,200. The dean offered her $8,500, which she accepted, only to find that others in a comparable situation were being offered $10,000, $12,000, and $13,000. Shortly afterwards, at the completion of her PHD, she discovered that a man in the same position was being paid 30 per cent more than she. In this instance, she was able to mobilize the support of her male department head in a successful bid to rectify the discrepancy.[86] She, like almost all the women, welcomed the introduction of defined criteria and published salary schedules after unionization.

Despite the deterrents, some women became and remained university teachers. The reasons lie partly in the pleasure they found in their work. Some enjoyed their work with other women.[87] Many liked the contact with students. Since there was a constantly changing body of students, they could "avoid getting stuck in a time warp."[88] "The intellectual exercise and mental keenness of teaching" was the explanation given by one survey respondent.[89] "The thrill I got out of the authors I was teaching," said another.[90] Similarly, another mentioned the satisfaction of training a new generation of therapists, and by extension helping all their patients, rather than helping only one patient at a time.[91] "When you have control, things are a lot better," noted another woman. Although the situation varyed from faculty to faculty, university professors had a considerable amount of personal control over their daily and yearly routine and over course content, methods of teaching, and research.[92] This provided considerable satisfaction: "the environment permits greater difference and also allows considerable anonymity – you can get on with what you want to do."[93] Similarly: "I have a strong commitment that the information I give to people will help them have a fuller, more meaningful life."[94] And who could query the satisfaction of a woman in the Faculty of Medicine: "When I began, 90 per cent of the patients in my field of research died; now over 60 per cent live." [95] Significantly, the only interviewees who mentioned rewards such as salary or vacations as a satisfaction were widows and divorcées – those with a licence to be breadwinners.[96]

The work also brought its irritations. Time wasting in meetings was widely disliked, even though the proliferation of committees was understood to be partly a consequence of a welcome move away from executive arbitrariness. The lack of long-term government planning, which had an impact on research funding, was a frustration for some, especially those who would have liked to be able to publish more.[97] Another problem was that it was not always possible to master the teaching material.[98] One woman expressed an explicit gender analogy: "I could have done more had I been two people rather than one ... or a man." But in that case, "with more ruthlessness, there wouldn't have been the other half of my very schizoid existence."[99]

The situation in one area illustrates a widespread condition that most women had to accommodate in a less obvious form. In the practice of dentistry as a profession, the men were the protagonists, the women auxiliaries, and the status issue was duplicated within the faculty. In the dental hygiene department the women were continually confronted with this model of the woman only as helper, the dental hygienist. In order to be accepted as a partner, one woman thought: "All I had to do was to prove I did the job well, and for the program to be good." But as she noted in retrospect, her "naiveté" was in believing that performing an essential job in a partnership situation would bring recognition as a colleague. It did not do so. The idea of women as equal colleagues was too difficult for dentists to accept. The women university teachers in that faculty had to learn to work with this status barrier or around it. It percolated through to the students, who during their training period became socialized to accept an unequal, noncollegial relationship as part of the work.[100]

For all their actual shared experience, the women on faculty at the University of Manitoba before 1970 had very little to do with one another. There was no overt solidarity, political or social. There were no formal or informal associations beyond the personal gatherings of a few friends. There was a Faculty Wives' Association, but faculty women were not members and few recognized any identity of interest – quite the reverse:[101] "We none of us went to it. Our director thought that we were professionals in our own right, she didn't go, and we agreed with her."[102] Some consciously avoided the company of other women: "I had a contempt for women's groups. I wouldn't be caught dead in them ... These feelings lasted a long time."[103] Others had not the time, even if they had desired stronger connections: "My hands were more than filled," and after a day at the university "you want to get away from work."[104] A single mother appointed in the 1930s stated, "I had to bring up two children and I had a heavy workload."[105] Several questioned the assumption that an organization of academic women was desirable. One thought it was "not sensible" to have women's support groups; it was better to integrate women into the existing structures and work "in the big leagues" – in the major university committees, in administration, and in executive positions.[106] Another gave it as her opinion that many of today's feminist groups are not very realistic, wanting both to have their cake and eat it.[107] No respondent identified the absence of a women's academic association as having any bearing on discrimination.

Many women were active outside the university, involved in professional groups, many of which were exclusively or mainly female. Only a handful, of the oldest generation, were involved with the University Women's Club – but for social reasons, not in the expectation of professional advantage.[108] One, who joined the Business and Professional Women's Club, which in the 1950s was in the vanguard in Canada in a fight for equal pay for equal work, did so not for political reasons but because she directed plays among the membership.[109]

### THE MODEL PROFESSIONAL

All the women described themselves as busy, but none more so than those with children at home. In this respect, there was a clear generational difference. Until well after the World War II, it was rare to find a married woman employed as a full-time university teacher at the University of Manitoba. In 1921, when the director of home economics "resigned to be married," such a course of action was commonplace.[110] One woman employed in the mid-1930s at St John's College was married, but she emphasized how very unusual it was for a married woman with a husband to be working for pay.[111] In the 1940s and 1950s, single women (either those who had never married or those who were widows) were still more common than married women. Only in the 1960s were married women hired to any extent, and this trend then continued.

For the years of this study, the vast majority of academic women had neither a husband nor children to care for. Some were expected to care for parents, but several lived with a mother who effectively worked as a housekeeper.[112] There was a distinct demographic difference between the earlier university women and those hired in the 1960s and later. Those of the older generation who were married were expected to run the household and look after their husbands, but they tended to be childless. The very real double burden experienced by working mothers was uncommon for most of the women in this profession before 1970.

Working mothers did not always complain. There was a beneficial side. While domestic responsibility limited a woman's physical time, it also served to provide a broader perspective on the demands of other age groups. "You are more human as a teacher." Personally, "you are forced out of your introspection."[113] One woman who continued to work throughout the infancy of her children sensed a sharp tension between those with and those without a family. When a university professor was also a mother, the tendency was for other people (and for her too) to consider that this was very much her own personal business. A widow teaching home economics, hired in 1964, was told that her job must come first and her children second and that there was to be "no excuse."[114] The private, individual nature of motherhood was thoroughly accepted by a woman who returned to university teaching in 1962 after a gap during which she had raised three children, who by then were adolescents. At a social event, her department head jokingly asked her husband what he would do if she came home from a day's work cross and bad-tempered. Before her husband could reply, the woman interjected that if it ever came to that, she would quit her job: "My family came first." Thirty years later, this woman says that she would still give priority to her family, but she has come to regret the smugness of her comment.[115]

The dual demands of family and profession could set up a tension in relations with others. One mother observed that in the 1960s single women "rather resented those of us who were trying to do the job and be mothers – they had done without, why should we have more?" This mother commented that the latent resentment, perhaps jealousy, "didn't make for much solidarity." She based her insight on the singular experience of having a woman mentor, a professor who encouraged and fussed over her – until the intolerable occurred: she became pregnant and was therefore no longer "professional."[116] There were so very few women in a position to act as mentors that it would be unwise to make too much of this one example. Nevertheless, it affords a glimpse of one facet of a society that penalized professional women who were parents, while rewarding men who had wives.

A woman professional was by definition in a position of conflict. Widows or divorcées with children did not flout public opinion quite so much, in that the breadwinner role of a woman with dependants was acceptable. She was working from necessity. But a woman who went out to work when she had a husband and children was flouting convention twice over; hence, the haste with which one of them insisted that her family came first. The apparent ambition and self-seeking of the professional had to be subordinated to the self-sacrifice of the wife and mother. The experience of women university professors at the University of Manitoba indicates that before 1970 the existing models were scarcely questioned, at least by behaviour.

These women's experiences also confirmed their belief in the model of the married woman who – like their own mothers (with a few exceptions), like the wives of their colleagues, and like their own married women friends – considered marriage a full-time career. Their observations about the fatigue experienced by the increasing number of women professionals who after 1970 no longer accepted the necessity of choice – marriage *or* a profession – in many ways strengthened their conviction that choice was necessary.

Most of these university teachers were single. They believed that the difficulties of combining career and motherhood were almost insuperable. "It would have been impossible for me to do the amount of work I did and be married and run a house," stated one. "My mother was always supportive and provided the home background, so I could concentrate entirely on university work, as men do."[117] Another typical remark was: "You learn to make a lot of compromises. We – my women colleagues and I – wish we had a wife."[118] Observing students and women professors with children – a rare phenomenon before 1970 but increasingly the norm afterwards – most expressed misgivings about the inevitable fatigue suffered by those trying to do too much: "Some stretch themselves out too thin – it wears them out";[119] "I can't believe people can cut themselves in two successfully without great trauma, guilt, and stress."[120] One woman remarked that the new generation of students "wants it all. Something has to give."[121] The few university teachers who did combine career and motherhood recognized the problem, but they neither magnified it nor exaggerated their own efforts: "You cannot operate full time in both fields. I have learned every shortcut in the book."[122] One woman, herself single, noticed how well organized her married students and younger colleagues were: "They're the ones that get everything done" by developing efficient support systems.[123] Even though the professional woman who is married has become more common than the single in the 1990s, these women interviewees accepted no new norm integrating career and family. The old dualities lingered powerfully.

## MANITOBA WEATHER

Discrimination was not frontally challenged. It was either denied or accommodated, and sometimes it was even promoted. Around the time of World War II, the few women university teachers tended to share a general social attitude not only towards working women but also towards members of any group that was different from the majority. One woman's story about a student friend illustrates a widespread attitude towards ethnic discrimination. The friend was a "powerhouse of intellect" and as a graduating student wanted advice from a woman faculty member about doing postgraduate work in her discipline. The professor told her that as a woman, moreover as a Jewish woman, she had no hope at all.[124]

"We almost accepted the experience of being excluded, as a woman, as ethnic ... there was not much overt protest."[125] In sexual discrimination, individual women were ready to excuse discriminatory practice on the grounds that the men did not know what they were doing. A single mother was concerned about insurance. When she came, in 1964, women were insured for only one year's salary, while men were insured for two – until she initiated a change: "They don't think about it until it's brought up."[126] With respect to salaries, many women were not surprised to know that theirs were lower, but they rarely took any initiative to improve matters. Concerning promotion, they tended to put the blame for slower promotion on themselves, mainly identifying a smaller research output or, particularly in the professional schools, the lack of a research degree.

Awareness was dawning, however. In 1971, when a woman with a PHD and a research career was appointed to staff, she was chagrined to discover that her name in official documentation was prefaced by "Mrs," while a male colleague without a doctorate was dignified by the title "Professor." This she challenged successfully.[127]

The idea of a chilly climate, of an atmosphere inhospitable to women, was recognizable before 1970. It was almost impossible for each woman not to feel a stranger in a private men's club. Yet, the women did not invariably feel rancour. One graphically and genially described the antics of her colleagues on the rare occasions when she went to the Faculty Club. The men would instantly change the topic of conversation "away from what it usually was, sport, or hockey, and jump up out of their seats – which they did not do for each other. Of course, it's changed now."[128] Inevitably made to feel intruders, most women kept away from the Faculty Club and from informal gatherings of men, even though they knew that much university business was conducted in such informal settings, particularly before unionization. "Networking works in their favour ... Men relax, they have coffee, they tell jokes, they have wives at home so they can come in at eight and read the newspapers."[129]

In Manitoba, the existence of a high proportion of women university teachers in home economics served to reinforce existing notions about women's place in society. Both by pedagogy and precept they reinforced the existing attitudes. Their course content emphasized domestic responsibilities as a woman's primary obligation. Almost to a woman, the home economics faculty women were single or widowed and did not challenge the notion that a normal family had a husband as breadwinner.

A composite picture of women university teachers would carry distortions. Yet certain generalizations can be made about their shared conditions. Most were aware that they were not being treated like the men on faculty, and each found her own way to accommodate the unfairness. Many suffered personal hurt. Only a very few made a fuss. Evidence suggests they calculated that the game was worth the candle. Before 1970 they had no alternative but to accept the university's conditions. Although they were frequently resentful at their subordination, their small numbers and lack of collective awareness did not allow them to contemplate strategies of resistance or reform. Modest in scholarly achievement, concerned not to appear personally ambitious, and, with few exceptions, in agreement with the dominant cultural domestic demands on a woman, they were neither the academic superperformers nor the innovators of the *Unequal Colleagues* thesis. Nor were there signs of the magical enchantment discerned in *Outsiders in the Sacred Grove*. If the university teachers were gratified by the notion of belonging to a "key profession" central to "economic survival and to cultural progress," there were few signs of it.[130]

Material elicited from Manitoba women contributes little to a celebration of academic success measured by traditional criteria. The data display little of the epic quest described by historians who have discerned myths in the lives of female academics. The respondents' testimony puts into question the relevance of attributing conscious career management to women who had little direct influence over their career progress. If there was heroism, it was not in any ambitious attempt to refashion academic discourse; it was in the individual strategies that each woman made for herself in coping with the thoughtless and sometimes deliberate sexism that was built into the system. Particularly difficult were the juggling acts of those women (few for most of the period but increasing in numbers towards the end of the 1960s) who balanced their academic work with motherhood – at a time, moreover, when research performance was becoming a more insistent demand of the job. Here in their homes were superperformance and innovation, hidden from the workplace professional history of university women.

### CHAPTER THREE

# Medicine: "Tough Old Birds"

In mid-nineteenth-century Canada, "the most widespread provider of medical care was the wife and mother of the family."[1] By the turn of the century, Manitoba still contained "many districts in the west that had no medical help whatsoever, and our grandmothers and grandfathers seemed to get along very well." Ida Armstrong, a Winnipeg physician giving a series of radio talks on medical emergencies during World War II, similarly identified the women as the primary health-care givers: "So, Mothers, try to make yourself prepared to look after these emergencies."[2]

In the nineteenth century, some women capitalized on their reputation for healing and sold their services, but groups of formally trained male physicians organized in each province began to make inroads into the informal female structures. Laws bestowing a monopoly on physicians for medical services and confining licensing authority to such groups were passed in Upper and Lower Canada and in the Maritimes. These laws could not be fully enforced, however, because the physicians were not united. "Each medical group had its own approach and offered the medical 'consumer' something different." There were Thomsonians, eclectics and homeopaths, their ideas and training emanating from the United States. Thomsonians used only botanic compounds in their prescriptions; eclectics used nonvegetarian products as well; homeopaths thought that disease was cured by drugs that could produce effects closest to the symptoms of the illness. Training was primarily by apprenticeship. At the same time, private schools and universities began to teach medicine in an academic way through anatomy, physiology, surgery, pharmacy, and chemistry.[3] Mirroring developments that favoured "scientific" medicine in the United States, Canadian graduates of academic training, supplemented by clinical practice, eventually gained the upper hand.[4]

Provincial Colleges of Physicians and Surgeons established their ascendancy as the monopoly organizations established by law to regulate admission into the profession, along with the standards of operation. By the end of the century, "the medical profession was a group on the rise but not one that had arrived." Its position was not yet entirely secure.[5]

In this chapter, I first describe the historical context for medicine in the province. Then, using three time divisions (pre-1941, World War II, and postwar), I consider the size of the group of female physicians and describe the women's training and work experience. I examine the importance of family concerns and then analyse women physicians' views of gender and the profession of medicine. Finally, there are summary comparisons in relation to other places.

The records of the College of Physicians and Surgeons furnish the statistical basis for this study. All lawful practitioners had to register with the college, so its registration receipts provide a complete list of women physicians. In addition, the college kept index cards on all who registered.[6] These data are supplemented from the records of the Faculty of Medicine and the Alumni Association of the University of Manitoba, which was Manitoba's single major training institution for doctors.[7] Along with census reports, these sets of lists provide an outline of the number and proportion of women physicians and show where the doctors trained. There is further information to be drawn from these lists, but it is not comprehensively available: not all marriages, for example, were recorded, nor were all deaths noted. In addition, a very small number of women left records, published or unpublished, on aspects of their careers.[8] The major qualitative primary source is a survey of thirty-nine women doctors, ranging in time from eight who qualified in the 1930s to ten who graduated in the 1960s.[9] This combination of statistical and descriptive sources bearing on the education, demography, work, and mentality of medical women permits a limited comparison with women doctors and other professionals in other places.

PIONEERS

The College of Physicians and Surgeons of Manitoba was incorporated by the legislature of Manitoba on 28 February 1877. The first women to whom it accorded licences to practise medicine were trained elsewhere. Lillian Yeomans, licensed by the College of Physicians and Surgeons in 1882 and her mother Amelia, licensed in 1885, were both graduates of the University of Michigan who came west to Winnipeg in 1882. The two Yeomans doctors specialized in "Midwifery and Diseases of Women and Children." From the beginning, Amelia was interested in more than medicine. She concerned herself with improving social and economic conditions for immigrants and for women. Her interest in reform and a social gospel led her to the Woman's Christian Temperance Union. She travelled about the province lecturing against drink and served as the organization's president. She was also an organizer of a mock parliament in 1893, in which she took the part of the premier and argued that women should have the vote. After the defeat in 1894 of a women's franchise measure in the Manitoba legislature, she founded the Equal Franchise Association, whose objectives were as much educational as activist. Amelia left the province and moved to Calgary in 1905 and Lillian joined her mother in 1906.[10]

While the Yeomans were practising in Winnipeg, a third woman, Charlotte Whitehead Ross, an 1875 graduate of the Woman's Medical College of Pennsylvania in Philadelphia, was working as a physician in rural Manitoba for some years without a licence. In 1881 she had left the province of Quebec to join her husband David at Whitemouth, a wooded community 110 kilometers east of Winnipeg, where he was establishing a timber mill whose products could supply the new railway construction of western Canada. The night after Charlotte Ross arrived, she treated her first patient.[11] She held no licence from the College of Physicians and Surgeons. There was doubt about whether Whitemouth was within the boundary of Ontario or Manitoba, and Ross wanted to be sure of her own credentials. In an attempt to secure her position, in 1887 she applied to the Manitoba legislature for registration as a practising physician. She instructed a Winnipeg legal firm to file an application for a private act that would authorize her "to practise Medicine, Surgery and Midwifery in the province of Manitoba."[12] In the event, the bill did not proceed into law, and no licence was issued by the College of Physicians and Surgeons, but Ross nevertheless continued to practise until 1912 when, after her husband's death, she moved to Winnipeg.[13]

The College of Physicians and Surgeons took no initiative to clarify Ross's authority even though, like all medical licensing bodies, it normally closely guarded its right to license physicians, according to ever-tighter criteria, and to prosecute unauthorized practitioners. The college's jealousy of its privilege was demonstrated in the training of Elizabeth Scott Matheson, who eventually registered in 1904. As a young woman, Elizabeth Scott trained to be a schoolteacher but left the province in 1887 to attend the new Women's Medical College in Kingston, founded in 1883. After one year she went to India to work on a Presbyterian mission.[14] She returned to Canada to recover from malaria and married an old suitor, John Matheson, who in 1892 was appointed Anglican missionary and schoolmaster on an Indian reserve at Onion Lake, which was then in the North-West Territories. He encouraged his wife to continue with medical training, and in 1895 Elizabeth enrolled for her second year of medicine at the Manitoba Medical College.

The Manitoba Medical College was established in 1883 to offer instruction leading to a degree at the University of Manitoba. This represented a victory for local practitioners over a newly arrived Toronto physician, who had plans to found a private school issuing its own degrees.[15] Although the college was "in theory, co-educational from the beginning," no woman was in fact admitted until 1890.[16] Its first woman student was Harriet Foxton, who had already studied two years at the Woman's Medical College, Toronto, which was established in 1883 (and in 1895 became the Ontario Medical College for Women).[17] Foxton graduated from Manitoba in 1892. She did not work in the province, for she married a fellow doctor and with her husband practised first in Detroit and then in Billings, Montana.

Elizabeth Scott Matheson therefore was not the first woman student at the Manitoba Medical College. Before she completed the course, a friend paid for her to study in the single-sex environment of the Ontario Medical College for Women, and Matheson graduated in 1898. In order to be licensed in the North-West Territories, a doctor normally had to take an examination set by the provincial College of Physicians and Surgeons. Because she did not want to subject herself to "trick questions" supposedly asked in an oral examination, Matheson applied for registration without the exam. She was refused. Despite her lack of formal registration, on her return to Onion Lake she worked as a physician and was even appointed government doctor by the Department of Indian Affairs. In 1903 her practice experienced competition from licensed physicians in new settlements nearby. To recoup her position, having again failed to gain registration without sitting an exam, she enrolled for the final year at Manitoba Medical College and graduated in 1904, whereupon she was immediately registered by the Manitoba College of Physicians and Surgeons. Her famous missionary husband signed a cheque for her North-West Territories registration fee, and Elizabeth was eventually accorded full official recognition as a physician at Onion Lake, where she continued to work until her husband's death in 1916. Moving to Winnipeg, she then took up another career, 1918–43, as a medical inspector in the city schools. There she joined the first doctor appointed as a medical inspector, Mary Crawford, who was registered in Winnipeg in 1903.

Crawford graduated in 1900 from Toronto and, like Amelia Yeomans, was very involved in campaigns for social reform and women's franchise in Winnipeg. Founder member of the University Women's Club in 1909, Crawford also helped found, and presided over, the Political Equality League of 1912, whose highly efficient activism brought women's suffrage to Manitoba first of all Canadian provinces in January 1916.[18]

Doctors Yeomans and Ross trained in the United States; Foxton and Matheson trained both in Ontario and Manitoba; Crawford and another early doctor, Ellen Douglass, trained in Toronto. Ellen Douglass, registered by the College of Physicians and Surgeons in 1909, was a native of New Brunswick and a graduate in medicine of the Ontario College for Women in Toronto. In Winnipeg she maintained her own practice and worked also as medical examiner for the Manitoba Government Telephone Company until World War I, when she organized a Women's Volunteer Reserve and served overseas as a medical officer. Like Yeomans and Crawford, she worked for women's rights and later was active in women's organizations and in municipal politics.[19]

That these women had become doctors at all showed their ability, determination, and sense of adventure. In addition, many were sustained by a religious faith, which some did not hesitate to declare publicly. Amelia Yeomans in her WCTU lectures pointed out, "Christ, when on earth, never gave any example to the men to keep the women silent for many women followed and helped Christ while on earth."[20] Elizabeth Scott Matheson served as a missionary in India before working as her husband's missionary partner in northern Canada. Ellen Douglass showed both her own faith and her confidence in Charlotte Ross's when she spoke on Ross's life in a radio talk: "She carried religion into her daily life ... in Whitemouth she kept a Church and Sunday School going ... Their home life was ideal and the Christian atmosphere in it spread to the surrounding district so that crime became unknown."[21] Yeomans, Crawford, and Douglass worked for women's rights. These pioneer physicians were prominent as community leaders, but two of the first women doctors were more aloof. As noted above, Harriet Foxton married and left the province before working as a doctor; and the second woman to graduate from the Manitoba Medical College, Lavinia McPhee (in 1898), left no registration with the College of Physicians and Surgeons and no further record behind her other than the fact of her marriage.

Besides the few who followed the professional rules of training and admission, there were in Manitoba an indeterminate number of women practising medicine beyond the jurisdiction of the Manitoba College of Physicians and Surgeons.[22] Even well-established and prosperous villages and farms were often isolated in rural Manitoba and

had no resident doctor, and the inhabitants often had recourse to un-
licensed practitioners, who included women. A 1922 rural survey of its
members by the United Farm Women of Manitoba (an organization
representing farm families with "greater capital assets than the average
farm family") revealed that many were far from professional medical
help. One-third of the survey's 364 respondents lived 15 kilometres or
more from a doctor, and two-thirds of them lived 15 kilometres or
more from a hospital.[23] In such circumstances, midwives especially
were in demand. In new immigrant farming communities, newly settled families were usually poor and were rarely fluent in English. In
Eastern Europe there was a flourishing tradition of sick people consult-
ing women who had served informal apprenticeships as midwives and
healers, and in the new Canadian communities this practice continued.[24] Because such women were operating outside the monopoly of
the College of Physicians and Surgeons, they and their customers
found it advantageous to be discreet, and there is no way of assessing
their overall numbers and influence. But an occasional local history
refers to their presence. Anna Kaczmarski, for instance, was "Gretna's
first midwife" in the 1890s.[25]

Within the confines of their community, healers enjoyed considerable recognition:

When travelling women "doctors" visited Mennonite communities men made
special note of their presence. In February 1884 a certain Frau Baerg arrived
in the East reserve and men dutifully spread the word that patients could see
her in the village of Steinbach. Later in 1884, it was a Frau Neufeld who arrived
to practice medicine and once again men put out the notice that she could be
seen for consultation at her rented room in Steinbach. When Neufeld visited
the settlement again in 1892 and attended church in the village of Bluenort,
the village mayor, Abram M. Friesen, noted the event in his diary. When another woman doctor, Frau Thiessen, visited Steinbach in 1888 a local farmer
noted how she set up shop "here at A. Reimers' where she lectured and doc-
tored for three days." He also noted how men and women from the surrounding villages came for "medical remedies." The observer himself saw the doctor
and jotted down her recipe in the family diary.[26]

Such women were the bane of local formally trained physicians, who
wanted the field clear for themselves. From its early days, the Council
of the College of Physicians and Surgeons was regularly exhorted to
prosecute all illegal practitioners.[27] The college characterized unli-
censed healers as quacks and charlatans. In 1893 and 1903, for instance, the college used its authority to harass women "practising
massage" and people (three men and two women, in this instance)

"practising electricity without a licence," as well as women in rural areas.[28] Fines and prosecutions did not always succeed in stopping the women, however. When "the beloved Mrs Thiessen who is known as a doctor throughout southern Manitoba" was "fined by several English doctors," her community continued to patronize her. "It is very strange that a woman who has tirelessly worked to dispense her own wisdom should be persecuted," reported a Mennonite newspaper.[29] Into the Depression years, the college was still prosecuting women healers in Mennonite areas.[30]

### NUMBERS

In Manitoba, as elsewhere in twentieth-century Western society, the academically trained professionals were soon able to drive out competitors. Training was by law under the control of the Manitoba Medical College, which had been incorporated by the legislature in 1883. Before World War I, only four women graduated from the Manitoba Medical College, and two of them had received part of their instruction in Ontario. During the interwar period, there was a small but steady stream of female students and no year passed without at least two women graduates (see table 8, appendix 1).

Of the eighty-six women who graduated in medicine from the University of Manitoba between 1892 and 1941, altogether fifty-two were licensed to practise in Manitoba by the College of Physicians and Surgeons.[31] Of these, only about one-third (sixteen) proceeded immediately to registration on completion of their degree.[32] The rest waited. They had other items on their agenda besides working for a living as physicians. Twelve waited only one year;[33] another twelve waited two or three years.[34] Possibly, marriage and pregnancy provided a common if not universal reason for these relatively short intervals, and a few took further training before going into the workforce. The remaining twelve took longer before eventually committing themselves to medical practice in Manitoba.

Before 1941, fifteen women physicians who qualified elsewhere migrated to the province. These immigrants replaced only half the Manitoba-trained women physicians who left the province. Of the immigrants, six were trained in other parts of Canada,[35] five in the United States,[36] and four in the United Kingdom or Ireland.[37]

Thirty-four, or 40 per cent of the pre-1941 University of Manitoba female graduates did not register with the provincial College of Physicians and Surgeons.[38] They clearly had no intention of working as physicians in Manitoba. Exactly how many worked elsewhere is not known. Before 1941, twelve of them had moved to the United States.[39]

All save one of them were married.[40] Seventeen had moved to other parts of Canada,[41] and eleven of these were known to be married.[42] Of those who moved away from Winnipeg to other parts of North America, therefore, three-quarters at least were married.[43] Marriage was probably the main reason for their living away from Manitoba, but it did not always lead to retirement. At least five of the American residents worked professionally.[44]

Four of the Manitoba graduates used their medical training to work overseas as missionaries, two in China and two in India. There, they were among groups of women serving as "influential agents of British cultural and political imperialism," fortified by feminist sympathies as well as Christian faith.[45] Away from the control of the Canadian professional organizations, their mission was mainly to women; and in India, particularly, their colleagues were frequently women too.

Isobel McTavish, who in 1915 became the sixth woman to graduate, went on to be a medical missionary. She worked in Honan, northern China, as the only woman doctor in the mission hospital. Her work included surgery, obstetrics, and a clinic for women and children, and she trained nurses in the school attached to the hospital.[46] The other woman who went to China was Gladys Story, who graduated with the gold medal in surgery in 1923, the same year she married Eddison Cunningham, who was already a physician-missionary. Gladys practised in the large city of Chengtu, and she was also a professor of obstetrics and gynaecology in the West China Union University, an institution of the United Church of Canada.[47]

India attracted Jessie Findlay, who in 1920 went out to the Medical College for Women in Vellore, southern India, which had been established in 1917 by the American Dr Ida Scudder.[48] Findlay "had always wanted to go in for missionary work." Like Amelia Yeomans, Mary Crawford, and Ellen Douglass, she concerned herself with women's politics as well as healing. She welcomed the prospect of independence for India and an increasing independence of women. "The women of India had come a long way in the past quarter of a century," she said in 1945. "The women had fought in many ways against their old-time bondage. More and more their collective voice was being heard in the land. They had fought well against child marriage, against the law that when a husband died, the estate was willed to the next male member of the family and the wife ignored, and many more wars on behalf of their emancipation."[49]

Findlay was followed to the Vellore College by Dorothy Jefferson, a 1933 graduate, who founded its physiology department. Jefferson's career illustrates the faith and feminism of many other medical missionaries. These overseas missionary doctors have been described as cultural imperialists, but Jefferson was no simplistic flag waver.[50] On her retirement in 1957, she said that her lifetime mission had been in "helping the Indian people to help themselves" and that she had originally entered the Faculty of Medicine with that end in view. Jefferson noted that many of her working colleagues as department heads at the Vellore college were women. She noted with approval that "women of India [had] been carried forward to a position of ready equality on the crest of the wave of nationalist independence," and added, "Economic necessity has driven many married women to work and has aided in their emancipation."[51]

At least two other prewar Manitobans acknowledged the missionaries' example as their own inspiration to medicine. "Reports from missionary doctors" impelled one to apply in 1932.[52] Another, who applied in 1929, first planned to be a lawyer, "but an uncle steered her away from that ambition on the grounds that lawyers didn't make enough money and that India needed women doctors. She studied medicine at Manitoba Medical College, intending to specialise in gynecology, then to work in India."[53]

In one respect, the prewar women doctors who stayed to work in Manitoba resembled the missionaries: they tended to work more in institutional employment than in private practice. No fewer than six became anaesthetists in hospitals.[54] Work for a government department was undertaken by two, in addition to Crawford and Matheson, the school medical inspectors.[55] One woman was employed by a hospital as a pathologist;[56] one worked at a tuberculosis sanatorium;[57] one was active in child and community health;[58] and one became the principal of a girls' school.[59] Whereas most men went into private practice, there seems to have been a far smaller proportion of women who did so. Three of the few women who went into private practice in Manitoba did so as partners of their husbands.[60] By 1940, most (45 of 74) of the 1919–40 graduates had left the province. In the 1930s, during the Depression, it was not easy for anyone who was starting a career, and the type of experience that Elinor Black described may well have encouraged her classmates to seek a life elsewhere:

We were in college during the boom years. Work during the holidays was not too hard to find. The men took interesting jobs like sleeping-car conductors or waiters on the trains, stewards on the Great Lakes ships, salesmen of aluminum cooking ware, Fuller brushes, encyclopedias or magazines, foremen of road or railway gangs; they joined survey parties, became Government cream tasters, worked on farms, got office jobs, or, what was considered a really lucrative job, joined a Chatauqua troupe – some of the women did this too.

I had taken a course in stenography, so worked in a bank or office. One year

I got a job with the University in the Botany Department: from 9 a.m. to 5 p.m. I picked the germ out of wheat grains with a very fine probe and got paid 18 cents an hour. Probably this introduction to research is why I never got seriously interested in it. Then came internship when one did not have to worry about board or room or laundry because they were provided by the hospital, but there was no salary.

The depression was seven months old when our class graduated and was ready to make a living in an unhappy world. I was more fortunate than most of my classmates because an aunt in England sent me money to go to London for a year. I returned from those interesting months, full of enthusiasm, to start a general practice, which seemed the natural thing to do – one rented an office, furnished it from second-hand shops and any useful objects that were redundant to friends, and patients came. They did, but with alarming slowness while one watched one's cash reserves, never very ample, erode away. I realized then what many of my classmates had been experiencing for a year.

Each new patient who came into the office was a hopeful source of more to follow. It was obvious that if she were treated satisfactorily she would send her friends. Since the patients had no excess money either, one was careful not to put them to any extra expense. One waited, optimistically, sometimes for many, many months for bills to be paid. There was one sure source of money and that was from the patients on City Relief, which most of mine were. There were no baby bonuses nor unemployment insurance in those days: people who lost their jobs were just plain poor and went on City Relief. Some doctors were on Relief too. The City paid us 50 cents for an office visit, one dollar for a house-call, 10 dollars for a maternity case including pre- and post-natal care, but if a patient had an incomplete abortion which required a curettage 15 dollars was paid.

There was a great feeling of camaraderie because we were all in it together. One came to know one's patients and their families very well ... Our younger colleagues say the years of hardship gave us "a depression psychology" which made us over-cautious and unprogressive.[61]

Another student of Depression years was more aware of discrimination against women. Mindel Sheps (née Cherniack) was in first-year medicine, one of seven female students, in 1935. "The dean took me aside and advised me to leave medicine. 'You'll be much happier in Arts,' he told me. 'Besides, there aren't many openings for female interns.'" Thirty-six years later, when the University of Manitoba awarded her an honorary Doctor of Science degree for her distinguished career in medicine, public health, and academic work, Sheps publicly rejoiced that she had refused to follow the dean's advice.[62] Not only did she persist in her career choice, but as a Winnipeg school trustee in 1943–44 she was the first to challenge discriminatory practices against women teachers.[63]

## WORLD WAR II

The Depression ended and war came. War imposed particular conditions on the training of doctors, and the experience of women medical students was different from those of men:

When we were in the end of our second year [1942] they took us into the army. We went in as privates – this was to ensure that we would continue on in the army when we graduated. I had to join the Canadian Women's Army Corps, whereas the men went into the men's army. We all wore army uniforms for the next couple of years while we were at university. We had the odd parade just to make sure that we knew we were soldiers. The thing that really has always frustrated me is, the men were paid close to $90 a month to be a soldier and we were paid $33, which was the acceptable differential between male and female salaries at that time. When we graduated with our degree we were automatically Lieutenant, all in the Royal Canadian Army Medical Corps, and at that time we were paid equal pay. After we'd taken a basic training thing down at Camp Borden, we were then elevated to Captain and paid appropriately.[64]

This experience highlighted the armed forces' policy of paying the gender rather than the job. The Canadian Women's Army Corps (CWAC) "remained a segregated Corps, its members retaining a status different from that of the male members of the Canadian Army." Servicewomen throughout the CWAC complained that their pay was not equal to that of the men they relieved, but to little avail.[65] Women medical students in training were paid as women soldiers, receiving less than the men; but as qualified female physicians, they were paid on the same scale as male physicians. That the female physicians received equal pay was a considerable victory for the Federation of Medical Women of Canada, an organization that lobbied the generals in Ottawa.[66]

There was a second development in Manitoba during the war years which had the potential of transforming women's opportunities in medicine. This was the modification in 1944 of entrance criteria for the Faculty of Medicine. The prime focus of public attention at the time was the matter of ethnicity. Gender was treated almost as a diversion from the main point. Like the matter of equal pay in the armed forces, the fracas over medical admissions illustrated the contemporary attitudes towards women in public life.

In 1932, on the appointment of a new dean of medicine, Dr A.T. Mathers, the university reduced the size of the first-year medical class from sixty-four to fifty-four. Over the next twelve years, the proportion of Jewish students in the class fell from 28 to 9 per cent. This was the consequence not of fewer Jewish students applying but of a deliberate racial quota.[67] Applicants were sorted into four lists. One was for Jews, a second was for women, and a third for Ukrainians, Poles, Mennonites, and others. The fourth, the "preferred" list, was for Anglo-Saxon, French-Canadian, and Icelandic male students. During the selection procedure, students on each list were ranked according to marks.[68] A quota, usually of about twelve or thirteen, was established for the first three lists, and the remaining students were selected from the "preferred" list, which meant that quota list applicants with higher marks than "preferred" list applicants were excluded.[69]

This admissions process, developed in a university committee, was painstakingly reconstructed over the winter of 1943–44 by the Avukah Zionist Society, an organization of Jewish doctors and students. Most of the research was done by Shlomo Mitchell, a lecturer in the university's mathematics department. Word of the committee's findings leaked out, and in February 1944 a member of the legislative assembly rose in the legislature to say that he knew of discrimination against minority-group applicants to the Faculty of Medicine. The minister of education denied the charge, and the MLA was told to provide evidence within three days or withdraw his allegations. The Avukah Zionist Society then retained a lawyer, Hyman Sokolov, to present its findings. The matter was referred to a select committee of the legislature, whose hearings were reported in the press.[70]

University spokesmen denied racial discrimination and insisted that their admission criteria rightly "went far beyond mere scholastic requirements" and included "intelligence, scholarship, character and physical and ethical fitness." Dean Mathers referred also to interning opportunities for graduates: "It would be folly to turn out more students than can be accommodated in our hospitals. A deterring factor in admitting female students is that some of our hospitals refuse to accept women internes, and similar restrictions operate with regard to certain racial and technical groups."[71] This policy was generally well understood. Long before the Avukah Zionist Society made the fuss, and despite the unwritten nature of the quotas, the women were well aware of their existence: "We knew."[72] A 1944 graduate related in a matter-of-fact way that the faculty "took sixty men. Thirty girls applied and they took four: one Jewish, one French Canadian, and two Anglo-Saxons. This was widely known."[73]

The College of Physicians and Surgeons sent a committee before the university's Board of Governors in May 1944. The college insisted "that the ethnic origin should not come into the selection of medical students" but made no comment on gender as a criterion.[74] Its brief reaffirmed "that at least a full interne year in a properly equipped and properly staffed hospital is essential to the training of a man or woman prior to entering Medicine" – a comment that silently endorsed the dean's acceptance of discrimination against women.[75]

The university agreed to insert a clause saying, "Selection shall be made without regard to the racial origin or religion of the applicant," in the publicly declared criteria for admission.[76] For the academic year 1944–45, the previous practice was modified enough to permit the lawyer Hyman Sokolov to state, "For the first time in many years, merit has been recognised as the basis of selection of students to the Manitoba Medical College." However, he condemned the university for continuing to use what he called "humbug qualifications of personality and background." He predicted that this would result in "future evasion of democratic practice."[77]

No criticism of gender bias was made publicly. An idealistic interpretation of the hearings was that, as a result, quotas would no longer apply. One woman who entered the Faculty of Medicine in 1944 was still a science student in the spring of that year, studying in the Broadway buildings just a block away from the legislature:

We skipped classes to go over to those hearings. Women, of course, had no representative speaking for them. Now I thought that the law changed that spring and that we were the first class to come in with marks only as the criterion. I have subsequently read that it was the next year, but I think the Medical School saw the writing on the wall because certainly ten women came into Medical School in the fall of '44. I don't think they'd had that many before. Before, usually, there were about four women ... At the time, I wasn't consciously aware that [the Avukah Zionist Society was] fighting women's battles too. Looking back, we weren't organized, I don't think we thought of organizing.[78]

By the late 1960s, women medical students had the impression that there was again a cap to the number of women permitted to enter medicine. "Ten percent of the class was female during the sixties, until 1973," declared a woman who graduated in 1970.[79] "I have always understood that there were quotas," said a graduate of 1969.[80] "As female medical students, we thought there was an informal quota system – 10 per cent female, 10 per cent Jewish, and 10 per cent out of province," said another 1969 graduate.[81] A 1949 graduate understood that the 1944–45 reform was not so much an abolition of the gender quota as an enlargement to 10 per cent from the previous 4 per cent. She bluntly stated that "college enrolment quotas were the reason why there were so few women doctors before 1970."[82]

Table 8 showed that the average number of women graduating annually from medicine in the 1920s was 3.4 per year; in the 1930s, 4.0, and in the 1940s, 5.7. In the 1950s it was down to an annual average of 3.9, and in the 1960s it had increased to 4.8 per year, which was still less than in the 1940s. These statistics do not show the attrition rates of students accepted into medicine in first year who did not complete the course. Without an analysis of the relationship between the applicant pool and the number accepted into the faculty, it is difficult to determine whether a gender quota, tacit or not, lingered on after World War II.[83] It is true that there were more women accepted into and graduating from medicine in the late 1940s, but this increase was temporary. There was a lower proportion of female students in the 1950s than there had been in the 1930s. Perhaps there continued to be a gender quota; perhaps there were socially based explanations besides or in addition to a quota. It is possible that in the 1950s a lower proportion of applicants were women. The women physicians themselves suggested that "fewer women wanted careers outside the home"[84] and that "family considerations may curtail a woman's professional work to some degree."[85]

## WOMEN DOCTORS 1941–1971

After World War II, in contrast to the number and proportion of women studying medicine at the University of Manitoba, those actually working as doctors increased (see table 9, appendix 1). The proportion of Manitoba-trained medical graduates who did not proceed to register with the College of Physicians and Surgeons was slightly lower than in the pre-1941 period. Of the 144 women who graduated MD from the University of Manitoba, 1942–71, just 95 registered with the College.[86] This was 66 per cent of the post-1941 graduates, compared with 58 per cent of the pre-1941 number.

Two-thirds (sixty-five) of those registering did so within three years, during which time many did work-related training. The average wait between graduation and registration was one year. The thirty graduates who took longer before acquiring a licence to practise waited on average six years. The reasons for this, among the doctors involved in the survey, tended mainly to be family-related; they thought it was important to give priority at that time to servicing a husband's career, or to small children who demanded attention. A few of the women had health problems of their own which delayed entry into the labour force. A few worked as teachers in the Faculty of Medicine and did not take part in clinical practice. There is little information on the forty-nine women who did not register with the College of Physicians and Surgeons. Among the doctors surveyed, there was one graduate who did not register, but she worked a lifelong career elsewhere in Canada.[87] The balance between those who worked outside the province and those who did not work professionally at all is unknown.

After 1941, there were more externally trained women working as physicians in Manitoba than women trained at the University of Manitoba. Between 1942 and 1971, 118 women doctors who had trained outside Manitoba registered with the College of Physicians and Surgeons. This was more than twice the number of the University of Manitoba graduates who did not register, and it was actually more than the number of Manitoba-qualified doctors who remained to work in the province. Whereas externally trained female physicians had accounted for only one-quarter of the pre-1941 qualified women, they represented a majority, or 55 per cent, of the post-1941 number.

Most of them came in the 1960s: almost two-thirds (seventy) registered during the decade before 1971. During the 1940s there were twelve immigrant registrants, of whom eight were trained elsewhere in Canada[88] and two in the United Kingdom.[89] This pattern changed considerably in the next two decades. In the decade before 1961, only one of the thirty-six immigrants were trained in Canada.[90] Twenty-one trained in the United Kingdom,[91] and a further three in Ireland.[92] Of the remaining eleven, five trained in Eastern Europe and left during or after the war.[93] During the 1960s, when the number of immigrants (seventy) exceeded the number of Manitoba graduates (forty-eight), their countries of origin were more diverse. The largest group, eighteen, trained in the United Kingdom,[94] and a further nine in Ireland.[95] The next largest group, thirteen, trained in the Phillipines,[96] and a further three trained in the Far East.[97] Seven trained in the United States,[98] four in Eastern Europe,[99] one in Western Europe,[100] and one in Egypt.[101]

Four of the post-1941 respondents were immigrants to Manitoba. They thought that both the number and the status of women physicians in Manitoba were lower than in their native countries. "Teachers and parents discouraged women in Canada but not in Poland," said one.[102] "I think that G.B. was way in advance of North America," said another.[103] "In Northern Ireland it was not the case" that there were few women doctors, said a third,[104] while the fourth observed, "There were few women in medicine when I first started. Having come from Europe, I found this rather surprising and unusual."[105]

POSTWAR TRAINING

Those who trained in Manitoba remembered their years in the medical faculty mainly with affection. "Our class was a super class" was a typical comment,[106] as was: "I loved the camaraderie."[107] In comparison with the atmosphere in which nurses trained, medicine seemed much more free.[108] While many women noted only happy memories, some – both in the 1940s and then twenty years later – were more critical and considered that the men had received more pedagogical attention than the women. "A female had to be more outgoing to get attention," said a 1969 graduate.[109] Some had memories of a curriculum and behaviour they considered condescending and hostile, even vicious.[110] In the 1940s "there were certain things we didn't do: male urology," for example.[111] "The dean of medicine, Dr Mathers, thought it was a waste of college time, space, and money to educate women in medicine," noted one woman,[112] and another who trained under this dean pointed out that in the profession, to justify your presence in the faculty, "you were supposed to have a burning ambition, especially if you were a woman."[113] Another said that women were given to understand that they were "taking the place of a good man."[114]

Two women medical students of 1961 recorded their "views and grievances" in the article, "Medicine: The Female Point of View," for the university's medical journal. They cited a "maternal desire or instinct to comfort the sick" as a woman's natural qualification for medicine, and with some humour claimed to resent society's inability to recognize women as the "rightful inheritors of the profession." They then described the treatment meted out to the female student:

During the first days at the school, the poor medical girl is stared at by all the fellows in the class, who are obviously wondering what kind of monster she is. She doesn't really look like a freak but she must have something wrong with her head to want to crash this "man's profession." Now, and for the next four years, many boys feel it is their duty to keep the girls aware of their position as intruders ... We were only at school one week when the class decided to have a class party. We ... were mildly discouraged when most of the class referred to it as a stag. None of us had even been to a stag in her life, so it took a bit of courage to show up ...

We always try to appear at lectures and clinics well-dressed, combed, and with noses powdered. This effort is rarely noticed by the lecturers, who frequently refer to the whole class, not as "Ladies and Gentlemen" but as "Hey, fellas" ... When it comes to decide where our futures lie in Medicine, we become quite confused. This is because of all the advice we get. The majority will tell us that the best fields for women are in Paediatrics or in Obstetrics and Gynaecology. Then we learn that one clinician firmly believes that there is no place for women in Obstetrics ... We really don't expect you brain-washed fellows to agree when we claim that women alone are suited for Medicine.[115]

Being treated differently could work advantageously: "Dr Elinor Black was one of our Obstetrics and Gynaecology professors. We admired her. She gave the women medical students a private lecture on birth control methods. This was given in the evening in our common room. It was illegal to give such a lecture at that time [late 1940s]."[116] Another advantage was that some women interns were not required to work all night: "They thought we weren't strong enough."[117]

One bothersome condition concerning interning lasted into the late 1950s, when it shocked a newly arrived British-trained doctor.[118] The hospitals' reluctance to take women as interns had been used in 1944 as part of the university's rationale of the gender quota. Once they were in the hospital setting, women interns had a particular problem, which Elinor Black in the late 1920s also had suffered:

I was in the Internes' Quarters only three or four times. It was just east of the pathology Lab., but was for men only so the women internes had to find a room nearby. There were three of us during my internship and we were allowed to rent a suite on the top floor of the Elenora Apartments. The hospital paid our rent, gave us free meals in the Nurses' Residence, supplied us with uniforms and free laundry, but paid no salary. Furniture was not provided for the apartment but friends and family came to our aid.[119]

In the early 1940s, two women interns did not want to put up with such conditions: "We were not allowed to have a room in the interns' quarters. We were given $12.50 each to find a room within three minutes' walking distance [of the hospital], so we put our money together and our families each gave us more. We got a $35-a-month apartment in a block ... We had to eat with the nurses – we weren't allowed to eat with the boys." Unlike interns, the nurses had regular schedules; consequently meals were not always available for the women doctors: "We went to the head of the hospital to see if there might be a couple of rooms in the hospital – the district was very tough. He said, 'No. Quite frankly, if I had my way, there'd be no women interns.' So we just smiled."[120] Another woman pointed out that not only did women interns "miss out" on the comradeship, but at that time they also had no one to look after their laundry.[121]

By the mid-1950s, the official attitude towards women training in the profession was softening. In 1956 the *Winnipeg Free Press* carried a headline: "Dean of Medicine Spikes Taboos on Women Doctors." "We can forever dispel the idea that women in medicine are useless," announced Dr Lennox Bell. "When you analyse objections they all fall to pieces." He "noted with pleasure the overcoming of prejudices of other women against patronising a woman doctor – one of the greatest problems in the past," and concluded: "There is a wonderful field for women in social medicine as well as pediatrics and obstetrics."[122] Yet at the end of the period under study, a woman medical student referred to the "faint suspicion that a woman doctor is doing something somehow unnatural." With perspicuity, she wrote, "A medical woman's career has two facets, the professional and the personal, and it is the latter aspect of her life that often makes her a stranger both to her profession and to the other members of her sex."[123]

## WORK, 1941–1971

Newly qualified physicians of the postwar period, like prewar women physicians, frequently found work with institutions. Public health – in the form of municipally supported well-baby clinics, the medical inspection of schools, and city clinics in poor neighbourhoods – was a more prominent aspect of medicine in the days before medicare (that is, before the late 1960s) and employed more women.[124] Women physicians also sought salaried work with hospitals, mainly as anaesthetists and pathologists,[125] and with school boards (as child psychiatrists, for example).[126] This type of work, and work with provincial governments and federal agencies, was attractive for obvious reasons: all these forms of salaried employment carried regular office hours, minimal "on-call" responsibilities, and reasonable pay.

Men physicians were not as likely as women to find this work appealing. Women were not indifferent to the higher income prospects of private practice; but at the same time, money alone would not carry quite as much importance for married women whose husbands were employed. The regular hours and reduced likelihood of weekend and night work were more appealing than additional income to mothers, who expected to shoulder the responsibilities of domestic and parental work; whereas men, in normal situations, could assume that their spouses would relieve them of housekeeping and paternal concerns. There was a third economic reason. A salary from a government department or a hospital obviated the need to seek out patients, and many women doctors sensed a reluctance in the public to go to a woman doctor. The 1970 medical student recorded some ambivalence when she wrote, "The public has accepted ('as long as my son doesn't marry one') the women doctors."[127]

One doctor said, "The male population had a great fear of female doctors"; but few respondents sensed that their patients were prejudiced against women doctors.[128] A wartime graduate pointed out that a benefit of specializing in paediatrics was that a doctor did not have to cope with the problem of men patients not wanting to see a woman physician. But others failed to draw attention to this topic.[129] This does not necessarily mean that the barrier did not exist. Other explanations for this silence are possible. Perhaps respondents took the assumption of male reluctance for granted. Perhaps the perceived public reluctance evaporated over time. Those who were in private practice had clearly surmounted any barrier satisfactorily enough for their own business. A women in a practice with a partner – often her own husband – tended to specialize in the paediatric and gynaecological work while the male doctor dealt with most of the men.[130] This neatly accommodated any prejudice that might persist.

### FAMILY

Family considerations with respect to the type, location, and hours of employment were important among the thirty-nine respondents in the survey. Of this group, one-third were single, and most of these single women had family responsibilities. Four of them had adopted children or were responsible for children.[131] Several cared for older dependants. In five instances, one or both parents lived with the doctor, who was responsible for their emotional and material care.[132] Only four of the single women said they had no dependants.[133]

All save one[134] of the married physicians surveyed had children, and they had plenty: an average of 3.9 children each. Yet only one of the respondents found the dual role of mother and professional to be too much to cope with, and she retired from professional work when her second child was born. She also had a sick father and a sick husband to care for, and she was unable to find a housekeeper.[135] Most (seventeen) of the others continued to work through their children's infancy, but part-time. Part-time work while the children were small was the standard behaviour. The single women with children worked full-time; and two of the married doctors, each identifying herself as the primary breadwinner, worked full-time.[136] Three of the married doctors who were in a practice, either solo[137] or with a husband[138] worked "flexible" hours in the practice when their children were small. In every case, the doctor resumed full-time work when the children were considered not to need so much of their mother's time.

The women made it very clear that their families came first in their priorities. Their maternal sympathy was proclaimed in the almost universal move to motherhood (even among the single women), in the size of their families, and in their expressed ideology. There appeared to be no complaints at the busy combination of work and family. Positive repercussions could be seen: "You learn how to organize your time."[139] Family considerations gave a woman doctor "a broader understanding of any problems faced by the non-professional women."[140] Only a few made comments critical of this dual commitment. One of them explained, "It is very hard to be a professional career woman and a good mother and homemaker."[141] Another stated, "I would not have attempted" hospital employment "if married ... This would be a very difficult and stressful combination if one wished to enjoy a reasonable life. Neither occupation can be confined within the hours appointed to it."[142] A woman doctor is "two people: a professional person and a person who reproduces."[143] This truism and the social consequences were accepted and accommodated by the large majority.

One or two of the women doctors sternly noted that a professional is a professional, and they resisted the implication that female professionals require separate consideration.[144] For instance: "Flexible hours are a real difficulty. You cannot abandon a very sick patient halfway through!"[145] Most respondents agreed that women doctors had different needs, as one said, "mostly because of family considerations."[146] Several thought that "women should make the adjustments" themselves, personally, rather than expecting employers or governments to provide services.[147] "I have simply accepted the fact that we have to juggle many more responsibilities than most of our male peers," said another.[148] One doctor agreed that a professional should make her own "arrangements" but thought that some institutions could lobby for more tax benefits for a doctor's day-care or houskeeper expenses. Beyond that, "we don't need special favours, condescension."[149]

One physician, far from considering difference to be a liability, saw it (though she did not define what "it" was) as an advantage: "Medical women – vive la différence!" She was careful to assert that non-anatomical characteristics "tend not to be so much masculine or feminine, but a blend of the two and are more individual variations than sexual." Continuing the musical metaphor, she celebrated "the harmonious blend of the sexes ... Every aspect of our culture prospers with the participation of both men and women."[150]

## FEMALE PHYSICIANS' VIEWS OF MEDICINE

Only one or two of the survey respondents thought that women doctors practised medicine differently from men; for instance, that the women had more empathy and more of a "bedside manner"[151] or could offer women patients better service.[152] They were nevertheless not unanimous in the need for, or the desirability of, any special treatment, ranging from maternity leave to tax deductions and flexible interning hours. Most of them welcomed the post-1970 increase in numbers while expressing some concern about the heavy full-time workloads of doctors who were also mothers.

A wide range in age is represented among those surveyed, and it might be expected that there would be differences in working experiences and opinions expressed from either ends of the age scale. This was not the case. Instead, there were striking similarities in the doctors' reasons for entering the profession, their marital and maternal situations, the type of work they did, and their opinions about gender in the practice of medicine.

The appeal of missionary work for some early doctors was noted above, and altruism in other forms was important. A graduate of the immediate post–World War II period noted, "I was greatly influenced by a biography of 'Dr Mary' who had spent the last part of her professional career as a missionary doctor in Angola with the United Church. A biography of Dr Ida Scudder of Vellore Mission in India also inspired me."[153] This doctor worked thirteen years in Africa before returning to work in Manitoba. Two of the 1966–70 graduates also worked overseas in aid programs, one with the Mennonite Central Committee in Southeast Asia during the Vietnam War[154] and the other as a medical officer with the Canadian University Service Overseas in Uganda in the early 1970s.[155] They all said that "idealism" in one form or another was a motive for their entry into medicine. Some variation on this was identified by four more, who qualified in the 1930s ("I wanted to help children");[156] in the 1940s ("I wanted to be in a serving profession");[157] in the 1950s ("I always felt inclined to help the weaker or suffering one");[158] and in the 1960s ("You could save others").[159]

Other doctors identified a variety of reasons for going into medicine: early contact with it as a child, because of one's own illness or that of a close relative; the admired example of a physician friend; or, in the case of a couple of doctors, the desire "to give the orders, not to take them" within a health profession.[160] Some turned to medicine after dissatisfaction with nursing or teaching.[161] Only two of those surveyed actually referred to material expectations of high income or independence.

On the questions soliciting an opinion about gender in the practice of medicine, there were distinctions between those arguing for a recognition that female doctors were women and mothers as well as professional workers, and those arguing that gender should make no difference in training or work. There was also a difference between those who, while accepting a woman's double responsibility, thought that the woman herself should arrange for family-oriented services, and those who thought that employers, a group partnership, or a government agency could provide help. Generally, different ideological approaches spanned the entire period, although those who considered motherhood an entirely personal, rather than social, responsibility were found more among the older respondents. By far the majority of the doctors surveyed acknowledged that they had considered themselves to be different from the standard doctor, who was male. They argued, too, that the implications of this should be recognized and accommodated as a public, not a private, responsibility – though there was no unanimity on how child care, for instance, could best be achieved.

"Having graduated in 1941, I have an historical perspective and in addition I am female." So began Evelyn Loadman in a talk to the women paediatric residents of 1983 – thirteen years after the terminal date of this study, years during which women's medical training had changed considerably by virtue of an increased proportion of women students. "I remember over the years," recalled Loadman, "talking to quite a few young women about how hard it was to find a smooth path through the very conflicting demands that were made on us. On the one hand we felt pressures coming from the culture and from instinctive maternal feelings, whether realized or thwarted, with counter pressures created by the very human desire to achieve and the excitement felt from growing knowledge and competence." She went on to consider an American report on opportunities for women in paediatrics.[162] It led into those "vast controversial regions where we all wander vaguely trying to understand, to defy, or to deny the differences between men and women, their goals and desires." She continued:

Women cannot be lumped into a homogeneous group any more than men can. Some women will be comfortable only with part time work, some will want a career, and some will want full time work and manage homes and children and husbands as well.

The report suggests that women lack the depth and breadth of professional experience that men seek and achieve and women must change to do this ... It also suggests ... that men may have to broaden their horizons and modify their goals and philosophies, if they are to have true depth and breadth to their family and other experiences ...

For both men and women, the report advocates and supports the trend of major pediatric programs to re-examine their curriculae, to re-evaluate educational vs service rotations, and to question the educational value of 36 hours on call.

Also for both men and women, it advocates more flexible residency opportunities, with sufficicient leisure time, allowing both males and females to become better parents, better role models, and citizens at large. It points to the universal stresses for both men and women, the greatest single cause of stress being fatigue from long hours, heavy workload and responsibilities, with "one night on, one to sleep, and one to do the laundry."[163]

"Tough old birds, we are," said a 1950 graduate of herself and her class-mates. They had matured over the years:

I think we were so naive that we didn't recognize some of the discrimination. We were just so delighted to be accepted. I remember one time – I'm sure now the girls would flare up and rage, but we didn't, we just laughed along with the guys at some of the jokes, the female jokes – one lecture, the anatomy professor started off. The topic today, he said, is the female breast. And I want you to get a good grasp of the subject. Well, we just giggled along with the boys. We weren't feminist enough to realize that some of these things shouldn't be done, and were happening, and we ought not to take it, but we did. But you had to do it to get there.[164]

A few women did not see, hear, or notice that, as a group, women's professional experience was different from men's. They "dutifully up-held and transmitted" the precepts of professionalism: "individualism, scientific objectivity, rationality, personal achievement and career-ism."[165] Of the women doctors surveyed for this study, the majority were sceptical concerning the "normal" progression of a model career: it was premised upon a careerist with a spouse who would take care of all necessities outside the demands of a job. A normal doctor was one who could be single-minded in devotion to, and in pursuit of, his ca-reer. Women, on the other hand, recognized additional calls as entirely legitimate. A few were happy to be single, but most were married, and almost all of the latter had children. Indeed, some of the single women also went to considerable trouble to be adoptive mothers. Motherhood diverted some of the energy of the female physicians – usually for the years of their children's infancy. Among this study's respondents, how-ever, maternity by itself never disqualified a physician from work.

Most doctors were at a loss to know how conditions could be made more appealing for women when training, although several echoed Loadman's endorsement of flexible and shorter hours in hospital training. Only a few could identify particular organizations as effective advocates – the Federation of Medical Women of Canada, for example. In fact, with respect to their professional life, the doctors were remark-ably content. It was a rare woman who had no recollection of discrim-ination, but even those who smarted from barbed humour or from the inferior intern accommodation or the foolish exclusion of women from urology training – even they recognized that these were counter-balanced by the immense satisfaction brought by working with patients in the practice of medicine. Perhaps the respondents' memories had mellowed over time. Still, these doctors noted that they had usually been able to work when they wanted and in their areas of choice. None mentioned a deliberate exclusion or closed door on account of sex once they had managed to jump through the several hoops of academic training.

## OTHER JURISDICTIONS

Although the number of women working in the profession did not start to rise dramatically until after 1970, before that date women in Manitoba kept pace with women elsewhere in Canada, as tables 10 and 11 show (see appendix 1), and on five census dates out of six the proportion of women doctors in Manitoba exceeded the Canadian average. This percentage grew from 3 per cent in 1911 to 11 per cent in 1971 and was higher than the proportion of women doctors (about 5 per cent) in the United States.[166]

The British figures are higher. In 1921, when 1.7 per cent of Canadian doctors were female, 5.4 per cent of British doctors were. The British figures doubled by 1931, and at the end of World War II the proportion was 15 per cent. By 1971, when the Canadian percentage was 10 per cent female, the British figure was 18 per cent.[167] The structure of the British National Health Service, which employed most doctors on salary, was different from the situation in Canada and the United States, where most doctors were self-employed. Why the percentage of women in the medical profession should be almost double the proportion in Canada is unclear. In her analysis of why women doctors were not more numerous, British sociologist Mary Ann Elston identified social attitudes towards motherhood, opinions which influential bodies such as the British Medical Association also consider important.[168] Perhaps these attitudes were even more inflexible in North America. Possibly the fact that much secondary education for girls in Britain before 1970 was single-sex encouraged both girls and their academic advisers to be readier to consider professional aspirations. Whatever the reasons, after 1970 all three countries moved at a fast pace towards more equity in medical school enrolments for women.

Women physicians invested more time in their training than the other women professionals, and they reaped larger financial benefits. The doctor who said the women were "so delighted to be accepted" hit the nail on the head. The women physicians were grateful to be admitted into a men's club, there to share in the prestige and material benefits of the profession. In comparison with other women, these benefits were considerable.[169] Although the workload was heavy, it was possible to make it bearable. Either a woman physician could have employment with an institution or government agency, with regular office hours, or she could herself employ others to share in her domestic workload. Moreover, if she was in private practice, she had more autonomy over her daily work schedule and could accommodate other priorities and commitments if she chose.

Few suffered from any illusion that they had been admitted into the club as equal partners. In the years before 1970, clear-sighted women physicians recognized their inequality and actively lobbied to do what they could – a few through the Federation of Medical Women of Canada, and some through plain speaking to students. Until there was a conceptual framework of gender-conscious criticism, which was not forthcoming until the emergence of the women's movement of the late 1960s, there was little more that they could do.

### CHAPTER FOUR

# Law: "That There Woman Lawyer"

In May 1911 Melrose Sissons of Portage la Prairie, a prosperous and firmly established farming area in south-central Manitoba, made an application to the Law Society of Manitoba to be admitted as a student. Sissons was a farmer's daughter and a graduate of Manitoba College in the University of Manitoba, and she had won the university silver medal for her performance in political economy and history. She had wanted to be a lawyer "from earliest memory."[1] Anticipating refusal from the law society, she had already made inquiries in Saskatchewan, where the secretary of the provincial society assured her that although she was the "first woman to apply there he is quite sure she will be made very welcome."[2]

Sissons was following examples set in Ontario by Clara Brett Martin and in New Brunswick by Mabel French. In 1891, at the age of seventeen, Martin had petitioned the Law Society of Upper Canada for registration as a student member. She was refused: the statute incorporating the law society referred to "persons" seeking entry into the profession. In 1892 she persuaded a member of the Ontario legislature to introduce a bill that required the word "person" in the law society's statute to be so interpreted as to include females. The bill, in an amended state which gave the law society discretion to admit a woman, was passed in April 1892. Martin reapplied and was again refused. With the support of the premier of Ontario, she applied yet once again, and in June 1893 she was admitted as a student-at-law and began articling for the required three-year term. Her cause was again taken up in the legislature, and in 1895 an act was passed to give the Law Society of Upper Canada the discretionary power to admit women as barristers. Injured in an accident, Martin delayed until 1896 before making her formal application for admission as a barrister – whereupon the law society exercised its discretion and refused. However, on her appeal it reversed the decision, and in February 1897 Martin was admitted. At the age of twenty-three Clara Brett Martin had become the first woman admitted to the profession of law in the British Empire.[3] By 1911, when Sissons first applied in Manitoba, three women in addition to Martin had been admitted to the Bar of Upper Canada.[4]

Mabel French was admitted as a student-at-law in New Brunswick in 1902. She successfully completed the required articling and examinations and in 1905 requested the Council of the Barristers' Society of New Brunswick to admit her as a barrister. She too was refused, "her sex being under existing laws a bar to her admission." As in Ontario, it was considered that the "persons" eligible to practise law could not be construed to include women; there was also the wider allusion that women were largely incapacitated under "existing laws" anyway. At the next session of the New Brunswick legislature, an act was passed mandating the admission of women to the practice of law "upon the same terms and subject to the like conditions and regulations as men."[5] French was thereupon admitted into practice.

Six months after Sissons applied in Manitoba, the Law Society of Manitoba refused her admission, seeking no further than the by now obvious precedent that "the word person interpreted in this connection meant male person."[6] Before trying her luck in Saskatchewan, as she had intended, Sissons persisted in her home province and, following the example of Martin and French, she had her cause taken up in the provincial legislature. At the next session, the provincial treasurer introduced an amendment to the Law Society Act by which women would be enabled to practise as barristers in the province on the same terms as men. The amendment was passed in 1912, and Sissons began her articling and at the same time prepared for her Bar admission examinations. A second woman, Winnifred Wilton, started law studies at the same time.[7] The two completed their examinations together, in 1915, with Wilton gaining the highest aggregate marks of all students in the final examinations.[8] In 1916 Alma Graham (later Macarthur) was the third woman called to the Bar, and in 1917 Isabel Maclean (later Hunt) was the fourth. Maclean was the first also to have earned the LLB.

Between 1915 (when Sissons and Wilton were the first women allowed to practise law in the province) and 1971, fifty women were admitted to the Manitoba Bar. They were the successful ones: considerably more intended to be lawyers but left before qualifying. Thirteen women were admitted to the Law Society of Manitoba as students-at-law but did not complete their training.[9] A further thirteen earned the LLB degree from the University of Manitoba but were not subsequently admitted to the Bar in Manitoba or, so far as is known, anywhere else.[10] Whereas evidence for the non-graduates is unavailable, some information is known about the LLB graduates who did not proceed to the Bar. None of them worked in a legal capacity. One became a schoolteacher before emigrating to Palestine in 1920.[11] One worked as a journalist,[12] one as a university teacher,[13] one as a stockbroker,[14] and one was director for a social work agency.[15]

The terminal date of this study is 1971, a year after the *Report of the Royal Commission on the Status of Women* signified that the Government of Canada recognized discrimination as a problem for women.[16] Census data were recorded on the first year of each decade. The women lawyers considered here met two criteria. First, they were LLB graduates between 1917 and 1970; secondly, they were admitted to the Manitoba Bar in 1971 or before. In addition, four women without the LLB were included in the study: Sissons, Wilton, and Graham, who were admitted to the Bar in 1915 and 1916, and Mary Grant Wright, BA, who was admitted in 1948 despite the lack of an LLB.[17]

This is an examination of the working histories and the personal features of fifty or so women who at some time worked as lawyers in Manitoba. As far as possible, the women's careers are considered through the eyes of the women themselves. Using a variety of evidence – personal memoirs, written responses to surveys, interviews, and career histories built up from archives and newspapers – the case study seeks to discover what women thought about the law as a profession and also the reasons for their small numbers. By comparison with other jurisdictions, the study considers the extent to which the conditions in Manitoba were similar elsewhere.

First, I establish the size of the group. I describe the nature of their training and work. After examining the attitudes of the women towards their work, I develop a demographic profile of the woman lawyer. Finally, I compare the portrait of women lawyers in Manitoba before 1970 with men and women of other jurisdictions. The statistical infrastructure uses census documents and also the rolls and annual reports of the Law Society of Manitoba, together with the society's members' files and other collections in the Western Canadian Legal History Archive. Most of the qualitative evidence presented here is derived from two small collections of data and one large collection. The file assembled by Cameron Harvey, 1968–70, in the preparation of his study of women lawyers in Canada was made available; and the material assembled by Dale Gibson and Lee Gibson in the preparation of a history of law and lawyers in Manitoba before 1970 contained useful information, primarily in the form of newspaper clippings.[18]

The major source for the opinions expressed by women lawyers on their own work experience is the questionnaire, administered in person or through the mail, which was put to women lawyers who had earned the LLB before 1970. Some lawyers augmented the questionnaire material with longer accounts of their working lives. Survey or interview responses were received from twenty-four women. The span of their working careers was almost equivalent to the span of the period under study. One response was received from a woman who graduated in 1920. Two were received from those who graduated 1930–39, three from women graduating in the 1940s, six from the 1950s, and twelve from the 1960s.[19]

## NUMBERS

Tables 12 and 13 (appendix 1) show that women lawyers in Manitoba, like those in Canada generally, were during this period in a small minority. The women's education and training was the same as the men's. Four of them did not have an LLB degree. Of these, one was in practice for two years, until her marriage.[20] One practised for a year, then worked for the Canadian government in the Estates of the Overseas Military Forces during World War I. She later worked in Paris for the American Red Cross, married an American, and was subsequently admitted to the New York Bar.[21] A third married a lawyer and moved to Vancouver, where after World War II she worked in Japanese-Canadian claims.[22] Information on her is sparse, as it is on the fourth, who practised with her lawyer husband in rural Manitoba after World War II.[23] While all four are known to have worked as lawyers, there is incomplete evidence documenting the sequence of their work.

These four displayed some of the prominent features of the pattern that comes to light in an examination of the forty-six who were barristers as well as graduates of the academic discipline of law. Governments at the municipal, provincial, and federal levels provided employment for almost as many women lawyers as went into private practice. Women lawyers tended to work only briefly in a practice unless they were married to a lawyer in a partnership of two. It was usual for the woman to retire from professional work on marriage, and it was a commonplace that the women put their families first when family responsibilities conflicted with work demands.

Of the forty-six women who had both the LLB degree and Bar admission, most (thirty-three) were admitted to the Bar within two years of graduation, while thirteen experienced a longer gap. In six cases, this gap was twelve years or more; the longest was thirty-seven years. The other seven had an average gap of six years.[24]

## LEGAL WORK

Of the fifty women trained as lawyers, information is available on the type and length of professional work experience before 1970 for forty-two.[25] Seventeen worked in private practice alone;[26] three worked in government alone;[27] two, in business alone;[28] nine, in a combination of practice and government,[29] of whom two worked in business as well;[30] four worked in a mixture of government, business, and miscellaneous jobs;[31] one was an academic;[32] and six were not working in legal employment before 1970.[33]

The two largest categories of work were private practice and government work, or a combination of both. Government work ranged from strictly legal work for a department of justice, to work in social welfare agencies or in a municipal authority, or for the Canadian government overseas. In this category were five women who for at least part of their pre-1970 career were employed outside Manitoba.[34] Business also provided jobs for women lawyers. Two at least managed businesses which they owned or which belonged to their families.[35] Others worked for insurance companies, banks, and brokerages.

Before 1970, only two women had been appointed to the bench, both to the Family Court: Nellie Sanders in 1957, and Mary Wawryko in 1968.[36] If note is taken of post-1970 careers, four more were subsequently made judges, three of them in Manitoba and one in Ontario. This can be taken as an indication of success for the women whose careers began in the 1960s. But for those whose working lives began in the five previous decades, the picture is muted.

## TRAINING IN A MAN'S PROFESSION

Table 14 (appendix 1) shows that the overall numbers of women entering the profession were small. The number who attained the highest status within their profession was negligible. This study cannot examine the number or motives of women who were deterred from the profession in the first place. By its nature, it examines only those who as a minimum reached the point of committing themselves to training. The structure of the training system itself provides some explanation for the small numbers, for it presented a barrier that only a few women could or would surmount.

Legal education in Manitoba in the century before 1970 sometimes led – and frequently followed – the styles of legal education elsewhere in Canada. For most of the period, this could be characterized as an apprenticeship system organized and managed by each provincial law society, which was also responsible for establishing regulations concerning admission into, and the practice of, the profession. Before Manitoba entered Confederation, "anyone who chose to call himself a lawyer and to practise as such ... was entitled to do so," but acts of the Manitoba legislature of 1871 and 1877 outlawed such free enterprise. After 1877, the Law Society of Manitoba was established as the authority over legal education. Each would-be lawyer had to serve a five-year apprenticeship (three years for university graduates) under articles of clerkship to a practising lawyer and had to pass an examination set by the society. No formal academic education was provided except for occasional lectures. Students were given the names of legal text books on which they would be examined. In 1885 the University of Manitoba set up a three-year reading course in law leading to the degree of LLB, which provided an alternative to the BA for law students who wished to article for three rather than five years.[37]

The LLB became increasingly popular. Whereas in the five-year period beginning 1895, only eleven men graduated with a LLB, in the five-year period beginning 1900, twenty-nine did, and the numbers continued to increase: fifty-two in the five-year period beginning 1905, and seventy-four in the five-year period beginning 1910.[38] In 1914, for the first time, the Law Society of Manitoba made a purposeful attempt to provide systematic instruction for students by creating the Manitoba Law School. This offered a three-year lecture course leading to the University of Manitoba's LLB degree and to admission to practise. The classes were forty-five minutes in the early morning and forty-five minutes at the end of a business day, and for the intervening six and a half hours a student served articles in a law office. Seven years later, in 1921, the first official dean of the law school was appointed, and at the same time reforms were introduced making legal education "highly creditable," in the opinion of the chair of the Canadian Bar Association's committee on legal education.[39]

The Manitoba Law School became the first in Canada to adopt a new model curriculum proposed by the Canadian Bar Association. Articling combined with legal instruction lasted one year for university graduates. However, in 1931 a changed LLB degree re-integrated academic classes with practical instruction for each of four years. This pattern remained in effect for the next thirty years and contributed to what was described as "drowsiness and complacency" in comparison with other Canadian law schools.[40]

Reforms began in the early 1960s. In Ontario a new model developed whereby a student had three years of full-time study in a university law course, followed by one year of articling and further study in a Bar admission course operated by the law society. The same sequence was gradually introduced in Manitoba. The new regime was marked by the appointment in 1964 of C.H.C. Edwards as dean and by the transfer of jurisdiction over the academic degree to the University of Manitoba in a new Faculty of Law in 1966.[41] Academic instruction was physically relocated to a new building on the university campus in 1970.[42]

For almost all the years before 1970, legal education was dominated by the Law Society of Manitoba. Its essential feature was practical training. Students were required to find a law office that would agree to admit them as articling clerks. It was advantageous for them if they had contacts, generally through a family member or close family friend, within the number of established lawyers. Someone who had no ready-made contacts would have difficulty finding a law firm to take her or him at the age of twenty or twenty-one. The law firm would be testing the clerk as a potential long-term colleague. For women this was more of a problem than for men. Because there were so few women already in the profession, there was no regular network. Women were regarded as a risk and were widely expected to abandon the investment made in their training upon marriage: "The apprentice system ... was more into old boys, contacts, who do you know."[43] The difficulty was exacerbated for the woman who was exceptional on any other account. "I discovered I had three strikes against me from the start," said one who trained in the 1940s:

I was Jewish, I was a female, and I was from out of town without good contacts and he gave me a list of only Jewish lawyers and when I asked him why, he replied, "Well, you wanted to find out for yourself." He reluctantly gave me the list. I then obtained an appointment with a lawyer in the firm of — at 9.00 a.m. on a Saturday morning. I was kept waiting in the waiting room from 9.00 a.m. until 12.00 noon, when the lawyer came out and told me that the firm did not need a student. This was just one example ... I went from one Jewish lawyer to another, and the standard remarks were, "Why should we hire you? You are female and will get married and leave, and we will have wasted time and money in training you."[44]

Women tended to try and suppress pain while responding in a matter-of-fact way to their treatment. "I did have some difficulty finding an articling position in my first year," said one. "Most firms were reluctant to take in a female student. I probably would have had more difficulty had I not been able to type and do stenographic work." In retrospect, this lawyer felt that both she and the firm benefited from this working arrangement:

Although at the time [1951] I knew that I was being hired primarily because of my typing skills rather than as an articling student, nevertheless, I received more remuneration than my fellow students and also actually learned more than they did in the sense that I prepared all the documents relating to real estate transactions, court documents, wills, etc., and while typing them I learned how to draft the various clauses, and the various laws that governed the issues ... First-year articling students averaged about $10.00 per month – and the price of a bus pass. I was paid $25.00 per month in my first year.[45]

The majority were more sensitive to the difficulties: "It was very difficult to article as the offices didn't want women, particularly married women. They all thought you would get pregnant and quit." Even when a firm had experience with female articling students, this did not necessarily ease the way for others: "One of the bigger firms had had experience with women students and were not anxious to hire women."[46] One woman was prepared to resist exploitation: "There were not many openings ... and it was customary for women students to do their own typing." This woman had worked as a secretary before becoming a law student, but when the lawyer with whom she was articling made it clear that she was expected to do the typing, she told him, "I've forgotten how."[47]

The most common way for women students to surmount the universally acknowledged barrier was to article in the office of a relative or family friend. "Who else would have taken a woman?" asked one, who went to her uncle's firm.[48] "Another stated that the only firm she could get to hire her was the one she had earlier worked in as office staff.[49] By the end of the period, in the 1960s, some women found an ally in C.H.C. Edwards, the new dean of the Faculty of Law, who helped arrange articling positions: "I went to see Cliff. He had a list of offices seeking articling students. He picked [one of the largest Winnipeg law firms] and phoned someone there. He said he had a student with excellent marks, referred to 'this student' and got me an interview, and at the end of the conversation said, 'Oh, by the way, her name is ...'"[50]

After Dean Edward's appointment, the system changed. At this point, when training switched to an academic system, it was "a door opener for women. You didn't need to find an office at the start."[51] Even then, the reluctance of firms to take on women for their subsequent articling persisted. "After two interviews with law firms, it appeared that one didn't want a woman student and the other had specific (i.e., limited) jobs for women students," said one woman, who then turned to a government office for her articling.[52]

Another hurdle that the aspiring lawyer had to surmount was the personal approach of the law school's staff, who formally admitted students to the program and then provided academic instruction. For most of the period before 1970, there was little competition for admission. With money to pay fees, and academic eligiblity rather than good performance as a criterion, there is no evidence of women being refused admission on academic grounds. "All you had to have was your tuition and second year Arts," was the common observation.[53] However, the dean of the law school from 1945 to 1964, G.P.R. Tallin, took what opportunities he could to deter women.[54] As one woman described it, "When I began [in the early 1960s], the old Dean really had a lot of reservations about women going into Law. He called me in for a little chat and explained that although he knew that I was quite clever enough to do all these things it really wasn't suitable. I was baffled. He said, very embarrassed, Well, some times of the month you just might not be up to it."[55] Another woman said, "I went to pay my full year fee, and they suggested I pay only until Christmastime. I was intimidated." Nevertheless, she remained to finish the entire year.[56] The dean was "particularly hostile," it was noted, and was "unhappy to have women in the class – it was a man's profession."[57] One woman completed her two years in arts and applied to law, but as she was under twenty-one she needed the consent of the dean. "He refused. Because I was a woman. He didn't hesitate to say so."[58]

Once in the program, women were made aware of their minority status: "The atmosphere was definitely anti-feminine."[59] One of the women recalled: "A few [professors] would ask me to run an errand if a salacious joke was to be told. The men students were very anti-women. I was seen as a threat and as an embarrassment."[60] Another said, "I disliked the scepticism of my fellow male students about the seriousness of my intent."[61] One remembered the men as "just generally extremely competitive." The male students assumed that the women were there to get husbands.[62] One woman, married and a little older, perplexed them: "A couple of fellows couldn't figure out what I was doing there. One of them said to me (he was not a very smart fellow), You've already got a husband. What are you doing here? But most of them were fine ... I felt I was one of the gang."[63] Another observed, "The occasional off-colour joke made me uncomfortable – but this wasn't overwhelming. It was life."[64] Those who recollected some discomfiture also remembered the camaraderie, and a few remembered lasting friendships.

It was a considerable achievement for a woman to arrange for her own training and complete her course of study leading to the LLB, a course which, until the end of the period, also qualified her for admission to the Bar, since it included simultaneous articling. Nevertheless, thirteen women who earned their LLB degree never applied for admission at all and thirteen others, pre-1970 graduates, chose not to take their call to the Bar immediately after graduation. Their reasons were varied. Three cited family matters augmented by other considerations.

"I was not planning to work as a lawyer as I had my first child in December after graduating in May," said one, but she was disaffected on another count: "Women at that time [the 1950s] were 'encouraged' by the dean to specialize in family law – which was not my bag."[65] Another, who graduated in 1970, wrote, "Because I got married that stopped my career." Additionally, she noted that "in 1970 it would have been extremely difficult" for a woman to have a career in law: "We were made to feel very unwelcome. It was a very male-oriented career."[66] One-third were not particularly committed in the first place and were deterred by financial costs. For example, one woman explained: "My father was a lawyer ... he always said I was going to study law – so I just drifted into it ... I could not afford to be called to the Bar after graduation – it was during the depression – then I got married and had two children. Because of my husband's job we moved a great deal."[67]

### ATTITUDES TOWARDS LEGAL PRACTICE

Lack of enthusiasm was duplicated at another level. Among the women who managed to complete their training, many worked as lawyers only a short time and cited similar reasons for their retirement. The length of working career cannot be determined with accuracy since information is unavailable for eight of the fifty women who were admitted to the Bar. In those eight cases, it is likely that their working career was short or possibly (like those cited in the previous paragraph) nonexistent. The following generalizations apply to the forty-two for whom evidence on their working career is known.

One who qualified in the 1930s pointed out that "needless to say, [there were] no jobs for lawyers, male or female, in Winnipeg in the thirties." She worked in the book department of the Hudson's Bay Company store over Christmas and was able to find short-term employment before deciding to return to university for a further degree. She then worked for a government department. Like the women lawyers pre-empted from paid work by family responsibilities, she retired when she married: "No married women were then employed if a husband could support them."[68] This regulation, widespread in the civil service, was relaxed by the late 1950s when this woman returned to full-time government employment.[69] Another woman, although called to the Bar, never worked in a private practice but instead drafted policies for an insurance company. Her experience led her to the conclusion that a major reason for the small number of women lawyers before 1970 was the "lack of secure income" and lots of discouragement, despite the "expensive education."[70]

Two women who subsequently (after 1970) became very successful experienced initial disappointment in getting work. One "couldn't get a job as a lawyer," and during the 1960s she therefore worked in management training and as a library assistant.[71] The other, after her call to the Bar, was unemployed until she obtained a part-time research position. Her articling experience had served to discourage further effort: "I wasn't given much to do. I wasn't taken so seriously. I was put in the same place as the secretaries. I wasn't treated the same as the male articling students. It would have bothered me more had I cared more."[72] Later, both women were more fortunate, the first in finding congenial part-time work in the 1970s at the same time as raising a family, and the second in discovering a skill and liking for legal teaching.

Among the men in the profession, the dominant form of work was in private practice. It is noticeable that of the forty-two women, only seventeen worked in private practice exclusively, and over half of these (ten) had a father or husband with whom they practised.[73] Three of the twelve women who worked for government after, before, or at the same time as working in a practice also had close family connections with a male lawyer as a business associate.[74] Only a minority of the women who worked in a practice did so without benefit of a known family connection.[75]

For those few who completed training, found a job, and stayed in the professional workforce – three tests that seriously took their toll – law was a profession that had its rewards. An occasional lawyer admitted to a preference to research and administration. For example: "I liked law all right but was terrified of clients";[76] "I liked the intellectual satisfaction."[77] One liked "taking a mess, then tidying up and making sense of it."[78] This emphasis was unusual. Most preferred the work with people. Typical were comments such as: "I haven't had a client I disliked,"[79] and "I liked to solve problems to help make a better life – for example, for woman to get out of an abusive marriage."[80] There was also, for the woman who was self-employed in a partnership with her husband or in her own business, a flexibility in time that allowed her to combine law with parenting – or, as such women grew financially more secure, with extensive holidays.[81]

Working lawyers identified drawbacks in their profession with reluctance, pointing out that on balance these were outweighed by the benefits. Stress and responsibility for others were not welcome. A lawyer had to make a special effort not to take things too personally. In the practice, noted one woman, "I did have to demand that I not do all the family work. I liked it no more than the men did and had to make that clear. Usually, the women lawyers were landed with all the family work and not much else."[82] Some found that it was easy to get exasperated with the "administrivia."[83] Several disliked "the business side," particularly in terms of developing client networks. The pay was too low, said a few. While most considered that the work they did was remunerated at the same rate as men's, women who left the profession often did so for financial reasons. In the early 1960s, observed one woman, "salaries were beginning to increase and mine did not."[84] Another, who worked in several businesses, noted, "All paid less than one-half to females than to males. The fringe benefits were nil."[85] Financial reasons for taking retirement were reinforced by what one lawyer described as "the sexism, the clubiness, the old boys' network which one could never penetrate."[86]

## WOMEN LAWYERS

A composite portrait of the woman lawyer in Manitoba before 1970 would contain the following features. She trained under an apprenticeship system and had problems related to her gender with respect to articling and in academic class. The experience served to deter some women from proceeding to an immediate call to the Bar. Women who persisted found employment in a variety of settings. The smoothest way was work offered with a male relative – a husband, brother, father, uncle. Women who went into private practice independently of a male guardian were less common. Along with private practice, the other most common employment was government at various levels. Private-sector business offered salaried employment to a small number of women.

Many of the women who worked did so only for a limited time before retiring. There is information on the length of career for forty-two women who qualified as lawyers before 1971 and who worked professionally, many of them continuing after that date. Eleven of them are known to have worked professionally for some time, but it is not known for how long. Of the remaining thirty-one, about one-third (eight) worked for thirty years or more, and about the same number (ten) worked for twenty to thirty years. The remainder (thirteen) worked fewer than twenty years. When most of these women retired, they did so permanently. However, some returned to professional work after an interval.

As might be expected, the main key – though not the only one – to this history of a generally short career, together with, for some, an interrupted work history, is marital and maternal status. Certainly, before World War II it was normal behaviour for a woman to retire from employment upon marriage. Among the women lawyers examined here, there is no exception to this rule. The only married women who remained in or returned to the workplace subsequent to their marriage were those who had become widowed.[87] All others working at that time were single.

For women called to the Bar after 1940, the situation was different. This group numbered thirty-six.[88] The careers of five of these women – four of them married – are unknown.[89] A further nine are known to have worked as lawyers, but it is not known for how long. All of them, also, were married.[90] Information is available on the remaining twenty-two.[91]

Six were single. Before 1970, one was widowed, two divorced. Thirteen were married. Only one followed the prewar pattern and re-tired on marriage. Four retired at the birth of children, but all these subsequently returned to legal work, two promptly (within five years) and two after an interval of more than fifteen years. Eight therefore were married and continued to work without interruption.

It is likely that the reason why little or nothing is known about the careers of a relatively large number of qualified women lawyers is be-cause they practised for only a short time and retired permanently when they had children. One conclusion is unavoidable: that very few mothers worked at all and that even fewer did so when their children were small. Marriage had ceased to serve as a nonnegotiable disquali-fication of women from a working career, but maternity, for a married woman, served to render her virtually ineligible for paid work. Only a widow was not required to observe this taboo. For the period 1915–70, there were four widows working as lawyers, and three of them had chil-dren to support. Only towards the end of the period did any mothers with husbands violate the taboo against a working mother, and there were only three of them.

The collective impression of women lawyers would include in its de-mographic dimension a feature that changed over the two generations. At first, working female lawyers were single or widowed. In the second generation, they were mainly single, though some were married and there was the occasional widow or divorcée; but only rarely and re-cently (that is, just before 1970) were they mothers. The actual behav-iour of women lawyers would lead an observer to the conclusion that maternity and paid work did not readily mix. This was also the expressed view of most of the women themselves.

A lawyer who earned her degree in 1959 pointed out: "Few women worked full-time in the profession then. But I stayed home to raise my children, rather than hire other people to look after them."[92] One who qualified at the end of the period, in 1967, expressed it this way:

I feel strongly that women should have careers, but I also feel very strongly about the need of children to have at least one full-time parent at home until they are of school age. These two feelings are not easily reconciled. My choice not to work was the best one for my family. Even going into a full-time career when my children were older caused trauma and upset. The demands on my time were very great, despite the support of my husband. Somehow, the mother is still the primary care giver for day-to-day needs of the children and with that must also put in a full day at the office ... A legal career does not lend itself to "job sharing." Clients want *you* ... part-time in law is an 8-hour day ... If a woman is very "career oriented," it is my opinion that with law she has no time to raise a family. Others may have proved me wrong, but concessions would have had to be made along the way.[93]

"Family was my primary consideration," said a woman a little older. "A mother should be at home when the children are young. My husband didn't want me employed then."[94] "Domestic problems," said a woman without children, "seem to be what occupy my women colleagues all the time – they seem to take enormous time and energy."[95] The primacy of a mother's time allocated to small children was widespread. It is likely that family considerations propelled many women out of the profession altogether – perhaps those women about whose working career nothing is known. However, it should be noted that even when retirees cited children as a reason for their leaving paid work, this was generally accompanied by disaffection for other aspects of a legal career. Most frequently mentioned were low pay, lack of opportunity to work in a preferred area, and the deterrent effect of the old boys' club and network.

Absence from the workplace had serious implications for career progress: "If you take several years out [of your career], you never make it up."[96] One woman observed that if you get an itch and want very much to be best, you will sacrifice. The guys do that, therefore the women must do it too." She pointed out that any woman seeking the upper echelons of career reward had to be single or "an exceptional woman in an exceptional marriage."[97]

Such comments suggest that these women lawyers who worked before 1970 identified the fact that women were the primary care givers in a family as a major reason for both their small numbers in the profession and their relative lack of success in it. This is true, but it was not the only reason. Simultaneously, other reasons were advanced. The survey respondents laid most responsibility on public opinion. "A sign of the times," was how one woman put it.[98] "Families," noted another, "were not attuned to giving their daughters education ... At the end of the [second] war, few went to university, neither women nor men."[99] The following comments sum up the general viewpoint: "There was a belief that women did not have either the mental or emotional capacity to perform legal work";[100] "Women weren't encouraged to think of a career as lifelong but as an interim occupation, before marriage";[101] "Education was okay, but no one thought you would work full-time, if at all, once you got married. Thirty odd years ago, I don't think the male ego could take it!"[102] Law "was not a field women were encouraged to enter. You were either a teacher, nurse, secretary or waitress."[103] A woman who earned her degree in 1969 said that "it was not thought a 'suitable' occupation for women, to the extent that women worked outside the home."[104] Another commented, "Female lawyers are no longer [in 1991] considered an 'oddity' as they were in my time. I was frequently referred to by the public as 'that there woman lawyer,' whereas my male colleagues were referred to by name."[105]

Other women branded the existing cadre of lawyers as responsible for the small number and inferior status of women in the profession. "Lots of discouragers," noted one.[106] "Many women were discouraged from thinking, and intimidated by male lawyers," said another. "Women have been brought up to think everyone should like us. You can't be a lawyer and have that happen."[107] Outright prejudice against women was also a contributory reason for the small numbers. A woman using her law training in the private business sector identified "discrimination and people being afraid a woman might be better than a man" as reasons why women were held back.[108] "It is a very conservative profession and will take generations to change,"[109] was another opinion. "Opportunities for paid employment for lawyers (especially women) were few and far between," said a woman who had qualified during the Depression.[110] One woman voiced the opinion that women themselves were a problem: "'I would rather have a man lawyer' is still heard."[111] "Many women perhaps were not prepared to spend years at university to get a law degree and become self-employed."[112]

Women lawyers saw no advantage in pressure-group activism or in direct complaints. One woman who graduated in the 1950s recollected that when the final examinations came to be written, the women were separated from the other students lest the men be distracted: "I was told by the dean that ... their whole lives depended on their success in the exams ... It would have been funny if it hadn't been so sick. Creating a stink would have done no good at all."[113]

Intermittently over the years, women lawyers maintained their own organization. The Portia club was founded in 1917, during World War I, and at first had a service orientation beyond its purpose as a forum where women lawyers could meet. Its members offered free legal advice to soldiers' widows and dependants.[114] The first president was Isabel Maclean, who married a banker, Albert Hunt, and retired from practice. She was widowed and returned to work in 1929 as a solicitor for the municipal Department of Welfare in Winnipeg. The

Portia club met in members' homes. Hunt's daughter remembers "as a child lying in bed and listening."[115] "We discussed certain legal topics and had a nice social evening," recalled a former member of the club.[116] "There was a minimum of organization," explained another. "Essentially our personal relations with colleagues were simply translated into the club format on a very informal basis. The choice of name was perhaps inevitable although several of us (myself included) were never quite easy about the label ... We never managed to adhere to a regular schedule as to dates in spite of our good intentions."[117]

The club later became primarily a social one. Typically, the 1953 annual meeting concerned itself with plans for entertaining women delegates who were expected at a forthcoming Canadian Bar Association convention.[118] Few of the women lawyers who were surveyed for this study recollected their own involvement in any women's organization. Two who were active in the profession in the 1950s remembered the Portia club's successor, the Women Lawyers' Association, but by the 1960s the younger women were uninvolved and even tended to avoid women's groups. Over the years, women lawyers did not use collective organization to strengthen or further their careers.

## COMPARISONS WITH ELSEWHERE

After 1970 the situation changed considerably. The number of women students in the Faculty of Law registered a sharp increase and women law graduates slowly began to make inroads in the profession. The number of women who continued their professional work after marriage increased, and motherhood no longer served to bar women from work. The post-1970s have been a dramatic contrast to the pre-1970 situation. If the pre-1970 picture is compared with other places, however, contemporary jurisdictions display many of the salient features that were evident in Manitoba.

Tables 12 and 13 showed the number of lawyers practising in Canada and in Manitoba. If these are seen as percentages, as in table 15, different jurisdictions can more readily be compared (see appendix 1). The Canada-wide figures show a low percentage with a small rise after World War II and with a faster pace of increase in the 1960s to what was still a low figure of 5.1 per cent by 1971. The Manitoba figures are roughly parallel to the national until the war. The provincial percentage then actually dropped from the 1941 level and did not rise again until the 1960s; the 1971 proportion is less than half the national figure. This is partly a function of the tiny numbers involved: when even one woman retired from the workforce her personal decision could have considerable ramifications in the calculations.

As table 16 (appendix 1) shows, in other provincial jurisdictions (with the exception of Ontario, which includes Ottawa, the capital city where many government lawyers were employed) the figures are so low that, again, an individual woman's personal circumstances could make a noticeable mark on the percentages. Of the three prairie provinces, Manitoba had the fewest women lawyers noted in the post–World War II figures (twenty-nine, compared with seventy-one in Alberta and forty-one in Saskatchewan), and although these ratios are paralleled in general by provincial poulation figures, Manitoba's figures are still proportionately lower.[119] During the postwar era, Manitoba's percentage of women lawyers was lowest in Canada in 1951 and 1971, and the next lowest to Newfoundland in 1961. This observation excepts Prince Edward Island, which had no women lawyers at all.

The comparable figures in the United States approximate more to those in Ontario than to the lower figures elsewhere in Canada. In England, women solicitors made up less than 2 per cent of the total in 1957. Women barristers that same year were 3.2 per cent of the total, and their number rose to 5.4 per cent in 1967.[120] Low as these American and English figures were, the Manitoba figures were lower.

Manitoba's low numbers relative to other jurisdictions cannot be obviously explained. They may show how effective the gatekeepers of the profession were in excluding women. Certainly, the women who became lawyers testified to the misogyny of the law school's dean and the difficulty of finding articling positions. Manitoba women were not alone in experiencing hardship in obtaining articling positions, but there would need to be historical studies made of other jurisdictions before one could conclude that Dean Tallin's fierceness was unique.[121] Women working as lawyers in Manitoba were also fewer in number than the women trained as lawyers, for even though women had braved the dean and the articling difficulties in order to earn the degree of LLB, not all of them went on to work in the province. Thirteen such graduates did not proceed to the Bar, and information on only four of them is available. Possibly, some of the other nine left to work elsewhere or never entered the labour market at all.

The motives of male lawyers in defending their profession – or as many parts of it as possible – as a male bastion were expressed succinctly as late as 1967 when barristers of the Midland circuit in England confirmed their refusal to allow women barristers equal opportunity to attend circuit meetings and dinners: "Those who opposed the admission of women in the Midland circuit did so because they would 'inhibit the atmosphere' and 'completely alter the character and nature' of the messes [meals]. Moreover, it was feared that some women might attend dinner because they felt 'that in so doing they are in some way advancing their professional chances.'"[122] The male lawyers had "a desire to preserve the all-male atmosphere, and fear of economic competition from a new and very large group of people ... These feelings persist in the profession in Canada today [1973] and are the cause of the rather striking difference in career patterns between male and female lawyers."[123]

In the group of twenty-four survey and interview respondents in this study, seventeen had noticed anti-female behaviour or attitudes, ranging from deterrence on entry to articling experience, to misogynistic comments in class, to discrimination in opportunities and discrimination in pay and working conditions in employment.[124] The phrasing of the questionnaire was intended to elicit each woman's own memories expressed in her own terms, rather than necessarily to prompt remembrances of discriminatory behaviour. Seven of the respondents gave no evidence of having observed or experienced treatment which they identified as discriminatory.[125]

Harvey's 1970 survey of women lawyers in Canada recorded more women denying than admitting discrimination, but his questions had no necessary gender focus.[126] A respondent to Harvey's study remarked:

You may discover that some replies indicate an apparent lack of discrimination; in many cases I have found that women are unwilling to admit discrimination, either because they are trying to conceal the fact from themselves or because they must play the role of "Uncle Tom" and their chances of promotion depend absolutely upon their conformity to and acceptance of the existing patterns. In other cases, I found that women who have been subject to great discrimination in the government service and who have told me of it with considerable bitterness cope with the situation by escapism, viz. taking an early retirement and travelling or occupying themselves in more pleasant ways than by fighting against discrimination.[127]

These comments by a senior civil servant may apply to some of the seven women who made no record of discrimination when responding to the 1991 survey. There is also the possibility that none of the seven felt or saw discriminatory behaviour and that they were either unable to explain the small numbers and inferior status of women lawyers or could cite women's own behaviour by way of explanation. Over two-thirds of this study's respondents noted some acquaintance with discrimination, ranging from slight and tolerable to grossly unfair and painful. That discrimination exists and is suffered in other jurisdictions is incontrovertible.[128] However, there were other factors that combine with discrimination to provide a more comprehensive explanation of the small numbers and inferior status of women lawyers before 1970.

A Canadian jurist, Mary Jane Mossman, has reviewed current literature which notes that the post-1970 increase in the number of women lawyers does not automatically march in step with women's infiltration of the better-paid and more powerful positions in legal employment.[129] She draws attention to wider social explanations of a continuing inferiority in the status of women lawyers, who share with other professional women rewards less than those attracted by men of comparable performance. Citing the work of American analysts Carrie Menkel-Meadow, Cynthia Epstein, and Rosabeth Moss Kanter, she argues that professional men's deep suspicion of women remains in the 1990s.[130] Elements of this suspicion include an assumption of "women's 'inherent incapacity' to be assertive and dominant; social factors which 'direct women away from the public sphere to family-centred activities'; time problems and role strains flowing from 'women's sex-role associated duties'; [and] the lack of 'opportunity structures' for women to acquire appropriate skills."[131]

Kanter's insight was to show the importance of number thresholds with respect to the behaviour of women lawyers and other women professionals. She pointed out that when women comprise less than 20 per cent of the total in a firm or corporation, "the dynamics of tokenism are set in motion":

Tokens are more visible, which may lead to pressures to hide their achievements or to underachieve. They are more likely to be excluded from informal peer networks and to be constantly reminded of their "difference." They are also more likely to be trapped in stereotyped roles ... Tokens are faced with the choice of accepting isolation or becoming a member of the dominant male group at the price of denying their identity as women, and accepting a definition of themselves as "exceptional" ... [Such stereotypes] tend to eclipse demonstrations of competence and make it harder for a woman to show professional strength ... [They] have little to do with a woman's performance as a lawyer. But to the extent that women have to learn to ignore the comments they elicit or respond to them, and to the extent that they tend to trap women in uncomfortable roles, they create handicaps for women that men do not share.[132]

Since 1970, the increased number of women entering law have made "significant progress" in the profession, but according to a Florida barrister, Martha Barnett, women "have been unsuccessful in forcing those positions (hitherto closed to women) to change in ways that truly would accommodate their needs."[133] Barnett identified motherhood as the single major structural barrier for women's equality in the profession.

Maternity and its cultural demands were seen as incompatible with the practice of law. The Manitoba women themselves paid testimony to this, and studies of other professional women bear witness to it too. "The demands on female employees have been especially pronounced because of both the timing and the allocation of domestic demands ... The foundations for career development form between the mid-twenties and mid-thirties, a period that coincides with women's peak childbearing years." As the American law professor Deborah Rhode points out, "No matter which alternative the working mother chooses, whether dropping out or making do, she is likely to reinforce some of the stereotypes on which subtle forms of gender discrimination rest."[134] Retirement on maternity, for the pre-1970 women lawyers, should not be seen as personal failure. Rather, the profession's failure to accommodate trained lawyers who were also mothers should be seen as law's loss. Full-time motherhood could offer a woman a more satisfactory working life – albeit unpaid and not altogether litigious – than the dismal rewards offered by the legal profession.

Before 1970, only a few able, energetic, and lucky women managed to surmount these imposed stereotypes and expectations. Competence and merit exist and flourish only within a social context. It is important to understand the context and its history in order to allow for a more just assessment of the performance of the 2 per cent of the legal profession in Manitoba who were women.

### CHAPTER FIVE

# Nursing: "One of the Truest and Noblest Callings"

"The struggle of nurses is the struggle of women."[1] So declared one Manitoba woman, who as nurse, instructor, administrator, and activist has helped shape the profession in the late twentieth century. In her view, the fight continues. The goal – still to be achieved – is professional equality for nurses as well as social equality for women.

There is one obvious gender distinction between the professions of university teaching, medicine, and law on the one hand, and nursing and schoolteaching on the other. The first three professions were and still are male-dominated. Nursing and teaching were and are dominated numerically by women. Indeed, for most of the period before 1970, nursing was almost 100 per cent female. On the surface, nurses and teachers conformed to a stereotype of a nurturing woman who traditionally cared for the sick and the young. However, conforming in the selection of a profession did not mean that nurses and teachers necessarily conformed to female stereotypes of behaviour within the occupation.

Nursing as an occupation has had difficulty in persuading society and some of its own workers of a professional identity that deserves recognition and rewards that are commensurate with other professional work. The celebratory ideals and the more mundane conditions of nursing work can sometimes be confused, and at times it can be difficult for a historian to distinguish between the noble myths and the down-to-earth descriptions generated by nursing professionals. Just as traditions and myths have figured powerfully in the professions of medicine, law, and academic teaching, so have they in nursing. The monumental shape of Florence Nightingale towers over the development of this occupation.[2] The basic professional prerequisites of a formal training, with admission standards for entry and with certification tests at completion, began to be instituted in the second half of the nineteenth century.

Many chroniclers of the struggle have themselves participated in it. While most have been sympathetic to the goals of the leaders in nurses' attempt to consolidate professional attributes, there have been writers who have argued against the enterprise.[3] From an implicit vantage point of the superiority of a distinct women's culture, or alternatively from solidarity with other workers of an industrial proletariat, some observers have criticized nurses' agenda as professionals: "As women they could not hope to win the privileges of a profession, and as aspiring professionals they cut themselves off from the broader support that a more inclusive program could have provided."[4] One writer referred to "the lure of professionalism." Nurses, she implied, were mistaken in trying to improve their own working conditions, since such attempts militated against "an alliance between skilled and unskilled alike."[5] Another denied the scientific basis to nursing work and accepted a view of the occupation as a "mother-surrogate role for women" and "a glorified housekeeping profession."[6]

Nursing lends itself to contradictory interpretations.[7] Like much work performed by women, it accommodates a mixture of theoretical and practical work, and, bearing an almost completely feminine face, it appropriates behaviour assigned to the stereotypical female. Deferential, dependent, following rather than leading, selfless, and subordinate – such adjectives are not normal descriptions of the model professional. Serving both her patients and a physician, a nurse could be at the beck and call of two masters.[8] Nursing falls easily outside the segregated compartments of a professional labour force, which is assumed in sociological literature to be almost exclusively masculine, and it has been relegated to the ranks of a "semi-profession."[9] However, if we look beyond the traditional appearance of the workers in their erstwhile uniforms of skirt, cap, and cloak, and if we set aside their gender and examine the nature of the work performed and the structure of the occupation, we can discern most of the components advanced as "professional." As in other professions, the characteristics become clearer and stronger over time; as in other professions, some become deemphasized or more closely delineated in response to internal and external pressures; and as in other professions, professional organizations and leaders exercise a less than monolithic control over the ranks.

From the early days of hospital training schools, nursing has demanded academic (and other) tests for admission: a postsecondary training combining theoretical science and the practical application of skills; a certification test; and a code of ethics safeguarding service to the patient or the consumer. With the advent of state registration came the beginning of self-regulation. A failure to achieve autonomy should not be seen as the test depriving nursing of any claim to be a profession, for other professions also were less than totally independent.

In Europe, the characteristic of autonomy was almost irrelevant in the context of a professional structure where so many professionals were civil servants.[10] In North America, not all professions experienced the same degree of autonomy as American physicians, say. University professors enjoyed it in diluted form only. The collegial system of self-governing peers was rarely kept independent of the funders of university education, in the guise of private benefactors or governments, who populated boards of governors. Schoolteachers rarely escaped the managing supervision of school trustees and ministries of education. Even provincial law societies and colleges of physicians and surgeons thought fit to include lay members on their governing and disciplinary boards.

In North America, autonomy has been the most difficult standard component of professionalism for nursing to achieve. Other groups have always sought to control nurses (hospital administrators and physicians, in particular). Their success for so long has less to do with the work nurses perform and much more to do with the nurses' gender. Women were not supposed to be capable of full self-government. If women regulated their own profession, this would challenge the authority of other groups within a health-care system. It would also undermine the orthodoxy of women's dependence on men, socially, economically, and politically. Hospital administrators and physicians as groups therefore were not necessarily discriminating personally against women when they opposed attempts from nursing organizations to regulate aspects of the nursing profession or to have their own voice in the government of health-care systems. These men were manfully upholding the conventions of gender that permeated modern society, conventions that found their defenders among nurses as well.

Confrontation on the matter of authority was inevitable. The history of nursing in the last hundred years displays the several forays nurses have made in this battle. It is not surprising that the struggle continues; women still have inferior power in society, and men in positions of authority cannot be expected to surrender their power unless they have more to gain than to lose. John Stuart Mill's observation that "the concessions of the privileged to the unprivileged are so seldom brought about by any better motive than the power of the unprivileged to extort them" has been a lesson long in the learning.[11]

The story of nursing in Manitoba began in the same context of health care as the story of medicine – a situation in which men and women, informally trained in therapeutic skills, were consulted by their communities.[12] This practice did not cease with the advent of a large immigrant population and the institution of systems of formal training, but it rapidly lost its economic base of support. Nursing as a profession, actual or incipient, began with the establishment of formal training schools, which at first were directed by women who had in turn been trained in the first generation of hospital training schools elsewhere.

In this chapter, I examine the formation of training schools for nurses in Manitoba and consider the efforts that were made to achieve state registration of nurses. I analyse the structure of professional nursing in the years before World War II; and after a brief review of the change in the delivery of health care in the 1940s, I examine the reduced variety of options for nursing work in the postwar period. Finally, using primarily the testimony of women who worked as nurses before 1970, I look at the profession with a view to understanding its appeal to large numbers of women, and the subordination of its practitioners.

## HOSPITAL TRAINING SCHOOLS

By the time Manitoba's first training school for nurses was opened in 1887, the hospital to which it was attached, the Winnipeg General Hospital, had undergone several transformations since its foundation in 1873. At that date, the hospital was considered a kind of asylum for the sequestering and treatment of severely ill patients who could not afford private care in their own homes.[13] The first hospital dwelling was a single room containing twelve beds in a building owned by a physician. "The thought was that those who by misfortune got knocked out by sickness were lucky to have this primitive hospital to receive them. The patients would care for each other when able to do so, assisted by any help that could be obtained." After six moves in the first two years, a special building was erected and its board legally incorporated in order to qualify for dominion grants. Actually, the financing for the $1,818 structure came from voluntary donations, most of which ($1,345) were generated by women volunteers.[14] Nine years later, a larger hospital was built to accommodate seventy-two patients, and at that time it received both dominion and provincial grants towards its operation.[15] In 1887 a new medical superintendent was appointed, and he insisted on the establishment of a nursing school, with its own residence. It opened in November 1887, and the four apprentice nurses already working in the hospital were given credit for their previous service towards the two-year training course.[16]

By its existence and organization, the school acknowledged that nurses had to have prior education and maturity in order to be eligible; that a formal and systematic training was necessary in order to impart the required knowledge and skills; and that certification, through examinations, would result at the end of the training period. From the beginning, the nursing school was more than an educational institution. It was also an employer. The supervising authority was at first invested completely in the male physician who was medical superintendent of the hospital, accountable to the hospital board. This division of function – educational and economic – provided a context fraught with conflict for subsequent generations of nurses. Only after nurses-in-training ceased to be employees as well as students could nursing begin to resolve one of its major tensions as a profession.

The 1887 "Rules and Regulations" show how nursing was conceptualized both as a profession and as an occupation demanding cheap labour from its trainees: "The object of the School is to train women desiring to become professional nurses ... Regular lectures will be delivered and practical instruction given in the wards and at the bedside." While in training, nurses were not considered to be independent people; they were in the care of the institution, which served as a parent-substitute. Applicants had to be in good health and of good character, and to be so testified by a clergyman. They had to be older than school-leaving age – between twenty-one and thirty-four years old – and at least nominally pious: "Pupil nurses are expected to attend their own place of worship every Sunday." During training, students were provided with room and board, and with their uniforms, free of charge, and after one month's probation they received a nominal wage.[17]

In 1895 an improvement was made to the quality of training, which was extended to three years from two – at the same time extending the period during which the nurses-in-training could be paid at their low wages. In 1889 one small inroad was made into the absolute authority invested in the hospital board and the medical superintendent. A lady superintendent was appointed to supervise the graduate nurses and the nurses-in-training. She shared the supervisory authority, albeit unequally, with the medical superintendent. In 1900 Lady Superintendent Adah Patterson, a Canadian graduate of the famous Johns Hopkins Hospital School of Nursing in the United States, challenged the medical superintendent, to whom theoretically she was subordinate. She asked that questions relating to nursing service be considered not by him alone but by an advisory committee of physicians. Patterson's request was denied, and she resigned.[18] The problems posed by inequality, however, were not lost on some of the probationary nurses in the school at that time. Two of them, Isabel

Maitland Stewart and Ethel Johns, became staunch advocates of improved training and professional independence for nursing, and as leaders of the profession in Canada and the United States they forged links with other feminists.

The personal memoirs of one of the first graduates, Mary Ellen Birtles, indicate that the nurses, both graduates and those in training, had to work very hard and for long hours, and that they were often given heavy responsibilities for which they felt unprepared. At the same time, the training was rigorous in imparting the scientific foundation of nursing in antisepsis and asepsis:

Operations were performed in any part of the hospital, sometimes in the sun galleries and sometimes in the wards. In the latter case, Lister's Spray was brought into use to purify the atmosphere surrounding the patient. It fell to my lot on several occasions to have charge of it and to see that the steam and carbolic acid were properly diffused ... One time, a patient was brought in for ovariotomy. The large room ... was emptied and scrubbed and made as clean as possible for the operation. Everything used in the way of linen and mackintoshes had to be new, direct from the store, and placed in the room; new sponges, and these were real sponges (flat), were used over and over again after being washed in three different bowls of solution (carbolic) [19] ...

We were sometimes sent out. One night the medical superintendent called me at 11.00 p.m. to go out to nurse a maternity case. I told him I had never seen a case and didn't know anything, but that did not make any difference ... I was relieved of having to wash the baby. The doctor sent me down to tell the grandmother to go and wash the baby as he needed me upstairs; she never gave me another opportunity of displaying my ignorance. [20]

Joseph Lister in England had made famous his antispetic procedures, which involved the destruction of micro-organisms around a wound or incision by applying an agent such as carbolic acid. The aseptic method prevented new sources of infection from invading the weakened body of the patient; this was achieved by a rigorous cleansing of the patient's environment. Antiseptic methods and asepsis were known in Canada by 1870, but they were slow in spreading because of the resistance from doctors trained in alternate scientific theories. By the 1890s, they were being used in Winnipeg. [21]

Ethel Johns entered the nursing school in 1899, and with the benefit of hindsight gained by a half-century of working for improvements, she was uncomplimentary about the school's standards:

Could it truly be said that The Winnipeg General Hospital was conducting a school of nursing worthy of the name? There were no teaching facilities what-

soever. There was no one whose whole time could be devoted to theoretical instruction. The pupils had to work to the point of exhaustion. They were
ill-housed and ill-fed. And yet, in spite of it all, there was a school of nursing.
And its pupils were fiercely loyal to it. They knew that the woman at its head
possessed integrity and character. They knew that the medical staff respected
them and tried to teach them. They shouldered responsibility much too heavy
for their young shoulders and they learned ... by trial and error. But they did
learn.[22]

The obedient subordination demanded of nurses, already challenged
by one lady superintendent, was for a second time flouted in 1902.
Three graduate nurse positions were filled by nurses trained in the
United States and Montreal. The Winnipeg nurses held a meeting to
protest the injustice "when persons from outside and from another
country are brought in and put over our heads," and they drafted a resolution to place before the hospital board. William Hespeler, chairman
of the board, responded that the board "must retain absolutely its freedom to choose nurses."[23] The five nurses who had protested were sum-
marily dismissed,[24] but their cause was taken up by local labour leaders
and feminists. A woman who edited and produced a weekly newspaper
and who was later a strong suffragist wrote: "The diplomas and medals
were given as a guarantee that they had completed their training and
were qualified to attend the sick, not as a reward for politeness towards
the board or as a mark of their good behaviour."[25] Student nurses gave
support to the dismissed nurses by submitting "a round robin" protest
letter to the board, but to no avail.[26]

The episode is revealing because it demonstrates the nurses' lack of
power, and at the same time it shows their spirit; they did not allow the
intimidation of the board to blunt their protests. The episode also
reveals the links between nurses and other groups working to reform
society, connections that were strong at the beginning of the twentieth
century. Johns characterized the training system under the authoritarian board and medical superintendent as a cynical way of providing for
a "cheap, efficient and docile nursing force."[27] In 1902 and during the
following ten years, the behaviour of nurses at the Winnipeg General
Hospital was not as docile as the men would have liked.

### STATE REGISTRATION

Nursing Schools were soon attached to other hospitals in the province,
both in Winnipeg and in the country towns – all rapidly expanding because of the massive immigration around the turn of the century.
St Boniface Hospital, first opened in 1871, was owned and operated by

the Grey Nuns, and its nursing staff were at first sisters of the religious order.[28] They opened a school in 1897. By 1914, outside the metropolitán area, eighteen hospitals had been opened, of which ten ran nursing schools or participated in nurses' training. Of these, three (Brandon, Portage, and Dauphin) had a capacity of more than fifty beds, but the rest were small hospitals. Education offered in such circumstances was inevitably inferior to that in the larger hospitals, and much responsibility fell on inadequately trained student nurses.[29]

The contradiction between the two objectives of providing training and employment was early diagnosed as a problem by graduate nurses, who in 1904 resolved to reform the training system and the profession. The first step was the formation of an alumnae association of the Winnipeg General Hospital School of Nursing. Its constitution and by-laws were drawn up by Ada Newton, who had reviewed similar material from other training schools and "thought the lot of nurses could be improved." The association's aims were to provide mutual help among graduates, "to further the interests of our Training School," and "to place the profession of nursing on the highest possible plane."[30] Almost immediately, the association established its own independent referral agency for the most common form of nursing employment – private-duty nursing in a patient's home – and "the right of nurses to manage their own business affairs without undue medical interference was established in Winnipeg for all time."[31]

A second step towards consolidating the group of graduate nurses with a view to structural reform was taken in 1905. After hearing an Ontario nurse speak on the desirability of a provincewide organization, the Manitoba Association of Graduate Nurses (MAGN) was formed. As its immediate objective, the new association wished to introduce state registration. It felt that this would require membership and standards of training and professional conduct to be enforced by the nursing profession. This same objective was taken up in the Winnipeg General Hospital nurses' *Alumnae Journal*, which was founded by Ethel Johns in 1907 and edited by her. From the outset, the journal provided a lively forum for informed debate on nursing issues. Johns's business editor was Isabel Stewart. These two remarkable 1902 graduates subsequently exercised great influence in setting goals for nursing in two countries – Johns in Canada, both as editor 1933–44 of the national magazine the *Canadian Nurse* and as an educator and consultant; and Stewart as a professor of nursing in Columbia University Teachers' College, the foremost North American institution for nursing education. Both saw nursing as a lifelong commitment, which Johns stressed in an article addressed to newly graduated nurses. She deplored the tendency to use nursing as a prelude to marriage. A choice should be made between the two careers: "They are quite incompatible. Like iron and whisky, they are both most valuable – but you cannot take them in the same glass."[32]

Fortified by organizational support from a provincewide group and from hospital alumnae associations (St Boniface formed its own in 1905), the MAGN formed committees to draft and lobby for legislation to bring about state registration. The MAGN enjoyed support from the lady superintendent of Winnipeg General Hospital and the sister superior of St Boniface Hospital, who were honorary presidents, and from some doctors, notably Jasper Halpenny, who had been medical superintendent at Winnipeg General, 1901–04. During the registration campaign, 1905–13, the MAGN learned from the experience of other jurisdictions. Hospitals in Chicago had university affiliation, and this element was incorporated into the Manitoba proposals. The goal was to insist on satisfactory educational standards, to be enforced by educational institutions in partnership with nurses. This was a well-nigh impossible ideal for the time. Women suffered such widespread legal disabilities that the idea of them taking legal control of their own profession (when Canadian law did not even recognize women as "persons" until 1929) was almost unimaginable. The committee chosen to present the registration proposal to the legislature included five medical doctors and two lawyers – but not one nurse and not one woman.[33]

Opposition came from the rural hospitals, whose small size would disqualify them from having training schools and thus the low-paid labour of student nurses.[34] The draft legislation proposed to limit the schools to hospitals that had at least fifty beds. As well, it included proposals for a minimum educational standard for admission, a uniform length of training, a standardized curriculum, and examinations to be controlled by a provincial council. It also proposed to require nurses trained elsewhere to submit their credentials for licensing in Manitoba.[35] Support came from the local Council of Women, from Mary Crawford (one of the two women physicians then in Winnipeg), and from individual men connected with the University of Manitoba and the Winnipeg General Hospital.[36]

An act was passed in 1913, thereby making Manitoba the second province in Canada (after Nova Scotia in 1910) to achieve a measure of registration legislation. There were three positive aspects. First, the title "registered nurse" was recognized and protected by law. Second, all examinations were under the control not of the hospital or the medical profession but of the Council of the University of Manitoba, which had power to appoint examiners. Third, the foundation had been laid "upon which ... a substantial structure may be built."[37] Johns called the law "weak," observing that "this rather toothless initiative" enabled any hospital with a daily average of only five patients to have its own school of nursing. There was no compulsory educational qualification required for admission to training, and there were no provisions for the inspection of hospitals or nursing schools.[38] By 1929, there had been some improvements. Training schools had to have a minimum of twenty beds; and for admission into a program, an applicant had to have at least one year of high school education. The provincial association was renamed the Manitoba Association of Registered Nurses. Nurses were henceforward able to define who could identify herself as a registered nurse, but they still had no power to punish untrained personnel.[39]

### NURSING IN THE INTERWAR YEARS

By the early 1920s, the hospital was a very different institution from its asylum-type predecessors. It had become a modern, scientific, progressive laboratory where doctors could perform their new skilled techniques of surgical intervention. Until the discovery of antibiotics twenty years later, recovery rates after surgery depended primarily on the general health of the patient. Another highly important condition of the patient's recovery was the quality of the hospital environment with respect to the hygiene of the habitat and the personal care provided by watchful attendants. Both the vigorous cleansing techniques, which controlled germs, and the care were the responsibilities of the hospital nursing staff. Until later pharmaceutical developments, the new intrusive surgery carried many victims in its wake. That there were no more deaths than there were is probably due to the quality of the work performed by nurses in maintaining the aseptic environment and in providing care and comfort for the convalescent patient.

Nursing work was crucial within the hospital setting. In the interwar years, there were two additional areas for nurses' work: community health and private duty. The immense population influx into Manitoba in the decade preceding World War I revived fears of infectious disease, especially in the urban areas. Smallpox, typhoid, and tuberculosis were threats to the health of the whole community. Also, concern was expressed at the death rates in Winnipeg, which were frequently the highest in North America.[40]

Reluctantly and belatedly, the city council acknowledged a responsibility for health and appointed a city physician, passed regulations concerning sewage and water supply, and provided milk for babies in poor families. This mixture of ameliorative and preventive measures was continued during the interwar period. The delivery of health services was in the hands of nurses. Private organizations, directed by volunteers, and public governments at the provincial and municipal levels furnished funds for these services.

Although the hospital was the training ground for all nurses, in the interwar years it was not the single most important place of employment for registered nurses. As can be seen from table 17 (appendix 1), the Canada-wide distribution of nurses among the three major types of employment in 1930 and 1943 was mainly in private-duty nursing. In this type of work, a registered nurse was hired by a patient, often on the recommendation of a doctor. The nursing care was most often delivered in the patient's home, though it could also be delivered in a hospital, in a private or semi-private room. The patient was responsible for paying the nurse's wages, a charge that might be covered by private health insurance. As Kathryn McPherson pointed out in her study of interwar nursing, for the private-duty nurse, "the variety, choice and independence of one-to-one care captured the essence of what they valued in their working lives."[41] The type of work performed by private-duty nurses was categorized by George Weir in his study of nursing in Canada.[42] In comparison with private-duty nurses in other provinces and regions, prairie nurses were more likely to accept twenty-four-hour service jobs and to perform household duties.[43] One of the disadvantages of this work was the pay; the private-duty nurse was dependent on the patient for her fee and could not always collect wages that were due. Those working in an institutional settling had the benefit of the hospital serving as the collection agency, but in a domestic setting a nurse might be pressured into doing more work than she was paid for.[44]

A third problem for the private-duty nurse was that work was not always available. One Manitoba nurse preferred private duty to "floor duty" in a hospital, "but one might not get a case for a month," she stated. "Pay [for a 1934 RN] was $5.00 a day for 12 hours, $4.00 a day for 8 hours, $6.00 a day for 24 hours. Never sure of being paid."[45] "Long hours were often a minus factor," said a 1933 registered nurse.[46] Some took this kind of work because more agreeable alternatives were unavailable, as one nurse explained: "I did private-duty nursing – you were lucky to get work. There were so many nurses out of work during the Depression."[47] Private-duty nurses often found themselves in precarious financial straits, whereas those who managed to get hospital or public-health positions were at least guaranteed constant employment.[48]

The shortage of work caused many of the registered nurses of the 1920s and 1930s to emigrate to the United States, "where graduates of Canadian schools were welcomed. There was a feeling that standards in Canada were higher."[49] Of the three types of nursing work, median incomes for public-health work in 1930 were the highest: $1,574, compared with $1,022 for the private-duty nurse and $1,385 for the hospital nurse (taking account of the room and board supplied in institutions and private-duty nursing).[50] Public-health work was as "a travelling evangelist and teacher of health," and included welfare work as well as sickbed care.[51] Employed by a government agency at the municipal, provincial, or federal level, or by a welfare organization such as the Red Cross, the public-health nurse was secure. In Manitoba the range of public-health nursing work in the 1920s and 1930s included "health education carried on in schools, fresh air camps, summer fairs, teacher training institutions ... Services included maternal and child health, school health, adult health and communicable disease control." Specifically, the nurses organized and directed clinics related to dental and eye care, tuberculosis, and venereal disease. They supervised children's boarding homes, day nurseries, and maternity homes. They provided instruction on first aid to community groups.[52] Public health gave them the opportunity for organization and management as well as for the delivery of services.

One form of public-health nursing was practised in the Red Cross Outposts that were established by the Canadian Red Cross after World War I in remote areas with scattered populations. By the end of 1925, there were thirty-one outposts across Canada, five of them in Manitoba, each with accommodation for up to two bed-patients. (The outposts operated mainly by a system of "field nursing," whereby the nurse worked mostly in the homes and schools of the district.) By the late 1950s, the outposts were phased out, but for nearly forty years they offered opportunities of such great challenge – the nurses being "full of heroism without heroics" – that these women took on the reputation of gallant saintlike celebrities.[53] Financing was shared equally between the Red Cross and the provincial Department of Health.

In 1930 Hilda St Germaine took charge of the East Braintree Red Cross Nursing Station, some 60 kilometres east of Winnipeg, with "no doctors, no roads, and very little means of transportation." Travel was on a "jigger," a small unheated car that ran on the railway tracks and was propelled by a small engine. "Arriving at the nearest point to the patient's home on the railway line, the relatives would meet you with a slow-going team of horses and a wooden sleigh. Then followed a trip into the bush of anything up to ten or fifteen miles, over badly rutted roads, the same return trip after the patient had been attended."[54]

Primitive travel across the bush was likewise a common experience for Ruth Evans, who in 1951 was appointed nurse-in-charge at Alonsa on Lake Winnipeg, about 120 kilometres north of Portage la Prairie:

"The roads were not always kept open in winter and some of the people were quite isolated. The nearest hospital and doctor were fifty-five miles away at Ste Rose. The population at that time was roughly 2,000, spread over a large area. They were mainly farmers and fishermen near the Lake." Often a member of the patient's family collected Evans from Alonsa:

I was called out one bitterly cold night in January, shortly after my arrival. The man who came for me stated only that his little boy was very sick. I dressed warmly and packed my bag. It was a fifteen-mile trip across country through the bush. It was a beautiful night, with a full moon, but I was too cold to fully appreciate it! When we arrived at his small cabin, I found his small two-year old boy delirious with a high fever and pneumonia. I gave him penicillin and decided to take him to hospital in Ste Rose ... This time, we travelled in a caboose, or covered sleigh, back to town. There I was able to get a car for the rest of the trip.

Joint support from the Red Cross and the provincial government was provided for the Red Cross "car" on the Hudson's Bay Company railway in northern Manitoba between 1953 and 1958, as Evans described:

The car, an old day coach, had a large clinic room at one end, with a curtained off area for examinations. Next to the Clinic was the nurse's bedroom. To one side of the room a door led to a large storage room for drugs and supplies ... Off the hall was a small bathroom and galley kitchen ... The car would service the communities along approximately two hundred miles of the railway between Wawbowden and Gillam. In winter, the car was stationed for three months at Wawboden, and three months at Gillam, in order to be connected to the steam. In summer, the car travelled the line to the smaller communities.[55]

Health problems included accidents such as axe wounds, and gastro-enteritis in the summer, and the nurses carried on extensive immunization and nutrition programs. By the 1950s, the midwifery work was reduced, since "most women had become used to going to hospital" to deliver their babies.[56] But the nurses continued to see people in their own homes, which were often very poor and without services of sanitation and heating – services that were taken for granted in the urban settlements.[57] As Evans noted, "One never knew what would happen next! It was like 'playing doctor' without the necessary training, and no diagnostic facilities."[58]

These opportunities in the community were not exactly what most nurses wanted. Responsibilities more directly related to their hospital training were assumed by about one-quarter of the interwar nurses. A 1935 registered nurse described her response to the labour market: "When I graduated there weren't many choices. Private duty nurses were starving – public health didn't appeal. I found the psychiatric experience for six weeks during training very interesting and, as I expected there would always be humans going crazy, I was sure of a good living."[59] In these Depression years, work in a hospital, as in public health, held the attraction of security, regularity, and reasonable pay, as well as offering familiarity to someone who had spent three years learning all the routines.[60] The single most disagreeable aspect to the work was the lack of personal freedom. Other disadvantages were the "nerve-wracking responsibilities," the long and intensive hours of work, and the pay. Although institutional income was generally higher than private-duty income, in G.M. Weir's opinion it was not high enough.[61] He considered the pay to be "quite modest" in contrast to that of a high school teacher, whose educational standards and training he considered comparable.

Weir in 1932 had recommendations for a fundamental overhaul and a change in direction for nursing training and the delivery of nursing services. While many of his suggestions remained unimplemented until after 1970, some of the reforms were carried out during postwar reconstruction. He wanted hospitals to be staffed primarily by graduate nurses rather than by nurses-in-training; and as the other side of this coin, he wanted nurses to be educated prior to employment rather than having their untrained labour exploited by hospitals.[62] These reforms would make hospitals more costly to run and were also likely to reduce the control of hospital admistrators over the training of nurses. During the war years, developments on both fronts, at a time of national emergency, laid the groundwork for more thorough reform later.

## WORLD WAR II AND POSTWAR CHANGE

The increased demand for nurses in the armed forces absorbed the numbers of underemployed and unemployed nurses of the Depression years, and by 1941 officials in the government and in the nursing profession were recognizing "a possible shortage of qualified nurses."[63] Constitutionally, the provinces were responsible for health care, including hospitals. The war crisis gave centralizing power to the federal government, which in turn distributed financial support to encourage increased enrolment at hospital training schools.[64] Under pressure from a national emergency, training resources were rationalized to the extent of eliminating smaller schools and concentrating instruction in the larger urban centres. More new nurses were trained in fewer centres, and at the same time there was a concentrated effort to mobilize retired (or "inactive") registered nurses. The vast majority of this group had retired because of marriage, and recruiting propaganda went so far as to appeal to married nurses to return to work "for the duration." However, few hospitals went so far as to remove their normal prohibition against hiring or employing married graduate nurses.[65] The married nurses who worked professionally during the war were channelled mainly into private-duty nursing. This field of employment declined dramatically during the war years: "Whereas in 1930 the ratio of private duty nurses to institutional nurses was 60:25, by 1943 this had reversed to 29:48 and by 1948 had dropped to 15:67."[66] At the same time, hospital employment for registered nurses increased by 28 per cent between 1939 and 1943.[67] Working conditions for the hospital general-duty nurse slowly improved, though the hours remained long. In 1943 over half the graduate nurses in general hospitals across Canada worked more than ninety-six hours in a two-week period, but more institutions started to introduce an eight-hour shift.[68] By the end of the war, the hospital had replaced the private home as the major locus for nursing care.

Even though hospitals began to employ more graduate nurses, nurses-in-training continued to provide much of the labour of hospitals, and they were still subject to close supervision and rigid discipline. One nurse who trained during the war said:

Many classmates hated our training. We had a really tough time, obeying all rules, attending prayers before breakfast, having our rooms inspected daily. No overnights out, finally getting our first late-leave – 11 p.m.! – which we'd lose if we were late for prayers or signing in; our uniforms inspected suddenly during class to see that we had two straight pins attaching our collars to our dress, no safety pins in place of buttons, etc., hairnets to keep our hair off our collars, our shoes polished; plus lectures if we'd gone on an elevator before a senior student; lights out at 10.30 p.m.; no radios and no smoking ... I don't think it hurt us – but it wouldn't do today! You had to want to be a nurse![69]

The hours were long, as one woman recalled: "My biggest problem was trying to stay awake during lectures. We worked 7 a.m. to 7 p.m., six and a half days a week, with lectures from 1 to 3 p.m. ... The rules were overly strict. We were never allowed an overnight leave – even on Christmas Eve."[70] A 1948 graduate remembered the feeling "that we were 'slave labour'" as students.[71]

The hospitals did not monopolize nurses' employment, however. There was still a considerable number of public-health jobs in both town and country, and in rural districts with scattered populations these could offer work of great responsibility for the nurse. In Manitoba, the Red Cross nursing stations made the nurse the primary and often the only professional health-care giver in a community. In postwar society, nurses were divided between the field of public-health work and the larger (and, moreover, expanding) area of hospital employment. This reduction in variety of employment opportunities was more apparent than real. Within the hospital, developing technology and increasing specialization provided many different types of work. Gradually, many of the old deterrents to hospital employment were undermined, but improvement was slow and did not proceed uniformly across Canada. Reforms were linked to two other developments: the institution of health insurance, and a shift towards university-based nursing training. In Manitoba, the latter was still in its infancy before 1970.

The financing of hospitals, and of health care, was closely connected to the employment prospects for nurses. If a nurse could not be sure of getting paid, this was a clear disincentive to remaining in the labour force as a private-duty nurse; and if a nurse had to work long hours under rigid and repressive conditions in a poorly equipped hospital with unsatisfactory support systems, this did not encourage her to make nursing a lifetime career. New, larger, and more numerous hospitals, however, needed nurses for their staff, especially when the traditional supply of cheap trainee student staff was being reduced. In the generation following World War II, the nursing profession had an opportunity for transformation. In the event, nurses took two generations, not one, to achieve substantial change. The lengthier process was in part a result of divisions within the occupation and the retarding influence of the ethic of self-sacrifice. It was not easy to persuade nurses to take collective action at all, still less on their own behalf, when their training had stressed the duty to put others' needs and patients' comfort before their own.

The delay was also connected to the power of the purse. Hospital administrators continued to exert a very powerful influence – even, in many instances, a domination – over the training and subsequently the working conditions of the majority of employees: the nurses. The hospitals' income, in turn, came from a mixture of sources (fee-paying patients, charitable institutions, and municipal or provincial governments, which were perpetually strapped for funds), all of which were trying to maximize services and minimize costs. The bargaining power of the nurses depended on their willingness to withdraw their labour.

For many nurses and for their associations, this was construed as a trade union tactic, with which they were most uncomfortable, and it could be interpreted as a contravention of their commitment to service.

The funding for hospitals changed in 1957.[72] Henceforward it was derived almost totally from public funds – from federal and provincial governments – and in a context in which the federal government aimed to deliver equality of service throughout the country. In effect, the federal government, accountable to the electorate, was not only assuming responsibility for the health care of patients, who were also consumers and taxpayers, but it was also taking on the role of a single employer responsible for providing just working conditions. These were no longer exclusively what the hospital administrators could get away with; they were supposed to resemble models of equitable treatment. Politicians were more susceptible to pressures of public opinion than unelected managers were, and public opinion included not only patients, physicians, and the healthy but also the sick and the nurses. As the monolithic power of hospital administrators over nurses was reduced, the situation of nurses improved, albeit slowly and not always in the direction of complete professional autonomy.

In Britain, which in the nineteenth century provided many of the early Manitoba nurses and which continued to supply many models of training, nursing as an occupation went through three phases. In the first, "lady" nurses acted as hospital housekeepers, as the unequal partners of doctors. In the second phase, during the interwar period, nursing was made much more subordinate to the profession of medicine, which was becoming more linked to engineering and pharmaceutical knowledge. "The third phase was marked by state intervention," accompanied by a transformation in hospital-labour relations, which became polarized between management and workers, with a consequent appeal in collective action through unionization for nurses.[73] Just as British nurses became more militant towards the 1970s, Manitoba nurses and their organizations were more inclined to insist on the practical and public recognition of their indispensable contribution to the health-care system.

Weir in 1932 had recommended that nursing training should not continue under the aegis of hospital administrators but that, like training for other professions, it should be organized, administered, and delivered by universities.[74] Model institutions in Canada already existed. The first was the School of Nursing at the University of British Columbia, established in 1919. By 1947, ten other universities, including the University of Manitoba, were offering nursing programs. Most were postgraduate programs in nursing education, administration, and supervision, and in public health. The vast majority of registered nurse training continued to be offered through the hospital nursing schools. When in 1963 the University of Manitoba introduced the bachelor of nursing degree, it did not meet with universal approval from within the profession. Many nurses regretted the shift in emphasis away from direct nurse-patient care and questioned the need for a more theoretical training. Within the university, educational administrators were slow to accord full academic status to the School of Nursing and its instructors. Yet this shift, accompanied by much soul-searching from nurses and by ambivalence from university officials, was the way of the future. The nursing profession, twenty years later in the 1990s, became officially united behind the goal of university training for all nurses by the year 2000.[75]

## NURSING WORK, MANITOBA, 1950–1970

The working habits of nurses after the war were closely connected to family responsibilities. There was a significant difference from the pre-war experience, when most nurses retired from the labour force at marriage. In contrast, after the war, more and more married nurses continued to work. Two dominant patterns emerged. One was a nurse's retirement at the birth of her first child and her withdrawal from the labour force until her children were older, probably teenagers, at which time she would return to work, either full-time or part-time. The other pattern was a nurse's shift in employment, on maternity, from full-time to part-time work, which was most often at night or weekends. This usually lasted while her children were small and needed attention during the day, and it coincided with the early formative years of family establishment when expenses were high and a husband's starting income was often low.

Notwithstanding the willingness of married nurses to work for pay and the corresponding change in hospital practice to employ married nurses, a cultural expectation that a woman would retire on marriage, or at least at maternity, persisted. The statistics show that this expectation, although strong, became weaker. In 1946, 11 per cent of the registered nurses working in Manitoba were married; by 1951 the proportion was 29 per cent, in 1961 it was 52 per cent, and in 1971 it was 64 per cent.[76] As a 1950 nurse explained, "Very few stayed with nursing once they had their families. A greater majority married well so didn't have to work at nursing."[77] This was true, but as time went on, more of the married nurses worked for pay. Moreover, her analysis that "marrying well" saved a qualified nurse from "having to" work was not the only reflection to be made on nurses' continuing participation in paid work. The nurses who responded to my survey displayed various patterns of behaviour.

Invariably, the family came first. Yet many nurses found a way of continuing to work, albeit with interruptions. Twenty-eight nurses who were registered between 1950 and 1968 participated in the survey, and of these, only two (both of whom registered during the 1950s) retired completely from nursing when their children were born. Two others were single and always worked full-time. The remainder were evenly divided between those who interrupted their working career to withdraw temporarily from the labour force when children were small, and those who continued to work, always on a part-time basis, during their children's infancy. Postwar employers wooed the married nurse with the flexible hours and shift work that the nurses wanted, as their comments reveal: "When I worked part-time, I worked nights so I didn't have to leave my children in the care of a sitter";[78] "I worked evenings – husband and I took turns looking after first child";[79] "Working shift was acceptable to me: it allowed me to spend time at home with my children when they were young";[80] "Chose to work evenings or nights or weekends when spouse could assist with childcare. This ceased to be a problem as the children became teenagers";[81] "Nursing was ideal with small children as shift work was flexible – husband helped and I worked 6–12 p.m."[82] Some arrangements demanded complex organizational skills: "Worked part-time twice weekly when children 1–5 years old: neighbour babysitter 3–6 p.m. and husband picked up when he came home – I worked 3.30–11.30 when children 5–8 years old. I arranged a team of junior high seniors (grade 8–9) to come in from 4–6 until husband came home."[83]

The type of work nurses performed while their children were small reflected the type generally available. Hospital work dominated. During World War II, married nurses had still found themselves excluded from institutional employment and had tended towards private-duty nursing. After the war, there was very little private-duty nursing at all; hospitals no longer maintained the bar against marriage; and although public-health and community nursing still offered some jobs, the vast majority of nurses, regardless of marital status, were employed in hospitals (see table 19, appendix 1).

Many nurses identified the flexibility of hours and the availability of employment as a positive aspect to nursing work; it seemed tailor-made to permit a working mother to design an accommodating routine. Not that everything was ideal. Nurses identified problems with pay, the lack of fringe benefits, poor pensions, and fatigue, as well as systemic problems related to patients and physicians.

Among the nurses surveyed, there was a tone of diffidence in identifying drawbacks. Pay was thought satisfactory by some, or at least not an issue to complain about. "It is a relatively well-paid job after a relatively short period of education," said one.[84] But her perception was not general. More frequent were comments such as "The pay could be better so as to beat out Safeway cashiers";[85] "Nursing is underpaid for the hours and work required";[86] and "Nursing is on the bottom of the heap, especially the general duty nurse."[87] Criticism of low pay could be expressed obliquely. Referring to "quite a few who have left nursing," one nurse explained: "The main reason was, they could make a better living with a lower stress level."[88] "I was fortunate not to have been the breadwinner," said another.[89] On this point, a divorced nurse wrote, "Hours and pay always seemed adequate when I was married. Now that I am responsible for sole support, pay seems very inadequate for the responsibility of the job."[90] Although few explicitly noted that fringe benefits and pensions were unsatisfactory, one who did so felt strongly about it. "Pensions should be transferable from one position to another," she wrote. Picking up the theme that the struggle of nurses was the struggle of women, she continued: "Women should be more knowledgeable about the fringe benefits ... Disability and group insurance are important ... Your retirement years should be happy and comfortable with all the health benefits possible."[91]

Few of the surveyed nurses stated that pay and benefits were satisfactory. Most were silent on the subject, but some drew a direct link between low pay and collective action of a trade union type, suggesting that union activity brought more costs than benefits. This was one of the two topics to excite strong statements, and they were mainly in condemnation of unions, for example: "I think nurses aren't paid as well as other professions, but I don't think striking is the answer."[92] "I'd like to think ... that their pay cheques would reflect [their] training," noted one, but she did not consider that union militancy was a satisfactory way to accomplish improvements. "I guess I'm out of touch but I'd rather see talk than blackmail. Too many people suffer."[93] A retired nurse regretted "unions being formed" but felt that it "may have been necessary to get the higher wages."[94] Another nurse, who was still working in 1992, said that she resented "the militant approach" of their union talks: "I believe in co-operation rather than confrontation."[95]

The nurses who participated in the survey had extensive working careers before 1970, except for two, who retired completely when a first child was born. Many indeed continued to work after 1970. None of the respondents could avoid seeing union militancy from a post-strike perspective, for in January 1991 Manitoba nurses were on strike for one month before achieving an advantageous monetary contract. The sight of nurses on picket lines was unsettling to the nurses who had qualified before 1970. Some were disturbed at inroads on an image of professionalism. They held that unions had "not elevated our profession" but that, on the contrary, they had "lowered the standards and the entire meaning of nursing."[96] A similar view was: "Nurses should never have been unionized. They lost a lot of their professional dignity."[97] Another stated: "I hate to see strikes happening. Hopefully, there will be some better way, looking at ... the upheavals they cause for patients and all others concerned."[98] One nurse regretted "the need for a labour union. Nursing was considered a profession, and our professional organization developed reasonable guidelines for education and work and salaries."[99] A typically rueful remark was, "Although unionization has helped nurses attain better salaries, benefits, etc., I feel it takes away from the essence of professionalization."[100]

One respondent included an analysis of the relationship between the delivery of health care and union militancy:

The Manitoba Association of Registered Nurses and the Manitoba Nurses' Union must join closer ties and develop mutual goals to maintain both the professional and the monetary standing nurses have obtained, or patient/client care is going to deteriorate. Nurses must fight to maintain the health care system. The four year Bachelor of Nursing program associated with hospitals ... is a big step forward and should make great nurses ... I have seen the development of unionism in nursing ... Unfortunately, without the union movement and collective bargaining, nurses would still be making $400 a month. I feel the health care system never recovered from removing the 300 nurses from the Health Sciences Centre (and all other hospitals) who gave free service for educaton prior to 1970. When nurses (women) finally have been able to obtain adequate salaries to compensate them for their education and responsibility, the system can't pay them, and there are no jobs ... Tragic![101]

### WHAT NURSES THOUGHT OF NURSING

The surveys elicited information from nurses on how they viewed their profession, particularly with respect to their own training and to the differences they noted in the profession as it had developed since the time of their own registration. On two issues the respondents were agreed; on two others there were differences. There was almost universal agreement about the value of their own training (though some aspects had been problematic) and on the development of a different relationship between the nurse and physician. On the matter of a differing emphasis given to bedside patient care vis-à-vis theoretical knowledge of health care, there was disagreement, as there was about the "essence of professionalization," as suggested above.

The nurses were graduates of a hospital school of nursing, the dominant form of pre-1970 training. Although rules and routines had been modernized since the first Manitoba schools were established at the end of the nineteenth century, the central features remained. Students lived in residence for three years; there was a heavy reliance on learning by doing; the practical was emphasized over the theoretical, though the latter became more important over the years; direct bedside patient care was at the centre of the nurse's purpose; and the nurse was expected to tread a tightrope between a readiness to take responsibility and a deferral to other professionals and managers.

The years in residence resulted in impressive bonding among the nurses who lived and worked together intimately over three years. Looking back, the nurses valued "a great school spirit,"[102] and "the camaraderie of the students."[103] In the school, "there was a feeling of purpose of support."[104] Friendships lasted a lifetime, and alumnae meetings were well attended.[105] For many post-1970 nurses, this experience was unknown and enviable. The nurses were not uncritical, though. "Too much autocratic, senseless discipline," said one.[106] Similar comments were: "I found the regime sometimes strangling ... but that created good personal disciplines in my later life";[107] "Often we weren't treated as adults";[108] "Live-in residence not for me – when to brush your teeth, etc."[109] The fond recollections and "feminist support groups developed from living in residence together"[110] were at the cost of infantilization and military-type subordination during training.

A symbol of the hierarchy typical of the two original religious and military models for the nursing profession was the formal reverence accorded to the physician. Even though there was an occasional regret for the disappearance of "strict adherence to rules and protocol,"[111] no nurse expressed regret that "there is less treating doctors as gods."[112] "Am glad to see doctors don't look down on nurses now as second-hand citizens," said a 1934 registered nurse.[113] "Doctors were overbearing in my time and deserved to be hauled off their pedestals," said a wartime RN, but she continued equivocally, "We still need privates and generals and discipline."[114] Into the 1950s a nurse was supposed to stand when a doctor entered the room, to give up a place in an elevator, and to serve as his mute handmaiden.[115] This attitude persisted even later: "Back in the sixties one just followed orders and never questioned why."[116] Nurses were obliged to conform; yet, in retrospect, none expressed dismay over the passing of this era. They simply noted that things were "changing for the better as nurses and doctors now can confer about a patient's conditions and a nurse is asked for suggestions for care."[117] It was also observed that nursing students "are more direct, honest and self-confident."[118] By the 1990s, one nurse could go so far as to claim that "doctors are now considered colleagues, rather than superiors,"[119] but none made such an observation about the pre-1970 days.

Working nurses were mostly pleased with the training they had received and with the displacement of the physician from his status as a superior being. (Few physicians were women.) On the other hand, there was disagreement about the changing balance of practical and theoretical work. Many nurses thought that the emphasis should continue to be on practical training and considered that the tender loving bedside care given to a patient should loom largest in a nurse's job description: "Here is a nostalgic wish to return to the uncomplicated, non-technological world of yesteryear, with its more personal approach."[120] Nurses, it was said, have forgotten "the caring component and nursing love in all dimensions."[121] One nurse stated that she regretted "the lack of time spent with patients in explanations and treatment ... A relaxed patient is much easier to treat and has shorter recovery time, which is the object of nursing care."[122] Some resented the recent "emphasis on degrees in order to advance."[123] On the other hand, one stated: "Nurses today are much more highly trained ... They have much more to learn. Penicillin still hadn't been discovered when we were in training."[124] Similarly: "I don't think a nurse needs as much hands-on experience as I had, to become competent ... I do believe that learning theory and principles is a priority as there are so many changes in technology that affect nurses all along the continuum, from intensive care to in-home care."[125]

Among the nurses who worked before 1970 there was no single view of the appropriate academic/practical balance in nurses' training and work. Nor was there unanimity on what constituted a professional nurse. There were also differing viewpoints on the notion of vocation. Utilitarian responses were not uncommon: "Nurses are generally looked up to in the community ... you can usually arrange to work part-time or hours to fit in with the family."[126] Nursing had practical benefits for day-to-day living.[127] However, many working nurses viewed their work as if it were a calling: "I envisioned myself as an 'angel of mercy' nursing one and all back to health."[128] "I always wanted to be a nurse," was a common recollection of nurses spanning the years from the 1920s to the 1960s.[129] Others saw nursing as the least unattractive of the alternatives. One became a nurse "because I didn't want to be a teacher or stenographer or work in Eaton's or The Bay."[130] Said another, "I actually wanted to go into medicine but the discipline terrified me as a young teenager."[131] A 1960 registered nurse stated, "Most girls at that time were going into teaching, nursing, or secretarial work. I'm not sure why I chose nursing."[132] Once in the profession, there was evidence of a strong emotional commitment to the work, reinforced by a conviction that women, because of their nature, were particularly suited to nurturing care. "Women are caring by nature" was a common response to the question "Why do you think nursing as a profession has always been able to attract so many women?" This was true of the registered nurses of the 1960s as well as those of previous decades.[133] One nurse noted a problem at the heart of the nurturing stereotype. "Women often feel they need to take care of people to validate their worth," she observed, adding that it is "often hard for women to take care of themselves."[134]

This, of course, was why so many nurses had difficulty with the use of union tactics that openly put at risk the objects of their care. Patients could clearly suffer if nurses withdrew their labour as a tool of collective action. Nurses could not contemplate this possibility without shrinking from it. The apparent selfishness of nurses concentrating on their own working conditions could be offensive: "The *me* syndrome sems to have taken over."[135]

Although the survey elicited hints of nurses who found the work fatiguing, underpaid, stressful, and exploitative of gender stereotpyes, dissatisfaction was not expressed in any sustained way. Those women who trained as nurses and were later disappointed or disillusioned by the work tended to quit the profession rather than complain. Some moved to other occupations. Women before 1970, unlike men, could choose the socially approved option of youthful retirement at maternity. Those who remained or returned as working nurses were obviously reconciled to the major features of nursing as a profession. This does not mean that they saw no room for improvement. But among these pre-1970 registered nurses, there were multiple voices regarding the directions for improvement after 1990. As a historian has commented about *One Strong Voice,* an official history of American nurses, "there has always been a chorus."[136]

Since 1970, substantial changes have taken place in nurses' training and in the structure of health-care delivery. Pride in the profession is no longer necessarily interpreted as self-denial. The wartime nurse who "*loved* nursing" ("I loved the swish of my heavily starched uniform and I loved trying to cheer up the patients")[137] was a product of her time. So were the many nurses who entered the profession not because of the aura of service but because of the lack of alternatives. More than one said that she became a nurse because she didn't like typing, she thought she wasn't clever enough to be a teacher, but she wanted to be sure of earning her own living. With a greater choice of occupation, modern nurses are likely to be more rather than less committed to their profession. The feminist connection that nurses enjoyed in the early days has returned as a resource against sentimentality for the largest profession dominated by women.

### CHAPTER SIX

# Teachers: A Majority in the Margins

Teachers formed the bulk of the female professional labour force. More women worked in teaching than in any other single profession. Yet within teaching, men dominated the positions of responsibility and status. They were more likely to be superintendents, principals, and high school teachers. In Manitoba, women monopolized elementary teaching until after World War II, but they were few in number in the high schools and were scarce in administrative positions. Women's absolute majority in numbers, juxtaposed by a virtual absence from positions of authority, displays dramatically how gender was an organizing principle of this profession.

Some women teachers organized in order to defend and promote their interests. In 1933 the Winnipeg Teachers Association, the largest unit within the Manitoba Teachers Federation, split into two locals, the Men Teachers and the Women Teachers – separate organizations, which remained until 1966. The records of the Winnipeg Women Teachers show the women's attempts to advance policies aimed at protecting their position. These were not always obvious. Whereas the interests of male teachers throughout Manitoba were readily identifiable, women's viewpoints, because of tensions based on differential training and marital status, were not always united.

The structure of the profession mirrored gender relations in society. Just as mothers nurtured infants and children in the family, women were responsible for teaching elementary grades in the schools. Just as men monopolized positions of authority both in the family and in public life, so were they the principals and teachers in the high schools and in many elementary schools.[1] In the Province of Manitoba, women were principals in many rural schools, which were mainly confined to grades 1 to 8, and in some urban elementary schools. Elementary schools carried pay scales lower than the rates of senior and junior high schools. Women were found in the ranks of high school staff and in the junior high schools, grades 7 to 9, which in Winnipeg began to be separated as institutions after 1919.[2] Even where women taught the same subjects in the same school, their inferiority was indicated by a differential pay scale until the early 1950s. All men, both single and married, enjoyed a higher rate of pay than all women, whether the men had dependants or not. The pay schedule was designed to reward not only the work performed but also the status of the worker, in the sense that all adult men, actually or potentially, were expected to support a family, whereas all adult women, at the time or in the future, were expected to receive financial protection from a man. This situation was, of course, not unique to Manitoba.[3]

The social expectations of gender similarly governed the imposition of a marriage bar against the employment of married women. There was a widely shared assumption that a woman would retire from teaching at marriage. In the 1920s, when a married woman resisted enforced retirement, the Manitoba Teachers Federation refused to stir on her behalf. During the Depression years of the 1930s, the prohibition was rigorously policed in Winnipeg. A married woman had to show cause for entitlement to employment and was obliged to submit to a close scrutiny of her personal and financial affairs. As a result, after 1930 only the very small number of married women – those who could show either that they possessed irreplaceable skills or that their family conditions failed to meet the normal expectations for a male breadwinner – could remain employed as teachers.[4]

Gender issues in the teaching profession thus included differential pay scales, differential appointments to administrative positions, a marriage bar, and differential support from the teachers' professional association. From the early days of Manitoba as a province, women teachers learned how to accommodate and to challenge the ways in which these issues affected men and women differently. During the thirty-three-year life of the Winnipeg Women Teachers Association, many – but not all – of these issues were confronted directly, and by 1970 most – but not all – differential policies and conventions had been abandoned. Certainly, the Winnipeg Women Teachers Association developed a sophisticated rationale and strategy to promote their members' interests.[5]

The records of the Winnipeg Women Teachers Association, along with those of the Winnipeg Men Teachers Association and their parent body, the Manitoba Teachers Society (named the Manitoba Teachers Federation before 1942), document the attitudes of the teachers. Reports of the minister of education and records of school boards show what employers demanded of teachers. Individual autobiographies reveal different aspects of women in teaching. Together with the testimony of women teachers themselves, there is a rich repository of information describing the experience of women in the teaching profession.

In this chapter, I look at the number and proportion of women teachers, 1881–1971, and consider the levels at which teachers taught. Secondly, I examine their training and qualifications. Then, using published and manuscript records together with oral archives, I focus on gender issues in order to explore the differences in the working conditions of men and women teachers, and I show how women perceived the consequences of difference.

## NUMBERS

In the 1880s women teachers formed just over half of the female professional labour force. The huge and rapid immigration preceding World War I swelled the size of Manitoba's population and increased the number of teachers. Table 20 (appendix 1) shows that the proportion of female professionals who were teachers stabilized at around 50 per cent. After World War II, with an expansion of professional opportunities for women in occupations such as social work, the teacher proportion declined slightly. Nevertheless, teaching continued to attract more professional women than any other professional occupation.

Even in 1881, women formed a significant number of all teachers, but in those days they did not form a majority. As table 21 shows, only 39 per cent of the Manitoba teaching staff in 1881 were female. Already by 1886, the proportion had risen to 49 per cent. Between 1881 and 1911, the period of massive immigration, the province's population increased from 62,260 to 461,394, a rise of 640 per cent. The number of teachers increased much more – from 147 to 2,836 – reflecting the need for education among the large number of child immigrants and the children soon born to the adult immigrant women, who were predominantly of childbearing age. During this huge expansion, women teachers intensified their hold on the profession. Although the number of men teachers increased threefold between 1886 and 1911, the number of women teachers increased almost tenfold. By 1911, women formed 75 per cent of Manitoba teachers. After World War I, the proportion rose to 80 per cent. From then until 1961, the proportion remained over 70 per cent, and by the end of our period there were still 66 per cent who were female.

The phenomenon of the feminization of teaching was common throughout Canada and in the Western world generally. In the older parts of Canada it was the clear trend before Manitoba entered Confederation.[6] Table 22 (appendix 1) shows that the Manitoba experience bore more resemblance to the pattern of Ontario and the provinces farther west than to the Maritime provinces or Quebec, where the profession became even more feminized. Teachers everywhere in Canada in the twentieth century were mainly women, and as late as 1981 the majority (62 per cent) of all professional women were in teaching-related positions.[7]

How teachers were distributed among the various schools and grades is information that in Manitoba was not systematically reported on an annual basis. A general impression of the proportion of Winnipeg men and women teachers and principals can be gathered from figures culled from the period 1943–56, as shown in table 23 (see appendix 1). The proportion of women teachers was as high as 80 per cent in 1943, and although it fell after the war, by 1956 it was nevertheless 73 per cent. However, the proportion of female principals was never parallel. In 1943 only 46 per cent of Winnipeg schools had women principals, and the number fell to 33 per cent by 1956. Women overwhelmingly populated the ranks of the teachers, while men dominated the positions of principals.

A more detailed breakdown of the distribution of Winnipeg teachers can be constructed for the mid-1940s and is shown in table 24 (appendix 1). In the elementary schools, scarcely a male teacher was to be seen. Yet despite their general lack of experience in elementary teaching, men could be and were appointed to the elementary administration, and each year after the war saw an increasing percentage of male elementary principals. Nevertheless, women principals predominated at the elementary levels.

At Manitoba's junior high schools, which were established as separate units after 1919, women teachers dominated but not to the same extent as in the elementary grades, and with each year reported they lost ground to male teachers. In 1943 women were 75 per cent of junior high school teachers, and five years later their proportion had fallen to 58 per cent.[8] Without specific figures, one can only speculate that the high proportion of women during the war was at least partly due to the temporary absence of the male teachers who were in the armed forces, and that the women's postwar drop in numbers represented a reversion to the prewar practice. In these schools, boys were required to take industrial arts; girls, home economics. As there were roughly equal numbers of boys and girls in the schools, there was a prima facie case for equal numbers of specialist teachers, but this did not occur. There were always fewer home economics teachers (all of whom were women) than industrial arts teachers (all of whom were men). In administrative posts, men formed a large majority. A woman was first appointed principal of a junior high school in 1938.

In senior high schools, women formed just under half of the teaching staff, not only in the academic but also in the practical subjects, which at this level were elective rather than compulsory. No woman was a senior high school principal until 1964, when Agnes MacDonald was appointed to Elmwood High School in Winnipeg. Overall, women accounted for about three-quarters of the Winnipeg staff. In 1948 they made up 77 per cent of the classroom teachers and 36 per cent of the principals. All except one of the women principals were at the elementary level.

### TRAINING AND QUALIFICATIONS OF TEACHERS AND PRINCIPALS

The distribution of teachers was related to their training and qualifications as well as to their experience and gender. In order to teach in Manitoba, a teacher had to hold a certificate issued by the provincial Department of Education, and for most of the period 1870–1970 the department maintained an intricately stratified system of eligibility requirements for each level of certificate. Annually, the department reported on the total number of teachers by level of certificate held, and although these were not differentiated by gender, the reports give a general impression of the training and qualifications of teaching staff across the province. The department could also issue a permit, which allowed a person who was ineligible for certification to teach for one year, and it did so at times of severe teacher shortage.

Teacher training was provided by the department through the Manitoba Normal School, a Protestant institution created by legislation in 1882.[9] As well as providing courses for both men and women in Winnipeg, it offered short courses of teacher training at various centres around the province. The Roman Catholic school boards in the nineteenth century relied on religious teaching orders to train and provide elementary education to the Roman Catholic (mainly French-speaking) population of Manitoba.

After the fracas of the Manitoba Schools Question, 1890–97, the original system of denominational state-supported schools controlled by a bifurcated board of education representing the two founding cultures of French and English was abandoned. It was replaced by a system of nonsectarian public schools, in which the language of instruction could be other than English when ten students spoke in a non-English tongue. Because of the rapid and massive immigration from Eastern Europe in the years before World War I, there was a need for trained non-English-speaking teachers. After 1897 teacher training was available at St Boniface for francophones, at Gretna and other Mennonite centres for Mennonites, in Winnipeg for Ukrainians and Poles after 1905, and at Brandon for Ukrainians after 1907. This multiculturalism came to an abrupt end during World War I. Legislation in 1916 instituted compulsory education in the province and made English the sole legal language of instruction. As a result, all the non-English-speaking teacher training was abandoned. In the French-speaking Roman Catholic areas, elementary education was provided by laywomen as well as by the nuns of teaching orders; like all other teachers, they were supposed to teach in English.[10] All teachers had to be certified by the department.

There were various levels of teacher certification. A third-class certificate was granted to a person who had graduated from grade 10 and then completed a short course (generally lasting four weeks) of the teacher training that was available in various towns around the province. Third-class certificates were last issued in 1932. Over the years, eligibility for a second class certificate was tightened. By 1916, a person needed grade 11 standing, followed by a one-year course at the normal school in Winnipeg or Brandon. A first-class certificate could be attained in a variety of ways and carried several additional levels that allowed the holder to teach higher grades in the school system and also entitled her to more pay. For teaching grades 1 to 9, first-class certification was granted to someone who held a second-class certificate and had completed certain grade 12 subjects and a university-level summer session. For eligibility to teach higher grades, first-class certification was granted to a grade 12 high school graduate who had completed a one-year course at the normal school. Holders of first-class certificates who upgraded their qualifications with further university or normal school courses could improve their level of entitlement. A collegiate certificate, which allowed the holder to teach senior high school courses, was granted to a person who held a university degree and had also completed a one-year education course at "the university or its equivalent," or who already held a first-class certificate.[11]

As a result of recommendations from the 1959 MacFarlane Royal Commission on Education and the election of a new government in Manitoba, the system was modified. Teachers continued to be certified to teach in either elementary or secondary schools, but instead of the first- and second-class certificates, teachers were assessed to a certain level according to a mixture of academic qualifications (university) and professional qualifications (Manitoba Normal School or Faculty of Education programs or courses), combined with years of experience. The minimum requirement remained one year of postsecondary training.

The system was simplified when in 1965 the Manitoba Normal School was discontinued; thenceforth, the Faculty of Education at the University of Manitoba provided the professional training for all teachers. The target was set that before 1990 any teacher would require a university degree in order to be certified to teach in the province.[12] By 1974, 61 per cent of the province's teachers had one or more degrees. The average number of years of training beyond grade 12 was 3.6.[13]

During the period 1882–1970, the vast majority of women teachers acquired their training from the Manitoba Normal School. Students learned a mixture of theoretical and practical subjects. Nellie Hislop described her experience, beginning 1889:

I wrote the qualifying examinations for a Second Class ... Certificate during the first two weeks of July 1888. One evening in August Mr Blakeley arrived at our door to deliver my certificate personally into my hands. I had turned sixteen in May, and now I was qualified by age and education, if not by experience, to teach school. And I could upgrade the certificate to make it good for life by taking teacher training at Normal School. It was not unusual for sixteen-year-old girls to teach, even with lower educational qualifications than mine. They were always confined to country schools.

[After a year teaching], the greatest event in my school life was about to begin. I would have to attend Normal School for a term of five months beginning September 1, if I wished to continue teaching with my grade 11 background. Since there was no Normal School building then or for several years, we took our classes on the second floor of the empty Stobart Block on Portage near Main. We were a group of about thirty-five students. Most of us had some teaching experience, but the group included students newly graduated from country and city high schools. I met in this class a girl I loved all my life – Nellie Mooney from Wawanesa, not quite sixteen, lovely to look at, witty in speech, and altogether the brightest of our class ...

We had lectures on new subjects – logic, pedagogy, and psychology. We studied the old masters – Rosencrantz, Rousseau, Froebel, and Pestalozzi – who had formulated the science of child psychology. We received instruction in formulating a lesson, scientifically based in psychology. In time we visited city classrooms, mostly the junior grades, and observed how "good" teachers taught.[14]

Nellie Mooney in time became Nellie McClung, the novelist and famous suffragist and supporter of women's rights, who looked fondly back to her year at the normal school: "New books on psychology, history of education, school management and other aspects of the profession of teaching, all smelling delightfully of new paper and ink, were carried by me back and forth in a new leather bag, and studied with rapture ... I was learning how to think."[15]

Later students were apt to have kinder memories of their fellow students than of their instructors and the intellectual demands of the curriculum.[16] "Class at Normal School had 84 students – theory wasn't very interesting – not enough advice regarding practice," said a 1926 student.[17] "The theoretical training did not provide any training as to how to handle a classroom,"said a 1941 student.[18] "I found a number of the courses to be irrelevant," said a 1955 student.[19] Women who had graduated with a university degree and had then attended the normal school for their teacher training did not find all the instruction helpful. "I disliked the emphasis on primary grades by women teachers who were not university graduates and therefore had a tendency to want to pull us down a peg," said a 1930 student. The theoretical work "seemed to bear little relationship to what actually happened in classrooms," remembered a 1929 student. The university graduates were put among a section of the normal school's students, who "wouldn't have anything to do with us," recalled one woman. "They thought we were snobbish."[20] Misgivings about the quality of training provided by the normal school surfaced in the MacFarlane Commission of 1959, which criticized both the minimum eligibility requirements for student entrance and the qualifications of the instructors.[21] As noted above, in the mid-1960s all teacher training was put under the jurisdiction of the university.

Rarely did career teachers rely only on their initial training at normal school. More common was the habit of regular upgrading by taking evening or summer courses to acquire qualifications that enabled a person to teach higher grades or to go into junior high or senior high school. Often these courses, which were undertaken piecemeal over the length of a career, could eventually be combined to fulfil the requirements for a degree. This was commonplace for career teachers before 1970. Even in the nineteenth century, a noteworthy feature of teachers was their propensity to improve their qualifications, not only within the profession but also with respect to other occupations. An inspector's annual report of 1892, for instance, noted that "about 50 per cent of the men are fitting themselves for other callings, 20 per cent being medical students."[22] Male teachers were assumed to be upwardly mobile on the way either to better teaching or administrative positions within the schools or to better-paid careers outside teaching.

Female teachers were expected to marry, and until World War II were required to retire at the time of marriage, but single women who planned a lifetime career in education had some incentive – though not as great as men – to upgrade their qualifications. The pay for a junior high teacher was greater than for an elementary teacher, and greater still for a senior high teacher. Even if junior and senior high schools did not have women as principals, there were many female elementary principals both in the cities and in the countryside. After the prohibition against married women was lifted and when more women, both married and single, made a lifetime career of teaching, it was unusual for a teacher not to improve the initial qualifications that had been gained as a student. Teachers were rewarded with improved pay, but in general only the male teachers were additionally rewarded by access to the highest-paid positions, as school principals.

Superintendents kept an eye open for qualified candidates as management material and invited suitable teachers to consider such promotion. "We looked at teaching competence, educational qualifications, general suitability, and whether they could work with colleagues," said a superintendent of the 1950s. It was widely known, he said, that one of the Winnipeg superintendents of the 1940s deliberately discouraged women from getting the higher credentials that might place them in the pool from which principals were plucked: "He would say, 'You don't want to waste your time getting more qualifications,'" and consequently many capable women felt inadequate and in effect counted themselves out of the informal competition. "Women were slow in putting themselves forward."[23]

Women teachers corroborated this interpretation. "In my early teaching years," said a teacher who began in 1942, "it was just accepted that school principals would be male."[24] Another 1940s teacher said, "There were many more male principals, but many female teachers were also involved with families and had little desire to become administrators."[25] Beneath the surface of acquiescence lurked considerable discontent. "I was often very frustrated and had to compete somewhat aggressively even to be noticed. Any male could be considered for administration," said a teacher who qualified twenty years later, in the 1960s.[26] Even a teacher of the 1940s vintage expressed dissatisfaction with the conventional system: "I decided to go into administration and did not have a problem doing so. But, generally, women did not have the same opportunities. I know many good women who were discouraged from applying by male principals and superintendents."[27] Some who did become principals sometimes felt it necessary to insist that they had never put themselves forward, so great was the taboo against the notion of a women acknowledging that they had ambition. "I never applied for a job as principal ... I would never have applied," said a successful teacher who eventually became a high school principal.[28] In a wide-ranging 1974 study of women as teachers and administrators, surveying over 200 subjects, Linda Asper discovered that less than 10 per cent of the women teachers had ever applied for an administrative position.[29]

Sybil Shack in 1975 identified three prominent reasons for women's reluctance: "Lack of self-confidence, a felt clash with family responsibilities and an unwillingness to become involved with work that promises fewer satisfactions than the work they are already doing."[30] Women teachers confirmed that the virtual absence of women administrators outside the elementary schools until the 1950s, and then only rarely, had as much to do with women's attitudes as with discrimination. Shack overcame her own misgivings enough to be appointed principal of an elementary school in 1948, of an elementary and junior high school in 1964, and of a senior high school in 1975. Nevertheless, she understood what was then a common female antipathy towards assuming authority. Speaking of the 1933 split within the Winnipeg local of the Manitoba Teachers Federation, which resulted in the formation of a women's local and a men's local, she said:

It had good points and bad points. A good point was, it gave women opportunity ... They *had* to take office. Now the reluctance of women to take office is illustrated by what happened to me in the early 1950s. I had a telephone call one evening from a woman who was on the nominating committee of the Women's Local. She asked me if I would serve on the conference committee (the salary negotiating committee) and I said no. Well, she said, if you don't take this I don't know what to do. You're the *nineteenth* person I have asked. So I said yes, and it was one of the most important decisions I ever made in my life.[31]

## PROFESSIONAL ORGANIZATION

Teachers often saw themselves as hapless employees of the school boards' arbitrary power. Not only could the boards appoint and dismiss, but they could set salaries and could even prescribe behaviour appropriate for the teachers' nonteaching hours. Although the Department of Education certified a teacher and established the curriculum for students, each elected school board (with its own budget, raised from the local community as well as from the provincial treasury) exercised far-ranging control over the delivery of educational services. Consequently, there was great variety in the salaries offered, the terms of employment, and the overall quality of instruction. Over the years, the financing of education became more dependent on money and policies funnelled through the provincial government, and the quality became more homogenized. Before 1970, tendencies towards centralization and uniformity were apparent but were kept in check by local pressures intent on retaining influence over the education of their children.

One of the most compelling centripetal forces within education was the teachers' own professional organization, which was consulted frequently both by officials in the department and by local boards. After an abortive attempt in 1907, the Manitoba Teachers Federation was founded in 1918:

to enable teachers to take a more active part in the profession to which they belong, to grade themselves according to their qualifications and experience; to prevent the profession from being a mere stepping-stone to other "more remunerative" professions; to make it more attractive for the proper kind of candidates to enter; to see that those entering get an adequate training before being admitted; and that a salary adequate for the responsibility and the time spent in preparation is paid, as well as to insure to the rising generation a proper foundation for their future work ... In unity there is strength.[32]

Its founding was "a fairy tale."[33] But like all myths and legends, the federation contained demons as well as angels. Just as gender was one of the organizing principles of the profession and its bureaucratic structure, so too was the federation prey to the dominant prejudices of society with respect to the relationship between male and female power.

Its commissioned history relates how the scene was set. Leaders appeared in 1919: "Family men, all of them, with family responsibilities ... Many a teacher who went through the Depression ... blessed the founding fathers, especially E.K. Marshall, General Secretary from 1924 to 1945, who was a father to every teacher in the province."[34] Elements of a paternalist mythology included serious men looking out for their own interest and chivalrously protecting women – so long as the women were young, single, and imminently about to retire from the profession.

Married men turned to more than mythology to support their interest. Scarcely an annual convention went by without a resolution celebrating and encouraging the recruitment of married men. "Whereas the settled presence of married men teachers ... would be a stabilising and Canadianising influence in rural communities..." stated the preface to a 1927 resolution calling for appointments of more than one year at a time for teachers in rural school districts.[35] An editorial in the *Manitoba Teacher*, the official organ of the federation, in 1929 raised this concern to an issue of professional integrity: "It is somewhat disconcerting to find that the slight increase in male teachers which reached its peak (26.6 per cent) in 1923, has, since then, steadily decreased and now in 1928 stands at its lowest level (19 per cent) since 1920 ... So long as we find men drifting into teaching during times of stress and thrusting it beneath them when the business world offers greater financial inducements, we cannot hope to raise teaching to the rank of a profession."[36] The officers and voices of the federation identified the interests of men teachers, especially married men, as the interests of the federation.

During its first decade, the federation made no move to question the readier access of men to administrative positions, the differential pay schedules for men and women, or the exclusion of married women from employment. When a rural teacher requested the federation's defence in an appeal to her school board against dismissal at the time of her marriage, the federation declined to take the matter up: "Mrs Shewfelt not reappointed. Ratepayers objected to married woman teaching whilst her husband was earning a good living. Tenure Committee took no further action."[37] After the tough economic times following the financial crash of 1929, the competitive edge enjoyed by men increasingly caused discontent among women, and matters came to a head in Winnipeg in 1933.

It is significant that the women teachers themselves raised no explicit objection to the exclusion of married women. A campaign during World War II to abolish the prohibition was initiated and led not by teachers but by female school trustees.[38] Women teachers shared a commonplace view, intensified during the Depression, that a family unit was entitled to only one breadwinner.[39] However, women teachers differed from men concerning the pay to which the breadwinner was entitled. Women had long been used to differential pay schedules. One could find respectable arguments to support pay rates differing according to the academic credentials of the worker, her experience, and the supposed difficulty of the work (that is, the higher the level of certification, the longer the experience on the job, and the more demanding the supposed responsibility of teaching older children, then the higher the pay should be). Consequently, a second-class certified teacher was paid less than a teacher with a first-class certificate, who in turn was paid less than a teacher with a university degree; grade 1 teachers were not paid as much as grade 9 teachers, who were paid less than grade 11 teachers; and, usually, increments were added according to years of experience in the occupation. But within each category there was a male and a female schedule, which was justified not by the nature of the work or the expertise demanded, but by reference only to the status of the worker. A man was paid more. The differential was substantial; in many of the pay schedules (each school board maintained its own schedule), the maximum female salary was less than the minimum male salary.

Attempts to justify this inequality dwelt on the fact that men had dependants. A 1940 article in the *Manitoba Teacher* carrying the title "He That Hath Wife and Children" sketched a piteous picture of the married male teacher's deplorable financial situation.[40] Yet single men were not paid less – the supposition being that at some time in the future they too would have dependants. However, the reference to dependants was a smokescreen. Within this ideology, men were to be paid more because it was assumed that their work was worth more. Women who had dependants were ignored. They had failed to get a man to provide for them and they must shoulder the consequences as individuals. The *Manitoba Teacher* noted no objection to the differential structure, simply recording it as being "in accordance with the will of the public."[41]

Concerned women teachers acquiesced in this policy for only so long. When there was a proposal actually to intensify the inequity, the women withdrew from their sexually integrated Winnipeg local of the teachers' federation to form their own women's local. Much of their energy over the next thirty years was directed towards countering the insistence of the men's local that inequitable gender policies be maintained. This effort left in its wake a set of articulate records about women and gender within Manitoba's largest female professional occupation.

## WINNIPEG WOMEN TEACHERS ASSOCIATION

### Equal Pay

The Depression reduced the taxation revenues of governments, which in turn reduced the money available to school boards. In the rural districts, boards abandoned salary schedules and in advertisements for teachers included the request for an applicant to "state salary." Underbidding, whereby an applicant would offer to teach for a sum less than the salary paid the previous year, was common.[42] In the largest division, Winnipeg, the school board reduced its payroll in a more orderly way. In 1932 the city budget cut the teachers' salary pool by 10 per cent. However, each teacher was not to receive a 10 per cent cut. Rather, a new schedule was issued, which had the effect of softening (and in some cases annulling) a cut in the men's salaries while requiring individual women teachers to shoulder a cut of more than 10 per cent. At the same time, a new schedule with a greater differential between men's and women's pay for the same job was introduced. In 1933 a further 10 per cent reduction of the total teacher salary was inflicted. The combined effect of the 20 per cent cut resulted in the "Biggest Part of Burden to Be on Women," according to a newspaper headline.[43]

The differing impact on men and women was neither implicit nor incidental. "The schedule was passed chiefly to establish the principle of a wider spread between salaries of men and women teachers," one trustee said. Seeking to mobilize public indignation against the women, he added, "Undoubtedly the majority of the public would be surprised to learn that women high school teachers received as high as $2800 for a working year of only 10 months."[44]

Support for the intensified differential came from the Board of Trade, whose spokesman said, "It is generally conceded that the percentage of men on our teaching staff is too small. To reduce the men's salaries too drastically now would mean risking a serious scarcity of the right type of men in the years to come. Owing to the fewer better paid openings for women, there is much less danger of a scarcity of good women teachers." In other words, women had fewer career choices, and an employer therefore need not pay high wages to attract their labour.

This onslaught drove Winnipeg women teachers to analyse their situation and to conclude that they could not place complete trust in their federation as it was then structured. While not abandoning the partial security of solidarity with other teachers, they seceded from the Winnipeg local to form the Winnipeg Women Teachers Association, with a right to make representations directly to the Winnipeg School Board. Through these representations, particularly during the next fifteen years, the women's approach to differential treatment was forcefully expressed.[45]

In one of its first position papers, the women's local described the dimensions of the inequity. In Winnipeg, 123 women taught in the senior high schools, and there were 174 men working at both the junior and senior high school levels. Whereas the high school women stood to lose an average of $355 per annum, the high school men stood to lose only $100 on average. The women's local noted that some of the men were single, without a wife and children to support, and that some of the women, though single, had family responsibilites, notably in caring for elderly parents or relatives. In the new schedule, the maximum for a woman high school teacher was $2,400. However, the maximum for a man was $3,300, and his minimum was the same as the women's maximum: $2,400. Still, as the Board of Trade lecturer noted, "The basis of 'equal work, equal pay' raised by the women was evidently thought to be impracticable to work on."[46]

The women's impatience was confirmed in 1935. "For thirteen years I paid the membership fee," wrote Vera Patrick in a circular to the women's local, "believing the Federation was what its motto declared it to be, 'Quisque pro omnibus,' but during the past two years, to the disillusionment of many, it has been found to be, not each for all, but mostly for the male members." She had calculated the accumulated salaries of a man and a woman teacher with the same qualifications who started in a junior high school in 1924. By 1932 the woman had earned $16,200, the man $25,200, a differential of $9,000.[47]

The women's commitment to equal pay for equal work surfaced in another context in 1936. The local supported the board's proposal to open elementary schoolteaching to men, provided that the pay schedule was identical with the women's. The men's local insisted that if men taught in elementary schools, their salaries should not "be out of line with the present minimums of men in Junior and Senior High," which was a coded reference to the fact that men enjoyed a higher salary scale.[48] The incompatibility between the two locals resulted in two papers, which were presented separately to the board in January 1937.

The men supported their point of view by appealing to a notion that it was desirable to have more male teachers:

Low salaries make the teaching profession unattractive to men of the best type ... An increase in the number of men teachers in our schools is highly desirable to counterbalance the relative decrease of masculine control and companionship in the home ... A man is the head or the potential head of a family – on him, not on the woman, falls the responsibility of maintaining not only himself but his wife and his children, if he has any ... The question is not "Equal pay for equal work" but "Will the School Board offer such salaries as will attract men of fine character, adequate qualifications, men seized with a sense of the tremendous responsibilities that rest upon a teacher: will the School Board offer salaries that will bear comparison with those obtainable in normal times in other occupations and professions?"[49]

The women more briefly reiterated a commitment to equal pay, but in addition made two other observations. They stated, "No one – man or woman – wishes to bring down the salary of any individual or groups of individuals on the staff" in pursuit of equal pay. They would rather that women's salaries were raised. In a novel situation, in which men had not been used to receiving higher rates because no men had been employed at the elementary level, no inequity would be suffered, they said. Moreover, "an appointment can be made, based only on the qualifications of the applicants for the particular position," a principle that could in future be applied to women applying for administrative positions.[50]

In 1943 Dr Mindel Sheps was a newly elected school trustee who had herself suffered discrimination as a medical student. In her first action as a trustee, she recognized women's rights in two motions before the Winnipeg School Board, one concerning the employment of married women as teachers and the other to eliminate the salary differential.[51] Although both her motions were initially defeated, in January 1944 the board investigated the matter of differentials.[52] The men opposed elimination by a vote of 162 to 26. At the invitation of the board, both locals submitted briefs.

The men's local relied on a more sophisticated exposition of the family dependants argument. While acknowledging that a woman teacher might have dependants, the men stated that the actual average man teacher had more dependants than the actual average woman teacher. They redefined equal pay in terms of "standard of living and actual purchasing or spending power," and argued that since the group of dependants for whom a man was responsible was larger than a woman's, the man's group "must receive more dollars" in order to have equal pay. Moreover, a married man "performs an indispensable economic service for the community"; besides performing a "biological necessity," he maintains a home and educates his children to be useful citizens, and "his sons and daughters are speedily used in wartime."

The men noted that if women's salaries were raised to the level of men's, this would have the effect of widening the gap between elementary teachers (virtually all of whom were women) and women teachers in the junior and senior high schools, "with consequent dissatisfaction and injustice to the latter." They diverted the attention of the board by suggesting that the whole salary schedule structure should be examined, not merely the matter of differentials between men and women.[53]

For its part, the women's local reported that 96 per cent of the women supported elimination of the differential. To this the women gave priority: "We are not suggesting any increases in salaries at the present time, but we are asking that the principle of equal pay for equal work be recognized." The brief disadvantageously compared women's salaries in Winnipeg with those in other Canadian cities. It applied to women the men's argument about appealing to the "right type" of recruit: "The salary offered should certainly be adequate to attract the right type of man – and the right type of woman." The women pointed out that many more opportunities were opening up for women and that teaching should be made more attractive in order to compete with careers in scientific research, journalism, advertising, industry, the civil service, and (stated first) "the National Film Board." Equal pay for equal work was "the modern trend," they noted; and they shrewdly added, "Women members of the School Board receive the same honorarium as the men ... Men doctors, dentists, lawyers and architects would resent it very much if the women in their professions accepted smaller fees than the men do." It was surprising, they alleged, that the men teachers, like men in other professions, had not insisted on equal pay.

The women refused to acknowledge the force of the argument about the men's dependants. Women too had "parents or other dependants." The women did not dismiss the men's appeal to a satisfactory standard of living but turned it around: "The single man who receives the same salary as the married man has the opportunity to exercise this right ('to live pleasantly') equally with the married man. A woman, on account of her lower salary, is denied this right."[54]

The school board reported in March 1944 that it was "impracticable" to raise the women's salaries equal to men's at the present time, but the subcommittee chaired by Sheps continued to consider studying "all matters affecting the teachers' salary schedule."[55] There was a flurry of activity over the next eighteen months, with the women persisting in their demand for equal pay but recommending further upward adjustments in the salary structure as well. When in 1946 a new salary schedule was adopted in Winnipeg, the differentials remained;[56] but by the early 1950s, a single salary schedule was becoming the standard throughout the province. The 1951 negotiations in Winnipeg produced an agreement that recognized seven classes of teacher qualifications but no differential. In 1952 the Manitoba Teachers Society adopted equal pay for equal work as its stated policy.[57]

### Married Women Teachers

Mindel Sheps was more successful in her move to eliminate the prohibition on married women teachers. Here she had more public opinion on her side, but ironically the Winnipeg Women Teachers did not see the issue as a priority.

Since the early days, women teachers had been expected to retire on marriage, and if they did not do so voluntarily they were dismissed.[58] The 1931 census shows that a mere 4 per cent of women teachers in Manitoba were married, which was the same as in the female labour force as a whole.[59] Despite the small proportion, a forceful campaign to remove all married women teachers was instituted during the Depression. In Winnipeg after 1930 each married woman teacher was required to show cause why she should continue in employment.[60]

Only two excuses were accepted. Either the teacher had a special skill, such as the teaching of retarded children, which would have been difficult to replace, or she was deemed to have an abnormal domestic situation, which justified her earning a salary.[61] The number of women submitting to the annual inquiries into their private lives was small; the most was 30 in 1930, out of a total female staff of approximately 850.[62]

Ten years later the situation had changed. The economy had recovered, male teachers were enlisting in the armed forces, and there was more of a demand for teachers on the part of school boards. In Winnipeg, the matter was broached in the guise of women teachers marrying enlisted men. Although the policy of prohibition was reaffirmed, there was a relaxation in its administration. Married women were permitted to continue in employment, but on one-year contracts, even if their previous service had entitled them to be considered as tenured.[63] The numbers involved were small. Between 1940 and 1943 only eleven married women were confirmed "on the regular staff."[64]

In 1943 Sheps and the other female trustee, Etta Rorke, led a direct attack on the policy. Initially, they wished to maintain the security of women teachers who married members of the armed forces. They were unable then to get the policy changed, but increasingly the practice was followed of not requiring women to retire on marriage.[65] Already in 1943 the *Winnipeg Free Press* described forcible retirement on marriage as "ridiculous," stating: "Good teachers are hard to find, and hard to keep. So long as their work remains good, why should it matter to the school board whether they are married or not? What has marriage to do with teaching?"[66] The *Tribune* labelled the prohibition reactionary and antediluvian.[67] Sheps and Rorke were no longer on the board in 1946 when the policy was dropped, not without rearguard action from a large minority of trustees.[68] The board's action was not an isolated one. In the same year, Toronto rescinded its prohibition on married women teachers.[69]

Once the formal prohibition vanished, married women formed a steadily increasing proportion of the overall number of female schoolteachers in Manitoba. From 21 per cent in 1951, their numbers rose to 46 per cent in 1961 and to 67 per cent in 1971.[70] This was accomplished because of the political initiative taken by women trustees with the collaboration of educational administrators, who needed to staff the schools to accommodate the "baby boom" school population of the 1950s and 1960s. Many women teachers clearly found teaching a satisfactory way of earning a living after their marriage. Individual women teachers applauded the idea of married women working. To the University Women's Club, principal Aileen Garland quoted Elizabeth Garrett Anderson: "Unless all are free, none is free." But this was not the collective view of the women's local.[71] In 1946 the Winnipeg

Women Teachers asked the board to replace the married women with single women "as soon as single women are available for teaching positions."[72] They inherited from the Depression years a widespread but no longer majority view that working single women should not have to compete for jobs with their married sisters as well as with all the men.[73]

### Retirement and Pensions

In 1952 and 1953 the antipathy was so marked between the men's and women's locals that the men wanted to separate into a completely independent local.[74] The Manitoba Teachers Society refused to allow this splinter. Whilst several issues bothered the two locals, a major point of contention was the matter of retirement age and pensions. Men retired at sixty-five, women at sixty; and men and women were entitled to different pensions, the men's being larger.[75]

In 1953 the women informed the Winnipeg School Division that the membership of the women's local "was in favour of the age of retirement ... being extended on a voluntary basis," while the men wished "no change in the existing retirement ages."[76] The board initially agreed to individual voluntary exptensions for women, but the Manitoba Teachers Society did not like the practice of individual arrangements.[77] By 1957, the Winnipeg District Association – the parent body of both the women's and the men's locals – agreed on a single maximum retiring age of sixty-five for all teachers.[78]

### Impact of the Winnipeg Women Teachers

Between 1919 and 1959 there were thirty-five presidents of the Manitoba Teachers Society, twenty-five of whom were men and ten of whom were women. The first woman was elected in 1935. By the 1960s, much of the friction between men and women had begun to dissipate, and it is significant that the two Winnipeg locals decided to merge in 1965; they no longer considered it advantageous to remain separate. By then, the bothersome issues of equal pay, married women's employment, and fringe benefits had subsided, partly because of two external factors that contributed substantially to teachers' well-being. First, the rapid expansion in the school-age population of the 1950s and 1960s ensured an increasing demand for teachers, which allowed the teachers' professional society, recognized as a formal bargaining agent in 1948, to hold out for improved working conditions.[79] Secondly, in 1958 a Progressive Conservative government replaced the Liberals in a provincial general election. Benefiting from both local and national prosperity, the new premier, Duff Roblin, made education a priority and increased its funds. In 1959 teachers were reclassified, in a new schedule and the maximum level in the highest class was "doubled at one go."[80]

It is difficult to evaluate the impact of the existence of the separate Winnipeg Women Teachers local. Its major concern – to introduce equal pay for equal work – was implemented in the early 1950s. In this it benefited from a simultaneous nationwide campaign for equal pay led by the Canadian Federation of Business and Professional Women's Clubs, which by the end of the decade had achieved both federal and provincial legislation.[81] Recalcitrant jurisdictions were still able to argue that women were not performing "equal work," in order to circumvent the act; but Manitoba teachers implemented an undifferentiated scale. This was partly because of the presence on the Manitoba Teachers Federation's conference committee of a half-dozen articulate and experienced women who had served administrative apprenticeship as much in the executive positions of the women's local as in principalships. Also, the local's clear and coherent position papers probably contributed to an expansion of understanding and sympathy for its cause on the part of school trustees, administrators, and public opinion as expressed in the local newspapers. It would be interesting to compare the Winnipeg local's militancy and effectiveness with other jurisdictions, for example, Saskatchewan and Ontario, which had separate women teachers' organizations.[82] "Issues such as wages and pensions were the lifeblood and the main focus of these associations."[83]

The Winnipeg women's local was primarily concerned about equity and differentials. Born out of deliberate inequity and an exacerbated gender gap, the local promoted the interests of women teachers, who in the 1930s and 1940s were for the most part single. This caused them to be temporarily less than enthusiastic on behalf of the interests of married women. At the very least, the local helped to undermine the inbuilt sympathy for the male breadwinner posture, on which the men's local traded until the 1960s.

After the 1950s, without the cutthroat competition for jobs that had characterized the Dirty Thirties, and in an era when teachers could enjoy relative affluence and were secure both in terms of employment and improving credentials, there was less division along gender lines inside the profession. Nevertheless, one of the major differentials of the early years, whereby administrative positions were dominated by men, remained.

## TEACHING AND DIFFERENCE

The work of the Winnipeg women's local in the Manitoba Teachers Federation, together with the efforts of women school trustees, school boards, school administrators, and politicians, and shifts in public opinion, all combined to render teaching less sexually segregated in 1970 than it had been before. However, traditional male dominance remained in supervisory and administrative positions. Two-sided barriers to an integrated profession were still strong. On the one hand, many women were reluctant to assume administrative responsibility; on the other, some men worked deliberately and forcefully to maintain the status quo. At a personal level, a woman might well have calculated that it was not advantageous to carry a more stressful load in order to satisfy an ambition that in turn was only ambivalently sanctioned by society. A judgment that the administrative game was not worth the candle could have been a rational conclusion for people whose commitment to teaching was not without reservation.

Among the forty or so teachers surveyed for this study, the beginning of whose careers ranged from the 1920s to the 1960s, only a handful declared that from the outset they had been committed to teaching as a vocation, though about one-third were positively attracted by teaching; they had wanted to be teachers from an early age, or their love for children explained the career choice: "I was 'born' a teacher! I taught my dolls before I started grade 1"[84] ... "I always enjoyed working with children."[85] The other two-thirds tended to explain their entry into teaching more by default, for example: "I didn't really want to teach at first, but I knew I had to earn my living. The children soon taught *me*."[86] Some would have preferred another career but were prevented by circumstances. "I had no intention of becoming a teacher. Medicine was my goal ... the Depression was the deciding factor,"[87] was one explanation. Another was: "Not enough money to go to McGill to study medicine. Had worked four summers as a psychiatric nurse (untrained) so did not want to continue in nursing."[88] One woman's first choice was to be a writer, and her second was to be a lawyer; but she could not afford the training, and since she did not want to go into sales or be a nurse or secretary she "went into teaching."[89]

Most echoed this comment. A teacher of the 1920s said, "Years ago, the only career opportunities were teacher, nurse, and stenographer."[90] A teacher of the 1930s said, "I was refused admittance to nurses' training because I was too young. My father wanted me to have a profession and there were few options available."[91] The situation was much the same in the early 1940s: "When I completed grade 12 there was no money to go on to university or even take a business course, but there was the opportunity to teach on a permit and thus earn some money."[92] Similarly, in the 1950s, teaching "gave me an opportunity to earn a living after one year. I did not want to be a waitress or work in an office. My parents did not help me financially as I was a girl. Only boys were sent to university, so teaching was my only way."[93] Even into the 1960s, "there were no other options for women, especially in rural areas."[94]

When the teachers were asked more generally why teaching had always been able to attract large numbers of women, some referred to women as nurturers – women were gifted to be natural care givers and raisers of children. "Women are better at dealing with human nature, more tolerant and understanding,"[95] stated one teacher. "Basically, I think it is a woman's nature to want to mould and educate children, her own and others,"[96] observed another. Several placed themselves at arm's length from the nurturer stereotype: "When I was young, teaching was one of the three main professions that women chose ... Women were anxious to give and contribute and were considered to be more motherly, therefore better for the younger children."[97] Similarly: "We are natural care givers associated with children and are expected to be home-care people."[98]

Often, teachers who cited this reason for entry into the profession also referred to the limited options; of all the reasons cited, the lack of satisfactory alternatives was the most common. As historians of teaching in the United States have pointed out, women "entered teaching in large part because they needed work" rather than because they necessarily felt a calling.[99] Over and over in the survey, teachers echoed the sentiments of a woman who had trained in 1926: "It was important to earn money as soon and as quickly as possible and there weren't many choices ... Nursing and/or secretarial work did not appeal to me."[100] Despite the salary differentials and the unequal access to superior positions, the "alternative employment opportunities have been so much more limited" that teaching has long been able to attract large numbers of women.[101]

The women surveyed were able to find plenty of advantages in teaching. A short preparation was seen as a good thing: "Years ago it took less training."[102] One woman identified as an advantage "the respect and attention given to teachers."[103] Of the specific advantages, many women cited the hours: "The working mother had the same hours in the workplace as her children";[104] "Working hours may have been an incentive";[105] "The hours and holidays fit family responsibilities";[106] Another advantage was that, in the nature of the job, there was satisfaction. "In September you start with a class where most of the children cannot read and in June they leave you, able to do so,"[107] explained one. "I liked the kids,"[108] said another. As well, the variety was stimulating: "Young children are exciting and changeable, every class is different and needs to be handled differently."[109] One woman wrote: "Liked: association with students, subject area; disliked: administration, bureaucracy."[110] Similar views were expressed in a variety of forms. A positive dislike of administration was articulated frequently, for example: "I did not like much of the administrative end of things";[111] "I did not like supervising the playgrounds at recess";[112] "I disliked political influence in educational matters."[113]

By contrast, women who had served in administrative positions emphasized its positive side: "I liked administrative work and the opportunities to work in our Professional Organization";[114] "I particularly liked administrative work with children, parents, and teachers";[115] "I love administration."[116] As a principal, explained one, "I was a facilitator – a very important job. I like change and variety. I learned so much ... It was an asset, being a woman ... I was accessible for others' confidences. I could calm people down."[117] Another principal, who (like many) also served on the executive of the Manitoba Teachers Society, liked administration but "did not appreciate School Board decisions which were counter to the needs of the schools – or political appointees for superintendents."[118] Another principal disliked "very theory-bound inexperienced Social Workers who knew all the answers. These individuals seemed to feel that Principals and Vice-Principals who were dealing with 'their' clients needed to be educated in the ways of the world." But even she "thoroughly enjoyed" whatever she was doing.[119]

Clearly, once in the profession, whatever their initial reason for entrance, the women teachers were able to find considerable satisfaction. Women with the courage to become administrators could serve as vice-principals, principals, and, towards the end of the period, superintendents.[120] It is clear, however, that many women preferred to remain in the lower ranks. There was another factor which, in the years after World War II, operated to slow down the pace of women's infiltration into the higher ranks. This was the fact that an increasing number carried domestic responsibilities along with their teaching work. Whereas in 1974 women teachers remained in the teaching force "regardless of their family responsibilties," nevertheless, work in the home militated against their interest in promotion to administrative positions.[121] Among the teachers surveyed, those who became administrators before 1970 were all single.

On the general issue of the link between family and professional work, almost all considered it was inevitable that a woman's greater domestic responsibilities, compared to a man's, took a toll: "Parents should provide a stable home life for children. It has tended to fall to the mother";[122] "Who gets the larger pay cheque? Does wife sacrifice her aspirations on his account? Children – do we or don't we have them studying away from home? There are a lot of pressures put on women."[123] The consequences of a mother's work in the home were understandable: "She probably finds she cannot contribute as much as her male colleagues if she has sole responsibility for children";[124] "Many women enjoy their teaching but are limited in the time they feel able to give to their career because of family";[125] "Some women cannot accept promotions due to home responsibilities."[126] Some problems were intractable: "Women are in a very difficult situation when there are young children to be cared for";[127] "Most sick children have mother as the nurse during the night crises."[128]

A family could be a benefit as well as a drain, though only one or two mentioned this possibility; for example: "In teaching, your 'teachers' and supporters are right in the family."[129] One respondent had great confidence in women: "Women just work harder and longer. They have broad shoulders and bear responsibility quite willingly." This particular teacher, who served in administration at the end of her career, also noted, "Becoming a principal meant I had to be superlady. I worked with many mediocre male colleagues."[130] However, not everyone had the energy or the desire to be a superwoman.

The married teachers all agreed that marital and maternal considerations affected their personal decisions about employment. All who married before the mid-1940s retired immediately on marriage: "I left the profession when I married (1938). Married women were not hired as teachers";[131] "Upon marriage in 1942 I relinquished active teaching."[132] Although stories were told of teachers who kept their marriages secret in order to retain their positions, no specific examples came to light.[133] After the reversal of the marriage bar in Winnipeg and its disuse elswhere, women tended to defer retirement until the birth of children. Only two, who qualified in the early 1950s, continued to work full-time after children were born.[134] The same number retired completely on the birth of their children.[135] The remainder worked part-time, or as substitute teachers, through their children's infancy and resumed full-time work later.

Accommodations were accepted with varying degrees of acquiescence. Most found the need to juggle several responsibilities unremarkable, but a few were explicit about practical arrangements and their personal attitudes. "Of course" decisions about employment were affected by husband and children, wrote one. "I needed to be close to home – able to be there at lunch and soon after the closing time." There was a further dimension: "I stayed in elementary [teaching] because after fifteen years of being at home with small kids my confidence was not up to applying for high school. My training, interests, and ability would have enabled me to be an excellent high school English teacher."[136] Wrote another: "All courses, studying, teacher lesson preparation etc. were done around my family life. Summer schools meant delayed holidays. Because opportunities for *women's* advancement were virtually nil in my school division, I was 'deprived' of my one objective to go into administration as my husband's employment was in Brandon and one never considered moving to other cities for *my* career."[137]

On the difference between teaching and other professions, the women teachers spoke eloquently and with variety. Some thought teaching was better in the good old days, some that it had improved immeasurably. Some were quick to identify advantages unique to teaching, while others emphasized drawbacks. As might be expected from women who spent a considerable number of years committed to one occupation, most thought that, on balance, teaching was a good occupation both in its intrinsic rewards and in comparison with other professions.

One teacher who moved "ever onward and upward," in being the first woman teacher to achieve recognition at various administrative levels,[138] noted: "It was a very good job; but *now* you have to keep up to date more. *Then*, you could teach, drop out, and go back; now, you can't drop out so easily, you lose your place." She said that if she were beginning her working career over again, "it wouldn't be teaching."[139] Another noted the advantages of other occupations: "There have been tremendous changes in the attitude of the public over the past fifty years. Pay may be the reason, and yet ... law, medicine, business administration all command more respect."[140] Today, said another, "there are more opportunities for women in other professions. It no longer has the 'aura' it once had."[141]

A contrary opinion was voiced by a woman who thought that teaching compared "very favourably today, but it wasn't always so. The Manitoba Teachers Society is responsible for improvement."[142] Others welcomed the practical advantages: "By now our salaries are at a sound level. We have the perks of a good indexed pension, paid sick leave, health and dental group plans. We can accumulate sick leaves to use in a block when really needed. Teacher exchanges, possible every five years, and a sabbatical leave at half pay. In normal times, when jobs are available, people can re-enter the profession. Prestige has improved tremendously since I started (1941)."[143]

Specific features of teaching were considered beneficial: "Length of training has now increased to equal that of nursing but not that of a medical doctor or scientist ... The fringe benefit is the long summer vacation";[144] "Teaching is still one of the easiest professions to get into."[145] In a similar vein, one teacher stated, "Children are the best people you could work with. There's no desk sitting – it's active. Compulsory retirement is gone now." She added that one improves so much with experience that older teachers rightly keep teaching, and concluded: "Pay is good – best in world."[146]

Less enthusiastic views were also expressed, for example: "Discipline is becoming quite difficult, but there is stress in other employments as well."[147] Similarly: "I used to think teaching was an excellent profession for a woman. Now I believe that teaching in a city has become very difficult work. The pay is good, but the work demanding, and many very difficult families and disturbed children have made it a stressful occupation. School officials have cut funding and have placed very difficult children in regular public school classes."[148] Another teacher thought that after-school work was "often a problem."[149]

To another teacher, this represented an opportunity: "I could take my work home. Excellent hours for women. I could keep a tab on my kids as I had the same hours at school that they did. No other profession has such benefits. Lawyers and doctors have worse hours ... None of them get two weeks off at Christmas, two months in the summer, one week at the end of March ... If a lawyer or doctor misses a day, they don't get paid ... We have wonderful stimulating well-educated and nice colleagues."[150] A sober comparison stipulated: "The prestige is not as great; pay is not as good as some but better than others; security of tenure is better than most; length of training is less; employment opportunities are about the same; work is becoming more stressful, but holidays and working hours are better than many professions."[151] Another teacher drew up a similar checklist. The disadvantages were the work to be done at home, the extracurricular activities, the new course preparations, difficulty with discipline, and reduction in respect for the teacher. On the other side, there were "never two days the same (not even two minutes!)" and there were the summer holidays.[152]

On the vexed question of prestige and respect, Sybil Shack remarked: "Teaching has, unfortunately, never had the prestige that other professions have enjoyed ... Until the 1960s the qualifications for it were minimal and even now the Faculty of Education suffers from the academic snobbery of other faculties. It is much under-appreciated and misunderstood."[153] One very illuminating comment was made by a woman who retired permanently from teaching after the birth of her first child, in 1959: "The teachers were forerunners of equality for women in the workplace. Today [1992] the pay is equal for men and women with similar qualifications and years of experience. But in other jobs held by women, there is still a struggle to obtain equal pay for the same job done. Women teachers' length of training, pay, fringe benefits, opportunity to re-enter the work field, are ... superior to some other professions and jobs."[154]

### PROFESSING A PROFESSION

Teachers identified themselves collectively as a profession. When the federation's conference committees negotiated with school boards, they compared teachers' salaries with those in other Canadian provinces and cities, but they also compared their salaries with those of other professionals, notably doctors, lawyers, and engineers, most of whom were men. With rhetorical outrage, they also compared their pay in another direction – that of barely skilled labourers.[155] Yet in the 1950s teachers also saw in teaching some components of a profession that were still to be achieved, for instance, a higher minimum standard of entry, high salaries, and greater respect and prestige. Throughout the period, the *Manitoba Teacher* carried articles and reported speeches advocating "professionalism" with higher qualifications for entry and with more stringent codes of ethics, including greater solidarity and service.[156]

It was a strain for the male teachers in the Winnipeg men's local to accept that a female-dominated occupation could be a profession, and there were appeals for the recruitment of men as though of itself this would result in an improved image.[157] Commentators uncritically reflected the preoccupation that a profession by definition must contain more men. D.S. Woods in 1938 noted with indignation that "it is less than twenty years since girls of 16 could qualify with a Third Class Certificate to guide our schools."[158] Alexander Gregor and Keith Wilson alluded to the "troublesome fact" at the turn of the twentieth century of the "trend towards undue female dominance in the profession."[159] The stereotpyes were maintained by those in power in the profession, and in turn by the few historians who examined education in the province: "Mature and energetic males often stood in contrast to typically young and malleable female teachers; the latter, it was implied if not overtly stated, accepted low wages and therefore undermined the professional quest. If the former left teaching for greener professional fields, the latter departed to marry, both abandoning the schools once more to the second-rate – women and men who continued to perpetuate the 'low standards' so deplored by reformers of education."[160]

In the 1950s and 1960s, perhaps because there were several women presidents of the Manitoba Teachers Society, the *Manitoba Teacher* published more articles that avoided the use of a male model as a teacher, it showed more sensitivity to the female majority of the society's membership, and at the same time it insisted on "the increasing emphasis that the Society is placing on professionalism."[161] As an American analyst wrote, "The very notion of professionalization ... has been part of a complex attempt to win equal treatment, pay, and control over the day-to-day work of a largely female labour force."[162] Women, too, could be concerned about professional standards.

If control over one's daily work was a measure of autonomy within a professional occupation, then a teacher experienced it in some respects but not in others. The classroom autonomy of a teacher was limited by the curriculum she had to teach; but in her overall responsibility for the children's welfare and in her choice of teaching methods, she had considerable discretion. Indeed, the immense variety of a teacher's day and her ability to develop different skills were frequently regarded as a positive aspect of the work. In terms of the employer-employee relationship, progress was made, from the teacher's point of view, in the modification of an authoritarian power structure. Speaking of the hard Depression years of the 1930s, when there was a plentiful supply of teachers and too few jobs, one teacher described the powerlessness she experienced as a Winnipeg teacher fortunate enough to have employment. From one year to the next, teachers did not know to which school they would be assigned: "In the last newspaper before Labour Day [the school board] would publish a list of schools and teachers – not even the grades ... We were just told where to go, we had no choice. People were very very careful of their job, if they had one."[163] After the teacher shortages of the war, the high-handed attitude of the school board disappeared. The Manitoba Teachers Society took a more aggressive stance. Teachers credited the bargaining power of the society with improving not only salaries and fringe benefits but with giving teachers more control over their own working lives.

The achievement of a single salary scale, the major object of the Winnipeg Women Teachers, was a success story. However, it did not result in equal pay, for in the 1950s the male teachers were concentrated in the supervisory and higher-paid teaching levels, and the female teachers included a large number of women who were trained in only one year. The MacFarlane Report of 1959 pointed the way to a more rigorous future with respect to the qualifications of teachers. During the 1960s, with the transfer of Manitoba Normal School functions to the University of Manitoba, the MacFarlane reforms were already in process. At the same time, the demand for a greater number of teachers, together with a new political climate of support for education, resulted in increased government grants to schools. Salaries rose. More men were attracted into teaching. In 1971, 34 per cent of the Manitoba teaching force was male, up from 25 per cent in 1946. As the qualifications of teachers became more strongly academic, salaries rose, and it became less contentious to describe the occupation of teaching as a profession.

One feature of gender disparity that was evident at the beginning of the twentieth century remained constant until after 1971. In Manitoba, the pattern of men in positions of authority had been only minimally disturbed by 1971.[164] The relegation of women teachers to the margins of their profession must be explained by the attitudes and behaviour of the women teachers, by the concerns of the men teachers, by the organizations which both used to serve their interests, and, above all, by the "structural factors which served male dominance in the wider world."[165]

### CHAPTER SEVEN

# In Retrospect: "Delighted to Be Accepted"

No success awaits a search for a single representative figure, a type, of professional woman before 1970. Such a woman does not exist. There are too many individual variants for a historian to be able to identify one particular model as a type. Yet differences can be exaggerated. There were some common demographic, economic, and cultural conditions to which almost all conformed. The challenge is to identify common experiences while paying due regard to the different reactions of individuals. To acknowledge the broad common context in which individual choices may be taken is to recognize an ongoing dynamic of history. The difficulties for the historian, as for the professional woman herself, lie in deciding where the border lies between the given context, in which a professional woman had to fit herself or quit, and her own ability to shape the circumstances of her life. This territorial limit was generally flexible and porous. Consequently, the conclusions can seldom be comprehensive: they refer to some but not all professional women in the years before 1970. The following observations about the relative position of women working in the universities, law, medicine, nursing, and teaching illustrate the complexities of their lives.

Yet there were also some simple facts of prime importance. In none of the five professions were women as a group in control. In none of the professions were women paid at the same rate, or as much, as men. These two governing principles, which altered in intensity over the century, influenced the status of all professional women. By 1970 more women had more control, and more women enjoyed equal pay rates, though this did not mean that they enjoyed equality of income. Conditions had changed, but men were still in command. A third general convention applicable to all professional women was the constant expectation that women's primary responsibility was domestic. When this was combined with the relaxation of a taboo against the employment of married women after World War II, professional women who were mothers experienced the same divided responsibilities familiar to all working women. The three most significant conditions determining professional women's working lives were the same as those governing the female labour force as a whole. Professional women shared with all working women disadvantages vis-à-vis their male counterparts in terms of governance, pay, and demands on their time.

## GOVERNANCE

Governance concerns the composition of formal governing bodies and the population of positions of authority within the profession. In university teaching, medicine, and law the question of whether women exercised power within the profession is easily answered – in the negative.

Before 1970, the only women who held positions of authority in the university academic staff were directors of home economics and nursing, and, for some years, of social work. There was a dean of women, but her purview was not academic and had more to do with the welfare of women students. Even in these few areas, women did not necessarily value the authority they had. In 1966 the staff of home economics deliberately set out to attract a male director, who was then appointed the first dean – a more prestigious title, which was chosen explicitly because "in the upper echelons of the university," where "only men could talk to men in washrooms and corridors ... we could compete better in that milieu with a male Dean."[1] When an initiative was taken in 1972 to take stock of the status of women in the university, with a view to improvement, it came not from academics but from women members of the Board of Governors.[2]

In medicine there was one women on the staff of the teaching hospitals who was also a department head – gynaecologist Dr Elinor Black – whose singularity was celebrated and whose gender, to some, was invisible: "That's how Dr Black ended up with her picture in the paper under a heading 'Medical men gather in Winnipeg' and invited to the Manitoba Club (which everyone knew didn't admit women but it never occurred to them the rule would apply to Dr Black) to dine with the Minister of Health."[3] As well, women had appointments as hospital anaesthetists and pathologists. But few women were found in specialties other than obstetrics and gynaecology, and paediatrics; and as for the specialty carrying the most prestige, surgery, "No one told us we didn't *have* to go into surgery; but we just *knew*."[4] Women's move towards paediatrics was as much an effort to avoid discrimination from patients as from fellow physicians.[5] One physician, who practised in Winnipeg early in her career, later became a prominent expert in birth control with a distinguished international reputation, but she worked elsewhere.[6]

In law, the small numbers of women mocked even the suggestion that they might be in positions of authority. The occasional individual nevertheless was prominent in civic affairs. Mildred McMurray, for instance, would address women's groups, but her own legal practice was not a flourishing concern.[7] Before 1970 only two women had been appointed QC,[8] and two had been appointed to the bench (to the Family Court, in both instances).[9]

Nursing was a profession in which women decidedly were in authority. A nurse-in-training was under the direct supervision of women graduate nurses; in the years before World War II, when the majority of graduate nurses went into private-duty nursing, a private-duty nurse was to a large extent her own boss; after the war, when hospitals provided most nursing employment, nurses were in charge of nursing. In public-health nursing, women were both out in the field and in supervisory positions with the Red Cross or government agencies. The certifying body, the Manitoba Association of Registered Nurses, was staffed by women. Yet within the hospitals, the superintendents with ultimate authority over staff were male, and nurses deferred to physicians, most of whom were male. To escape this particular manifestation of male dominance, the nurses lobbied successfully, in Manitoba as in other provinces, to have nurse training removed from the aegis of the hospitals and transferred to universities. There, nurses had a different battle to fight in the same gender war as they strove to get academic instructors in nursing paid at the same level as other academic instructors. This fight was not begun until the 1970s.

Women teachers won some of their gender battles: equal pay schedules, for instance. Yet in terms of governance, only just before 1970 was there a female superintendent employed by the Department of Education, and in the entire period there were fewer than half a dozen women inspectors. The first woman principal of a junior high school was appointed in 1938, of a senior high school in 1964, and few followed them before 1970. Reforms made within the profession had come about partly as a result of the vigorous work of the Winnipeg Women Teachers and as a result of pressure brought by women trustees. Women undoubtedly held positions of authority within the classroom, with respect to their students, but with respect to their colleagues in the profession there was a "dearth of female administrators."[10]

## PAY

Of all five professions, only teaching maintained an explicitly differential pay scale for women. In university teaching, medicine, law, and nursing there was no formal separate pay scale for men and women, and, indeed, when the women teachers were canvassing for a single pay schedule, they looked to other professions as a model. "Men doctors, dentists, lawyers and architects would resent it very much if the women in their professions accepted smaller fees than the men do," the Winnipeg Women Teachers said in 1943. When the teachers achieved equal pay in the 1950s, they were understandably proud, and they continued to feel that teaching offered a salutary model for other occupations. Yet a single salary schedule did not result in equal average pay, neither for the teachers nor for other professions. Comparable wage data are not available at a provincial level for all professions; but at the national level, and at the provincial level for teaching, ironies come to light. The absence of a separate pay scale did not necessarily mean that women professionals on average were paid the same as men professionals on average. In all instances, even in nursing, men had higher wages than women.

Table 25 (appendix 1) shows longitudinal patterns for three professional occupations. Female physicians in Manitoba were paid 61 per cent of male physicians' salaries in 1941, 78 per cent in 1961, and 59 per cent in 1971. Clearly, women did not benefit as much as men from the move to medicare in the 1960s. Manitoba's female nurses earned 83 per cent of male nurses' salaries in 1941, 75 per cent in 1961, and 90 per cent in 1971. Figures for teachers show that the move towards an equal pay schedule scarcely affected average salaries. In 1931 the average wages for female teachers in Manitoba was 70 per cent of those of male teachers; in 1941 the proportion was 73 per cent; it was still 73 per cent in 1961, and in 1971 it was 74 per cent. The concentration of men in the more authoritative and well-paying positions accounted for the average higher salaries in each case. Equal pay for equal work of itself made little difference; what mattered more was access to the higher-paying positions. Even when women were not directly excluded from such positions, they often excluded themselves by virtue of other commitments to which they accorded a higher priority. Paramount among these loyalties was devotion to family.

## COMBINATION OF MARRIAGE
## AND PROFESSION

In the summer of 1919 the Canadian Federation of University Women was founded at a meeting in the Fort Garry Hotel, Winnipeg. There the Alberta delegate, Geneva Misener, "made a plea for larger professional life for woman, bemoaning the fact that so few made the professions a life work but were willing to forgo great opportunities for that of marriage when there should really be no necessity for so doing. Marriage and a profession may go hand in hand for a woman as for a man."[11] Developments in two organizations sympathetic towards professional women, the Winnipeg University Women's Club, and the Canadian Federation of Business and Professional Women, revealed more of an ambivalence towards the combination of marriage and profession.

In 1920 the University Women's Club of Winnipeg held a debate on the motion "that the Professional Life of Women should continue after marriage." Arguments ventilated during the debate indicated a mixture of hope and anxiety for the future, together with resignation about existing customs. They displayed the mind-set of educated women whose university degrees made them possible candidates for a professional occupation, and in a remarkable way they prefigured the concerns of women over the next fifty years.

The first speaker "deplored the economic waste of the present system," which encouraged a woman to see a profession merely as "a stepping stone to marriage." She thought that if a professional life was continued after marriage, this would result in more careful preparation for a profession. Within a family, "the salaries of two would aid the economic situation." Concerning motherhood, laws "would provide for birth periods," and child care would be no problem; for since "school hours practically correspond with professional hours, the children would not be deprived of the mother's presence." This speaker assumed that a professional life was synonymous with schoolteaching.

The negative viewpoint considered that marriage was a change of profession, which required undivided attention if home, health, and happiness were to result: "Good food, close companionships, maternal influence were dependent upon the mother's remaining in the home. Services of this kind, though unpaid, surpassed the paid services of professions." Moreover, the work of a conscientious mother "tended to prevent physically unfit children and race suicide."

The affirmative side then tarred opponents with the brush of "the usual question of opposition to women's rights, which denied to women the right to continue in their profession after marriage. Modern opinion ... favoured professions being open to women on an equal basis with men. Each person's life should be constructive ... Modern appliances, having relieved much of the work in the home, [put] more time ... at the disposal of the married woman ... The economic dependence which affects marriage would be eliminated."

The last presenter "confined her discussion to two questions, 'Does it work? ' and 'Does it pay?'" She thought not, referring to a "mechanical life ... at the sacrifice of social life, home comforts and properly developed children. The help situation prevents proper care of the children, and Juvenile Court cases result. Opportunities are lost to man and woman for becoming decent, calm, sympathetic human beings." Another contributor said that marriage need not "interfere with the professional life. Children should be cared for by experts carefully trained and all mothers were not experts along that line, and should continue their professional work leaving the cares of the home to specially trained assistants." Nevertheless, at the end of debate, the members of the club in attendance, all of them university graduates, decided for the negative.[12] In 1920 their conclusion was that the professional life of women should not continue after marriage.

By the 1930s, the leadership of the Canadian Federation of University Women was more ready to support the idea of married women in the labour force. The federation went on record as opposing the dismissal of married women from positions, and the federation's president, Mabel Thom, repeatedly argued against restrictive practice or legislation. "Women as individuals should decide the question for themselves," she declared.[13] During the war, in 1943, Margaret McWilliams, the first president of the federation, was appointed chair of the federal government's Subcommittee on the Post-War Problems of Women for its Committee on Reconstruction. In contrast to the conventional statements made by many other committees planning for the postwar era, her report went out on a clearly feminist limb.[14] It stated: "To women in each group (married, single, farm) the right to choose what occupation she will follow must be conceded as a right to which every citizen is entitled." The expected practical effects of this would not be radical, McWilliams thought: "We believe that the right to choose is not going to operate to make ... much larger groups of women want to leave their homes for the labour market."[15]

The Canadian Federation of Business and Professional Women was in some ways more prescient and certainly more sensitive to the pragmatic concerns of professional women in the labour force. Its first annual convention was held in Winnipeg in 1930. From the beginning, the organization was on record that it viewed "with disfavour any discrimination in the employment of women solely on the ground of their married status."[16] Thirty years later, its convention noted a "considerable change in the type of professions followed by women" and also noted a distinction in the marital status of women in the workforce. "In the days before World War II, numbers of women expected to work for a period of around five years before marriage, but the majority did not see themselves as re-entering the employment field when their families no longer needed continuous care. Today [1960] the average span of working years for many women will be around twenty-five years."[17] The organization's assumption in 1960 was that a mother would retire from her career to care for infants and would subsequently re-enter paid employment.

In 1920 there were in Winnipeg – and elsewhere – so few real-life examples of professional women who were also married that the University Women's Club debaters had to appeal to benefits and costs on the basis of faith rather than observation. By 1971 the situation had changed, in the directions already recognized by the Canadian Federation of Business and Professional Women.

The proportion of female professionals who were married had changed considerably. Comparable census figures are available for the period 1931–61, and select calculations can be drawn from the 1971 census, when categories were changed. Table 26 (appendix 1) shows that married women comprised only 4 per cent of all occupations of women in professional service in the province in 1931 and 1941, but after the war this proportion rose to 20 per cent in 1951, and to 41 per cent in 1961. Compared with married women in the labour force as a whole, the prewar incidence of marriage was similar. The postwar incidence was different. Until 1961, the proportion of married women in the total female labour force was higher than in the professions; that is, women who worked in manufacturing, sales, and clerical work were more likely to be married than women in the professions. By 1971 the proportion of married women in professional occupations was the same as the proportion in the total female labour force.

A review of the numbers of professional women before 1971 with respect to marriage indicates a division into prewar and postwar experience. Hardly any professional women before World War II carried on their profession after marriage, whereas after the war more married women worked in the professions, although by 1961 the majority of professional women were still single. By 1971, in three professions for which comparable statistics are available in the census – medicine, nursing, and schoolteaching – married women were a two-thirds majority of the women in those occupations, and the proportions of professional married women had become similar to the proportions of all working women who were married. The reasons for these shifts are complex.

From the perspective of professional women themselves, the small numbers and proportions of married women until 1971 were due to three main reasons: the difficulties of carrying the double burden of professional and domestic work; men's resistance to treating women professionals as partners; and widespread assumptions about the proper behaviour of married women, which included their retirement, at marriage, into domestic work and a leisured lifestyle (that is, receiving no pay). These reasons shifted in significance over the years, and there was a clear generational difference.[18]

Before and after World War II, most women academics were single. They believed that the difficulties of combining career and motherhood were almost insuperable. The few university teachers who did combine career and marriage recognized the problem of a double burden but neither magnified it nor exaggerated their own effort: "You cannot operate full-time in both fields. I have learned every shortcut in the book."[19]

Women doctors who were married were more numerous. In 1931, 22 per cent of the female physicians were married. In 1951, 44 per cent were, and by 1971, 65 per cent were. Of the thirty-nine physicians surveyed, two-thirds were married, and all save one of them had children, an average of 3.9 children per mother. Their maternal sympathy was shown in the almost universal move to motherhood, in the size of their families, and in their expressed ideology. Even the single women shared in this: among the women doctors surveyed, one-third of the single respondents had adopted children. There appeared to be no regrets at the busy combination of work and family, but presumably those who were out of sympathy with the combination quit work altogether. The physicians' training and socialization also inculcated a strong sense of career commitment. As several respondents noted, they were not allowed to forget that in the limited enrolment of the medical faculty they were occupying the place of a male, who would indeed be expected to work for pay for the rest of his days.

In the legal profession, very few mothers worked at all, still fewer when their children were small. Although marriage, after World War II, was no longer a nonnegotiable disqualification of women from a career in law, maternity rendered a married woman virtually ineligible for paid work as a lawyer. Widows did not observe the taboo, however. During the period 1915–70 there were four lawyer widows, of whom three had children to support. Only at the end of the period were three mothers with husbands able to confound the convention against a working mother.[20] The behaviour of women lawyers would lead an observer to the conclusion that maternity and paid work did not readily mix. This was also the expressed view of most of the women lawyers themselves.

A woman who qualified in the 1960s agreed with the view that "a mother should be at home when the children are young." She noted frankly a consideration that few others expressed – the authority and preference of her spouse: "My husband didn't want me employed then."[21] However, women lawyers who retired, temporarily or permanently, at the birth of children generally noted that their decision was based on other factors as well. Most frequently mentioned were low pay, lack of opportunity to work in a preferred area, the deterrent effect of an old boys' club and network, and, above all, public opinion.

These various stories from the professions of university teaching, medicine, and law confirm that the model professional was a man who had no direct daily responsibility for the rearing of children; that the model wife put the demands of her husband before her own; and that the model mother subordinated her own interests to those of her children. This book has shown how a woman professional, by definition, was a person in conflict. The breadwinner role of a woman with dependants was acceptable – she was working from necessity – but a wife who had a husband to support her must be working from ambition, and this did not conform to the model. The experience of women university teachers and lawyers indicates that before 1970 the existing models were scarcely questioned, at least by behaviour. Doctors, with their higher incomes and independent businesses, were in a better position to flout convention, but relatively few did so.

Nursing and teaching were different from the other three occupations in that they were female-dominated, but the married nurse and teacher experienced the same double burden of paid professional and unpaid domestic work as the other married working women. As with university teachers, physicians, and lawyers, there was a difference between prewar and postwar experience. After World War II, more continued to work after marriage. Two dominant patterns emerged. One was a woman's retirement at the birth of her first child, and her temporary withdrawal from the labour force until her children were older, probably teenagers, at which time she would return to work, sometimes full-time, sometimes part-time; the other pattern, displayed in nursing, was a nurse's shift in employment at the time of maternity from full-time to part-time, most often towards work at night or weekends. Nurses and schoolteachers, more than the other three occupations, conformed to a "bimodal" career pattern, discerned as "school–training–work–withdrawal–(possible retraining)–work–retirement," which was common in Britain before 1975.[22]

Of the five occupations considered here, nursing work by 1970 had become structured in such a way as to permit a working mother to design an accommodating routine. Yet flexible shift work in no way eliminated the fatigue generated by the double burden. For many married nurses, as for married university teachers, physicians, lawyers, and teachers, the attractions of professional work were outweighed by the deterrents.

Teaching, like nursing, was from an early date female-dominated, though never to the same extent as nursing. From the beginning, women teachers were required to retire on marriage, and most did so. Still, it can be seen from the census that, in 1931, 4 per cent of Manitoba's female teachers had avoided retirement on marriage. Partly because of pressure brought by the female school trustees, in 1946 the prohibition on married teachers was rescinded, and from then on, married women became a steadily increasing proportion of the overall number of female teachers.[23] From 21 per cent in 1951, married women accounted for 46 per cent of female teachers in 1961, and 67 per cent in 1971.

Victor Gollancz's declarations that "feminists would offer married women the possibility, but by no means impose the necessity, of combining other activities with the work of motherhood" and that "it is essential that married no less than single women should possess economic independence" were statements of faith in 1917.[24] From the point of view of the early professionals themselves, the difficulties in the way of the combination appeared overwhelming. Perhaps Gollancz and Geneva Misener underestimated the strength of a sexually segregated economy, combined with the social prescription of an adult woman's economic dependence.[25] The professions were a battleground where qualified women tried to defy both conventions. They wanted to work as professionals, on a par with men, within their occupations; and they wanted to be as free as adult men to marry without penalty. Women were prevented from achieving these goals partly, but only partly, by the practicalities of raising children. The internal structure of the professions, together with public perceptions about appropriate behaviour for married women reinforced the barricades against women.

It is important to consider these wider social conditions as part of an explanation for a continuing inferiority in the status of professional women. One barrier was the structure of male-dominated professions, which into the 1990s were still able to withhold equal opportunities and rewards from women.[26] When Geneva Misener stated that marriage and a profession "may go hand in hand" for a woman, she failed to recognize that the professions were not the meritocratic occupations she thought she saw. The social context in which professional work and marriage were embedded proved to be more than a match for the first few generations of women who wished to do both. Indeed, the present generation of professional women still find that "domestic and work structures interlock to constrain them."[27]

## FEMALE LABOUR FORCE

Despite women's lack of parity with professional men, there were advantages for a woman professional that were not enjoyed by her sisters in manufacturing, personal service, sales, and clerical work. A higher salary and greater security were two benefits normally endowed, but this was not evident until after World War II. In 1936, for example, among the twenty-seven occupations employing most women in Manitoba, there were seven in which the average earnings over fifty-two weeks were $10.00 or more per week. In order, these occupations were telegraph operators (average weekly earnings $22.71), schoolteachers ($14.11), office clerks ($13.48), bookkeepers and cashiers ($13.46), typists ($13.15), telephone operators ($11.21), and graduate nurses ($10.35).[28] At that date, training in clerical techniques for a relatively brief period would make economic sense.

After the war, as table 25 (appendix 1) shows, the average wage for the Canadian female labour force as a whole was considerably less than the average wage for the five professions. In the census years 1941, 1961, and 1971, nurses earned the lowest wage of all five occupations, yet the average female wage was lower: 61 per cent of the nursing wage in 1941, 61 per cent in 1961, and 74 per cent in 1971. Higher earning capacity carried a cost, most obviously associated with training.

Most professional occupations required higher admission standards and longer training than other women's work. Despite the serendipitous entry of most women university teachers into their occupation, all had a minimum of an undergarduate degree by way of postsecondary training, and many had graduate work by way of additional credentials. Medicine demanded a firmer commitment. Five years of university courses followed by one year of hospital internship were standard. Law was more balanced between practical apprenticeship and theoretical training, but it normally required four or five years training before admission to the Bar. Nursing demanded three years of full-time training. During this time, the apprenticeship component involved nurses in actual work for which they were paid a token wage. Nevertheless, a registered nurse had to be committed to the profession to the extent of three years of postsecondary training.

Schoolteaching demanded less of its practitioners. Until the mid-1920s, a beginning schoolteacher could be employed with only a grade 11 education supplemented by vocational training of less than a year. Not until after the 1970s was a university degree demanded as a minimum. Relatively lower standards of admission, together with the steady demand for schoolteachers, except in the Depression, were undoubtedly one of the attractions of teaching for a woman, who might calculate that there would be less investment of time and forgone income lost if she quit paid work and conformed to the model woman of pre-World War II, who retired permanently from the labour force upon marriage.

While university teaching, medicine, and law conferred higher salaries than nursing and teaching, the latter two offered security, in the sense that there were more nursing and teaching jobs available. Moreover, women were not treated as obvious interlopers. They could feel more comfortable in nursing and teaching with women as co-workers, for they were not the resented invaders of an old boys' club. As well, nursing and teaching carried higher salaries than the female labour force as a whole and could be wider avenues of upward mobility.[29]

One cost specifically associated with a professional occupation was the lack of earnings during the lengthy training period. Another was related to difficulties associated with maternity in the years after World War II, a difficulty shared with other members of the female labour force. In Manitoba, university teachers and lawyers generally left paid work altogether on maternity and followed the prewar pattern. On the other hand, a large majority of women doctors accepted the social consequences of combining motherhood and paid work with greater ease than other professional women, doubtless because of their high incomes and self-employed independence.

Nursing was unique in its accommodation of women's paid and unpaid workload by offering shift work. This was appreciated by some nurses, who were glad to earn money at night or on weekends when their husbands could help with babysitting, but it was resented by others, who found the dual burden immensely fatiguing. Married schoolteachers before 1970 had few complaints. They could care for their infants full-time and then return to full-time teaching without obvious penalty, and they could enjoy the same working hours as their children. The demand for teachers was high, and school boards were glad to employ experienced workers. It is true that any professional woman who withdrew from paid work took the risk of reducing her eligibility for a position of authority. The data suggest, however, that before 1970 few women identified themselves as being in the running for such jobs. Like women in the female labour force generally, they did not consider a managerial or administrative position to be a realistic prospect.

The authors of *Unequal Colleagues* examined the careers of nine professional women in the northeastern United States at the turn of the century. Those women's achievements were conditioned by their families, education, and social and cultural environment as well as by their personal energy. *Unequal Colleagues* concluded that women could choose among four strategies to promote their success. Separatism, superperformance, subordination, and innovation were the options.[30] The Manitoba data, derived from a more broadly based population, confirm the American thesis only partially.

Separatism, in the sense of participation in a women's culture that self-consciously nurtured women's values and primarily benefited women in society at large, was an option for some American (and European) women who were educated at single-sex schools and colleges and then went on to work in similar institutions as teachers.[31] This was not the case in Manitoba. Since the schools and universities were sexually integrated, no single-sex institutions (apart from a couple of low-enrolment private schools) could offer employment. Among the Roman Catholic population, most education was not in private convents but in co-educational public schools. Within the university, women were segregated to the extent that they were concentrated in domestic or nurturing faculties, but this was a system established by the men in power, not an option voluntarily chosen by the women. Separatism in the sense of women working in a woman-only occupation was no guarantee of "success," even in nursing, for even in that near-monopoly, male nurses made higher wages and men from outside the profession were in charge.

If superperformance means excelling to the extent that due recognition cannot be withheld, it is difficult to identify numbers in this category. Perhaps the one or two women physicians who were appointed to hospital positions or the half-dozen teachers made principals of junior or senior high schools, or the half-dozen women who served as directors or deans at the university, or the two women who were appointed judges can be considered as superperformers. These were exceptions – important as demonstrating that it could be done, and significant as role models for women later, but not representative of the career patterns of the overwhelming majority of professional women.

Innovation suggests that women could invent their own way of interpreting professional work, and it is true that some did feel they were able to work in a different way from men. Some university teachers believed they had a gift for teaching, as distinct from self-motivated research, and some physicians thought that women were more sensitive to the emotional needs of patients. But real innovation requires power and ambition: power to take a risk, ambition to test limits. Most women were more impressed by their powerlessness than with an awareness of opportunity; and as for ambition, even the most successful, by male criteria, would go to considerable lengths in my interviews and surveys to dissociate their achievement from any personal ambition. Rather, they insisted they had been chosen to serve by someone in authority.

Of the four strategies suggested, the one that makes most sense with respect to Manitoba women before 1970 is subordination. Almost all the women were subordinate. Some acquiesced, some were indifferent, some were resentful, a few resisted. Most notable of the fighters were the Winnipeg teachers who used their local to develop an ideology counter to the convention of the sole male breadwinner. They had the short-term satisfaction of abolishing differential salary scales, though this made little overall difference to the average pay. Their long-term significance was much greater. The Winnipeg women's local helped develop and confirm a mind-set which insisted that rewards be related to the work done rather than to the gender of the worker.

The actual experience of the women professionals showed that any presumptions of objectivity would be made at their peril. Other people regarded them more as women than as professionals. They could sometimes be seen as honorary men and, like women medical students, be greeted by their instructor's salutation, "Hey, fellas." The public had difficulty comprehending their existence as "two people: a professional person and a person who reproduces," as a woman doctor of the early 1950s put it.[32]

The absence of a double-sided or multifaceted model is a key to understanding both the women professionals and their society. The requirement to choose between options, once and for all, and live with the consequences was so much an ingrained habit of thought that it was almost impossible to consider any alternative moral economy. Another embedded assumption of western society was that a woman's mission was to serve and to consider others before herself. The idea that she might as well be able to consider other matters seemed difficult for mainstream moralists to comprehend.

So the women were in professional occupations partly on sufferance. They were allowed in, for the men could not totally exclude them without denying the ideals of merit that were enshrined in their assessment of performance and their codes of ethics. Once the women were in, the men in authority could not admit them into superior positions because there was no intellectual framework to account for women's capacity to juggle many oranges in the air at once. The common mentality assumed that single-minded commitment was the only model of professional work that existed. If you had resources of time and energy to allocate to leisure, voluntary activity, and family, then it was supposed that you were not a proper professional. The physician whose apprenticeship demanded "thirty-six hours on call" was being socialized to internalize this devotion as the desirable norm. When women started to question this in the 1980s, doubtless many male professionals were glad to share in a reassessment of the standard professional model.

In the meantime, as a woman doctor said, "We were just so delighted to be accepted."[33] Similarly, a woman university professor "felt privileged to be there,"[34] and a woman lawyer was glad to be "one of the gang."[35] In the male-dominated professions, the women's delight and gratitude took the edge off feelings of injustice and humiliation which, as there were so few women, were usually experienced in isolation. In university teaching, medicine, and law, women had neither the numbers nor the consciousness to develop alternative models of professional behaviour. Consciousness, in the sense of "reinterpreting and re-evaluating knowledge," and in the ability to imagine other ways besides conventional arrangements, came in the wake of 1960s feminism.[36]

Nurses and teachers had numbers, to be sure, but membership of an occupational majority by itself was insufficient to transform notions of nurturing. The nurse was expected to care for her patient and serve the physician and not pay heed to her own interests. The nurse worked primarily, though not exclusively, with other women and was rigorously socialized, during three years' residential training, into a straitjacket of routines which so locked her in that it was almost impossible to imagine alternative ways of working.

Teaching comprehended such a variety that no single model pertains. Many teachers were attracted precisely because they could fill a nurturing, maternal-type role of caring for children. Others went into teaching because, like some nurses, they cared even less for alternative occupations. In the years before the mid-1950s, all teachers were subjected to differential salary structures. It is true that during the Depression years of high unemployment, there was considerable support for the notion that a family unit was entitled to only one breadwinner and that women teachers were not averse to this idea. But to the vast majority of women, the idea that the same work should be paid according to the gender of the worker was odious. This was the issue more than any other that served to raise the ire of women teachers. Not surprisingly, it was the women teachers, in the Winnipeg Women Teachers local, who developed a critique of the male worker paid by virtue of his gender, a critique that led these women into a successful campaign of equal pay for equal work.

Even the women teachers, the most gender-conscious of all the professional women considered here, did not before 1970 undertake full-scale lobbying for women to enter the positions of higher pay and authority. As in all Western countries, "the results of … efforts to secure for women a permanent position in the emergent professional elite proved disappointing."[37] The teachers' numbers were high, but their mentality lacked an awareness of a generalized gender oppression until the Women's Movement of the late 1960s. Until then, each woman carried her own individual burden of acquiescence or negative resentment: "Although women have won political victories, they have not yet overcome their oldest and subtlest enemy, the inferiority complex. Diffidence has been too long identified with womanly virtue to be an easy foe to conquer."[38] Only after feminists showed that the personal was political, that a woman's discontent with her prescribed and circumscribed working conditions was not necessarily her own fault, was it possible for women to regroup their ideas and reconceptualize what had been happening to them.[39]

Listening to the voices of the professional women allowed me to understand their surface conformity to the male model professional. Yet I also heard dissonant tones beneath the tentative melody line, notes which declared that all was not in harmony. The feminism rekindled in the 1960s helped to provide a theoretical framework to justify resistance to the status quo. At the same time, a generalized "income shortage at the household level and a labour shortage at the production level" gave an economic incentive to more women to defy previous assumptions of dependency and to consider a lifetime career of working for pay as the norm.[40] More women therefore considered it worth their while to invest more resources in the extended training demanded by professional work. Fortified by greater numbers, women in professions in the 1990s have been disinclined to tolerate inequity and have been in a better position to effect change. Changes began after a new conceptual framework, designed to analyse oppression, could give support to insubordination. Foundations both of acceptance and resistance had been a century in the making.

# Appendices

# APPENDIX ONE

# *Tables*

Table 1
Women's Occupations, Manitoba, 1881

|                          | *No.* | *%* |
| ------------------------ | ----- | --- |
| Dressmakers & milliners  | 89    | 11  |
| Farmers, female          | 71    | 9   |
| Laundresses              | 24    | 3   |
| Midwives & nurses        | 10    | 1   |
| Nuns                     | 36    | 5   |
| Seamstresses             | 35    | 5   |
| Servants, female         | 471   | 59  |
| Teachers, female         | 58    | 7   |
| Total                    | 794   | 100 |

*Source*: *Census of Canada 1880–81*, vol. 2, table 14.

Table 2
Number and percentage of men and women gainfully occupied, selected occupational groups, prairie provinces 1891–1931

| | 1891 | | | | 1901 | | | | 1911 | | | | 1921 | | | | 1931 | | | |
| | Male | | Female | | Male | | Female | | Male | | Female | | Male | | Female | | Male | | Female | |
| | No. | % | No. | % | No. | % | No. | % | No. | % | No. | % | No. | % | No. | % | No. | % | No. | % |
|---|---|---|---|---|---|---|---|---|---|---|---|---|---|---|---|---|---|---|---|---|
| Agriculture | 47,184 | 66 | 410 | 7 | 78,906 | 64 | 436 | 4 | 279,724 | 56 | 3,748 | 8 | 370,350 | 59 | 5,216 | 7 | 435,169 | 56 | 8,478 | 7 |
| Manufacturing | 3,590 | 5 | 909 | 16 | na | | na | | 23,776 | 5 | 4,639 | 10 | 31,568 | 5 | 4,226 | 5 | 45,641 | 6 | 5,042 | 4 |
| Trade & finance | 3,993 | 6 | 123 | 2 | na | | na | | 37,600 | 7 | 3,212 | 7 | 51,115 | 8 | 7,366 | 9 | 59,821 | 8 | 8,911 | 8 |
| Professional service | 1,800 | 3 | 720 | 13 | na | | na | | 9,874 | 2 | 6,452 | 14 | 15,488 | 2 | 16,589 | 21 | 19,810 | 3 | 23,774 | 21 |
| Personal service | 1,504 | 2 | 3,132 | 57 | 3,642 | 3 | 6,758 | 58 | 14,057 | 3 | 22,366 | 47 | 16,793 | 3 | 25,679 | 33 | 25,424 | 3 | 47,025 | 41 |
| Clerical | 1,011 | 1 | 81 | 1 | 2,968 | 2 | 625 | 5 | 13,851 | 3 | 5,758 | 12 | 23,994 | 4 | 16,062 | 21 | 24,820 | 3 | 19,595 | 17 |
| All occupations | 71,479 | | 5,476 | | 122,684 | | 11,568 | | 500,834 | | 47,404 | | 622,179 | | 77,608 | | 779,941 | | 115,845 | |

Source: "Occupational Trends in Canada 1891–1931," Census of Canada 1931, bulletin M4, table 5.

Table 3
Number and percentage of men and women gainfully occupied, selected occupational groups, Manitoba, 1931–1971

| | 1931 Male | | 1931 Female | | 1936 Male | | 1936 Female | | 1941 Male | | 1941 Female | | 1946 Male | | 1946 Female | |
| --- | --- | --- | --- | --- | --- | --- | --- | --- | --- | --- | --- | --- | --- | --- | --- | --- |
| | No. | % | No. | % | No. | % | No. | % | No. | % | No. | % | No. | % | No. | % |
| Agriculture | 91,566 | 40 | 1,863 | 4 | 99,803 | 44 | 1,823 | 4 | 95,599 | 40 | 1,506 | 3 | 78,893 | 35 | 1,795 | 3 |
| Manufacturing | 17,678 | 8 | 2,811 | 6 | 18,651 | 8 | 2,878 | 6 | 27,784 | 11 | 3,883 | 8 | 25,531 | 11 | 5,382 | 10 |
| Trade & commerce | 18,036 | 8 | 3,775 | 8 | 18,257 | 8 | 3,861 | 8 | 19,556 | 8 | 5,089 | 10 | 8,720 | 4 | 5,807 | 11 |
| Clerical | 9,801 | 4 | 9,163 | 20 | 10,691 | 5 | 8,149 | 18 | 13,883 | 6 | 10,296 | 21 | 11,448 | 5 | 15,498 | 28 |
| Professional service | 8,017 | 4 | 7,835 | 17 | 6,411 | 3 | 7,783 | 17 | 7,386 | 3 | 6,644 | 13 | 7,838 | 3 | 7,597 | 14 |
| Personal, protective & other service | 1,167 | 5 | 17,525 | 39 | 11,623 | 5 | 19,665 | 43 | 13,492 | 6 | 20,267 | 40 | 24,308 | 11 | 12,611 | 23 |
| All occupations | 225,764 | | 44,908 | | 224,009 | | 45,811 | | 240,399 | | 49,912 | | 2,253,520 | | 54,609 | |

| | 1951 Male | | 1951 Female | | 1961 Male | | 1961 Female | | 1971 Male | | 1971 Female | |
| --- | --- | --- | --- | --- | --- | --- | --- | --- | --- | --- | --- | --- |
| | No. | % | No. | % | No. | % | No. | % | No. | % | No. | % |
| Agriculture | 70,430 | 30 | 3,397 | 5 | 46,533 | 19 | 1,558 | 3 | 38,535 | 14 | 10,265 | 7 |
| Manufacturing | 26,970 | 11 | 6,933 | 10 | 58,754 | 24 | 8,515 | 10 | 37,815 | 14 | 16,870 | 12 |
| Trade & commerce | 10,655 | 5 | 7,706 | 17 | 12,439 | 5 | 7,580 | 9 | 25,400 | 9 | 12,170 | 8 |
| Clerical | 14,221 | 6 | 20,044 | 30 | 17,384 | 7 | 27,577 | 31 | 19,350 | 7 | 44,235 | 30 |
| Professional service | 9,938 | 4 | 8,548 | 13 | 15,784 | 7 | 13,520 | 15 | 25,450 | 9 | 14,720 | 10 |
| Personal, protective & other service | 15,546 | 7 | 14,876 | 22 | 22,305 | 9 | 22,707 | 26 | 24,570 | 9 | 23,960 | 16 |
| All occupations | 232,296 | | 66,205 | | 239,806 | | 88,866 | | 268,015 | | 145,900 | |

Sources: Census of Canada 1931, vol. 7, table 4; 1941, vol. 7, table 4; 1951, vol. 4, table 4; 1961, vol. 3.1, table 20; 1971, vol. 3.2, table 2. Census of the Prairie Provinces 1936, vol. 2, table 7; 1946, vol. 2, table 3.

Table 4
Women in selected professions, Manitoba, 1911–1971

|  | 1911[1] | 1921[2] | 1931 | 1941 | 1951 | 1961 | 1971 |
|---|---|---|---|---|---|---|---|
| University teachers |  | 14 | 10 | 16 | 35 | 51 | 200 |
| Physicians | 14 | 13 | 18 | 40 | 50 | 74 | 145 |
| Lawyers |  | 4 | 4 | 10 | 5 | 9 | 15 |
| Schoolteachers | 2,125 | 3,465 | 4,288 | 3,688 | 3,985 | 5,998 | 8,075 |
| Nurses | 411 | 1,540 | 1,345 | 1,498 | 1,681 | 2,896 | 4,460 |
| Total professional service | 4,306 | 6,730 | 7,835 | 6,644 | 8,548 | 13,520 | 14,720 |
| Total female labour force |  |  | 44,908 | 49,912 | 66,205 | 88,866 | 145,900 |

Sources: For university teachers 1921–61 inclusive, University of Manitoba calendars 1920–21,
1930–31, 1940–41, 1950–51, 1960–61. For university teachers 1970–71 and other categories in 1971,
Census of Canada 1971, vol. 3.2, table 8. For all other categories, Census of Canada 1911, vol. 6, table 5;
1921, vol. 4, table 2; 1931, vol. 7, table 4; 1941, vol. 7, table 4; 1951, vol. 4, table 4; 1961, vol. 3.1,
table 20.
[1] Nurses category does not differentiate between graduate nurses and nurses in training.
[2] Nurses category combines graduate nurses and nurses in training.

Table 5
Full-time university teachers, Canada, Manitoba,
1920–1970

|  | Canada | Manitoba |
|---|---|---|
| 1920 | 2,225 | 198 |
| 1930 | 2,882 | 159 |
| 1940 | 3,169 | 149 |
| 1950 | 5,539 | 275 |
| 1960 | 7,760 | 410 |
| 1970 | 24,773 | 1,352 |

Source: Historical Compendium of Education Statistics, 1978, table 26.

Table 6
Numbers of female university teachers, by faculty, University of Manitoba, 1920–1970

| | Arts | Sc. | Phar. | Comm. | Eng. | Arch. | ID | A&HE | Ag. | HE | Ed. | SW | Mus. | Nurs. | PE | Art | Law | Total |
|---|---|---|---|---|---|---|---|---|---|---|---|---|---|---|---|---|---|---|
| 1920 | 3 | 1 | | | | | | 10 | | | | | | | | | | 14 |
| 1925 | 2 | | | | | | | 8 | | | | | | | | | | 10 |
| 1930 | 2 | | | | | | | 8 | | | | | | | | | | 10 |
| 1935 | 2 | | | | | | | 8 | | | | | | | | | | 10 |
| 1940 | 3 | | | | | | | 13 | | | | | | | | | | 16 |
| 1945 | 7 | | | | | 1 | | 13 | | | 1 | 1 | | | | | | 23 |
| 1950 | 5 | 2 | | | | | 3 | 16 | | | | 6 | | 2 | | | | 34 |
| 1955 | 5 | 4 | | | | | 2 | 12 | 1 | | 2 | 10 | 1 | 2 | 2 | | | 41 |
| 1960 | 5 | 4 | | 1 | | | 2 | 14 | 2 | | 2 | 10 | 1 | 2 | 3 | | | 46 |
| 1965 | 6 | 6 | | | | | 3 | | 1 | 20 | 14 | 14 | 2 | 6 | 4 | | | 76 |
| 1970 | 22 | 11 | | | | | 6 | | 1 | 28 | 18 | 19 | 2 | 23 | 3 | | 2 | 135 |

*Source:* University of Manitoba calendars, 1920–71.

Table 7
Percentage of female university teachers, by faculty, University of Manitoba, 1920–1970

| | Arts % | Sc. % | Phar. % | Comm. % | Eng. % | Arch. % | ID % | A&HE % | Ag. % | HE % | Ed. % | SW % | Mus. % | Nurs. % | PE % | Art % | Law % | Total[1] % |
|---|---|---|---|---|---|---|---|---|---|---|---|---|---|---|---|---|---|---|
| 1920 | 1 | 5 | | | | | | 26 | | | | | | | | | | 16 |
| 1925 | 9 | | | | | | | 20 | | | | | | | | | | 11 |
| 1930 | 8 | | | | | | | 21 | | | | | | | | | | 11 |
| 1935 | 8 | | | | | | | 40 | | | | | | | | | | 11 |
| 1940 | 11 | | | | | | | 48 | | | | | | | | | | 15 |
| 1945 | 17 | | | | | 25 | | 48 | | | 50 | 50 | | | | | | 16 |
| 1950 | 12 | 5 | | | | | 60 | 42 | | | | 86 | | 100 | | | | 17 |
| 1955 | 8 | 8 | | | | | 40 | 28 | | | 22 | 100 | 50 | 100 | 40 | | | 17 |
| 1960 | 7 | 6 | | 8 | | | 40 | 25 | | | 20 | 77 | 33 | 100 | 43 | | | 15 |
| 1965 | 5 | 7 | | | | | 43 | | 1 | 100 | 36 | 61 | 25 | 100 | 44 | | | 15 |
| 1970 | 8 | 6 | | | | | 55 | | 1 | 85 | 25 | 51 | 15 | 100 | 18 | | 10 | 15 |

Source: University of Manitoba calendars, 1920–71.
[1] Percentage of women among all faculty members.

Table 8
University of Manitoba medical graduates, 1892–1971

|  | 1892–1901 | 1902–11 | 1912–21 | 1922–31 | 1932–41 | 1942–51 | 1952–61 | 1962–71 |
|---|---|---|---|---|---|---|---|---|
| Male | 177 | 242 | 256 | 410 | 478 | 534 | 644 | 517 |
| Female | 2 | 1 | 9 | 34 | 40 | 57 | 39 | 48 |
| % female | 1.1 | 0.4 | 3.4 | 7.6 | 7.7 | 9.6 | 5.7 | 8.4 |

*Sources*: University of Manitoba Faculty of Medicine, Women in Medicine file, Natalia Pohorecki, "List of Female Graduates." University of Manitoba Alumni Association, "Nominal List of Graduates, Faculty of Medicine."

Table 9
Female physicians, Manitoba, 1911–1971

|  | 1911 | 1921 | 1931 | 1936 | 1941 | 1946 | 1951 | 1961 | 1971 |
|---|---|---|---|---|---|---|---|---|---|
| Male | 419 | 544 | 648 | 620 | 700 | 638 | 788 | 1,046 | 1,255 |
| Female | 14 | 13 | 18 | 27 | 40 | 28 | 50 | 74 | 145 |
| % female | 3.2 | 2.3 | 2.7 | 4.1 | 5.4 | 4.2 | 5.9 | 6.6 | 10.6 |

*Sources*: *Census of Canada 1911*, vol. 6, table 5; *1921*, vol. 4, table 2; *1931*, vol. 7, table 40; *1941*, vol. 7, table 4; *1951*, vol. 4, table 4; *1961*, vol. 3.1, table 20; *1971*, vol. 3.2, table 2; *Census of the Prairie Provinces 1936*, vol. 2, table 7; *1946*, vol. 2, table 3.

Table 10
Female physicians, Canada, 1911–1971

|  | 1911 | 1921 | 1931 | 1941 | 1951 | 1961 | 1971 |
|---|---|---|---|---|---|---|---|
| Male | 7,215 | 8,544 | 9,817 | 11,489 | 13,665 | 19,835 | 25,695 |
| Female | 196 | 152 | 203 | 384 | 660 | 1,455 | 2,890 |
| % female | 2.6 | 1.7 | 2.0 | 3.2 | 4.6 | 6.8 | 10.0 |

*Sources*: *Census of Canada 1911*, vol. 6, table 5; *1921*, vol. 4, table 2; *1931*, vol. 7, table 4; *1941*, vol. 7, table 4; *1951*, vol. 4, table 4; *1961*, vol. 3.1, table 20; *1971*, vol. 3.2, table 2.

Table 11
Female physicians, Canadian provinces, 1911–1971

|        |          | 1911  | 1921  | 1931  | 1941  | 1951  | 1961  | 1971  |
|--------|----------|-------|-------|-------|-------|-------|-------|-------|
|        | Male     | 395   | 597   | 714   | 896   | 1,306 | 1,990 | 2,925 |
| B.C.   | Female   | 21    | 12    | 15    | 21    | 69    | 160   | 335   |
|        | % female | 5.1   | 1.9   | 2.0   | 2.2   | 5.0   | 7.4   | 10.2  |
|        | Male     | 361   | 537   | 572   | 651   | 801   | 1,251 | 1,940 |
| Alta   | Female   | 8     | 11    | 11    | 20    | 39    | 105   | 245   |
|        | % female | 2.1   | 2.0   | 1.8   | 2.9   | 4.6   | 7.7   | 11.2  |
|        | Male     | 372   | 520   | 572   | 578   | 619   | 889   | 1,005 |
| Sask.  | Female   | 7     | 4     | 12    | 15    | 32    | 62    | 100   |
|        | % female | 1.8   | 0.7   | 2.0   | 2.5   | 4.9   | 6.5   | 9.0   |
|        | Male     | 419   | 544   | 648   | 700   | 788   | 1,046 | 1,255 |
| Man.   | Female   | 14    | 13    | 18    | 40    | 50    | 74    | 145   |
|        | % female | 3.2   | 2.3   | 2.7   | 5.4   | 5.9   | 6.6   | 10.3  |
|        | Male     | 2,947 | 3,383 | 3,828 | 4,486 | 5,038 | 7,406 | 9,535 |
| Ont.   | Female   | 106   | 76    | 106   | 212   | 325   | 632   | 1,135 |
|        | % female | 3.4   | 2.1   | 2.6   | 4.5   | 6.0   | 7.8   | 10.6  |
|        | Male     | 1,979 | 2,198 | 2,723 | 3,289 | 3,979 | 5,817 | 7,145 |
| Que.   | Female   | 21    | 18    | 24    | 59    | 118   | 350   | 775   |
|        | % female | 1.0   | 0.8   | 0.8   | 1.7   | 2.8   | 5.6   | 9.7   |
|        | Male     | 272   | 263   | 265   | 301   | 349   | 434   | 515   |
| N.B.   | Female   | 9     | 5     | 4     | 9     | 8     | 21    | 15    |
|        | % female | 3.2   | 1.8   | 1.4   | 2.9   | 2.2   | 4.6   | 2.8   |
|        | Male     |       |       |       |       | 140   | 219   | 365   |
| Nfld   | Female   |       |       |       |       | 3     | 11    | 40    |
|        | % female |       |       |       |       | 0.7   | 4.7   | 9.8   |
|        | Male     | 70    | 68    | 62    | 80    | 73    | 87    | 75    |
| P.E.I. | Female   | 2     | 0     | 1     | 1     | 0     | 4     | 5     |
|        | % female | 2.7   | 0     | 1.5   | 1.2   | 0     | 4.3   | 6.2   |
|        | Male     | 400   | 444   | 433   | 508   | 572   | 673   | 910   |
| N.S.   | Female   | 8     | 13    | 12    | 7     | 16    | 33    | 90    |
|        | % female | 1.9   | 2.8   | 2.6   | 1.3   | 2.7   | 4.6   | 9.0   |

Sources: *Census of Canada 1911*, vol. 6, table 5; *1921*, vol. 4, table 2; *1931*, vol. 7, table 4; *1941*, vol. 7, table 4; *1951*, vol. 4, table 4; *1961*, vol. 3.1, table 20; *1971*, vol. 3.2, table 2.

Table 12
Lawyers and notaries, Canada, 1891–1971

|  | 1891 | 1901 | 1911 | 1921 | 1931 | 1941 | 1951 | 1961 | 1971 |
|---|---|---|---|---|---|---|---|---|---|
| Total | 4,332 | 4,713 | 5,204 | 7,209 | 8,058 | 7,920 | 9,038 | 12,068 | 15,535 |
| Women | 24 | 0 | 7 | 64 | 54 | 129 | 197 | 309 | 780 |

Sources: For 1891–1931, *Census of Canada 1931*, vol. 1, table 83. For 1931–61, Canada. Dept. of Labour, *Occupational Trends in Canada 1931–61*, 1963, 40, 45. For 1971, *Census of Canada 1971*, vol. 3.2, table 2.

Table 13
Lawyers, Manitoba, 1881–1971

|  | 1881 | 1886 | 1911 | 1921 | 1931 | 1936 | 1941 | 1946 | 1951 | 1961 | 1971 |
|---|---|---|---|---|---|---|---|---|---|---|---|
| Male | 39 | 148 | 376 | 655 | 653 | 598 | 546 | 462 | 536 | 606 | 680 |
| Female | 0 | 0 | 1 | 4 | 4 | 4 | 10 | 8 | 5 | 9 | 15 |

Sources: *Census of Canada 1881*, vol. 2, table 14; *1911*, vol. 6, table 5; *1921*, vol. 4, table 2; *1931*, vol. 7, table 40; *1941*, vol. 7, table 4; *1951*, vol. 4, table 4; *1961*, vol. 3.1, table 20; *1971*, vol. 3.2, table 2. *Census of Manitoba 1886*, table 11. *Census of the Prairie Provinces 1936*, vol. 2, table 7; *1946*, vol. 2, table 3.

Table 14
Female law graduates, Manitoba, 1902–1971

|  | 1902–1911 | 1912–1921 | 1922–1931 | 1932–1941 | 1942–1951 | 1952–1961 | 1962–1971 |
|---|---|---|---|---|---|---|---|
| Male | 94 | 195 | 194 | 151 | 231 | 350 | 409 |
| Female | 0 | 9 | 2 | 10 | 6 | 12 | 17 |
| % female | 0 | 4.4 | 1.0 | 6.2 | 2.5 | 3.3 | 3.9 |

Source: University of Manitoba. Office of Institutional Analysis, "Numbers of Graduates by Faculty, 1891–1989," March 1990.

Table 15
Percentage of women lawyers, Manitoba, Canada, and the United States, 1911–1971

|  | 1911 % | 1921 % | 1931 % | 1941 % | 1951 % | 1961 % | 1971 % |
|---|---|---|---|---|---|---|---|
| Manitoba |  | 0.6 | 0.6 | 1.8 | 0.9 | 1.4 | 2.1 |
| Canada | 0.6 | 0.8 | 0.6 | 1.6 | 2.1 | 2.5 | 5.1 |
| United States | 1.1 | 1.4 | 2.1 | 2.4 | 3.5 | 3.3 | 4.7 |

Sources: *Census of Canada 1911*, vol. 6, table 5; *1921*, vol. 4, table 2; *1931*, vol. 7, table 40; *1941*, vol. 7, table 4; *1951*, vol. 4, table 4; *1961*, vol. 3.1, table 20; *1971*, vol. 3.2, table 2. For U.S. figures, Cynthia Epstein, *Women in Law*, 1981, quoted in Cott, *Grounding of Modern Feminism*, 1987, 219.

Table 16
Women lawyers, Canadian provinces, 1921–1971

|  | 1921 | 1931 | 1941 | 1951 | 1961 | 1971 |
|---|---|---|---|---|---|---|
| **BRITISH COLUMBIA** | | | | | | |
| Number | 13 | 7 | 12 | 27 | 44 | 90 |
| % female | 1.9 | 1.1 | 1.7 | 3.0 | 4.6 | 4.9 |
| **ALBERTA** | | | | | | |
| Number | 9 | 2 | 11 | 5 | 16 | 50 |
| % female | 1.6 | 0.3 | 2.1 | 0.9 | 2.3 | 4.2 |
| **SASKATCHEWAN** | | | | | | |
| Number | 4 | 4 | 5 | 8 | 8 | 25 |
| % female | 0.6 | 0.7 | 1.1 | 2.0 | 1.4 | 5.8 |
| **MANITOBA** | | | | | | |
| Number | 4 | 4 | 10 | 5 | 9 | 15 |
| % female | 0.6 | 0.6 | 1.8 | 0.9 | 1.4 | 2.1 |
| **ONTARIO** | | | | | | |
| Number | 23 | 32 | 73 | 107 | 161 | 345 |
| % female | 1.0 | 1.1 | 2.3 | 3.1 | 3.2 | 5.0 |
| **QUEBEC** | | | | | | |
| Number | 9 | 4 | 5 | 30 | 58 | 225 |
| % female | 0.4 | 0.1 | 0.1 | 1.1 | 1.7 | 5.1 |
| **NEW BRUNSWICK** | | | | | | |
| Number | 1 | 0 | 5 | 8 | 5 | 10 |
| % female | 0.5 | 0 | 2.1 | 3.5 | 2.3 | 2.9 |
| **PRINCE EDWARD IS.** | | | | | | |
| Number | 0 | 0 | 0 | 0 | 0 | 0 |
| % female | 0 | 0 | 0 | 0 | 0 | 0 |
| **NOVA SCOTIA** | | | | | | |
| Number | 1 | 1 | 8 | 5 | 5 | 15 |
| % female | 0.3 | 0.4 | 2.6 | 1.7 | 1.7 | 3.7 |
| **NEWFOUNDLAND** | | | | | | |
| Number | | | | 2 | 1 | 5 |
| % female | | | | 3.1 | 1.3 | 5.2 |

*Sources*: *Census of Canada 1921*, vol. 4, table 2; *1931*, vol. 7, table 40; *1941*, vol. 7, table 4; *1951*, vol. 4, table 4; *1961*, vol. 3.1, table 20; *1971*, vol. 3.2, table 2.

Table 17
Distribution of nurses by type of work, Canada, 1930
and 1943

|  | 1930 | | 1943 | |
|---|---|---|---|---|
|  | No. | % | No. | % |
| Private duty | 6,370 | 60 | 6,387 | 31 |
| Public health | 1,521 | 14 | 13,959 | 69 |
| Hospitals | 2,639 | 25 | | |

Sources: G.M. Weir, Survey of Nursing Education in Canada, 1932,
55; Kathryn McPherson, "Skilled Service and Women's
Work," 1989, 250.

Table 18
Nurses, Manitoba, 1911–1971

| Year | 1911[1] | 1921[2] | 1931 | 1941 | 1951 | 1961 | 1971 |
|---|---|---|---|---|---|---|---|
| Number | 411 | 1,540 | 1,345 | 1,498 | 1,681 | 2,896 | 4,460 |

Sources: Census of Canada 1911, vol. 6, table 5; 1921, vol. 4, table 2; 1931, vol. 7, table 4; 1941, vol. 7,
table 4; 1951, vol. 4, table 4; 1961, vol. 3.1, table 20; 1971, vol. 3.2, table 2.
[1] Does not differentiate between graduate nurses and nurses in training.
[2] Combines graduate nurses and nurses in training.

Table 19
Percentage distribution of registered nurses by field
of employment, Manitoba, 1966 and 1970

|  | Hospital or institution % | Public health % | Education % | Other % |
|---|---|---|---|---|
| 1966 | 82 | 7 | 4 | 7 |
| 1970 | 85 | 7 | 4 | 4 |

Source: Countdown: Canadian Nursing Statistics, 1967, table 5, 13;
1971, table 4, 13.

Table 20
Teachers and professional female labour force,
Manitoba, 1881–1971

| | Women teachers | Women professionals | Women teachers as % of female labour force |
|---|---|---|---|
| 1881[1] | 58 | 104 | 56 |
| 1886[2] | 227 | 358 | 63 |
| 1911[3] | 2,125 | 4,306 | 49 |
| 1921 | 3,465 | 6,730 | 51 |
| 1931 | 4,288 | 7,835 | 55 |
| 1936 | 4,020 | 7,783 | 52 |
| 1941 | 3,688 | 7,591 | 49 |
| 1946 | 3,666 | 7,597 | 48 |
| 1951 | 3,985 | 8,548 | 47 |
| 1961 | 5,998 | 13,520 | 44 |
| 1971[4] | 8,075 | | |

*Sources*: *Census of Canada 1880–81*, vol. 2, table 14; *1911*, vol. 6, table 5; *1921*, vol. 4, table 2; *1931*, vol. 7, table 4; *1941*, vol. 7, table 4; *1951*, vol. 4, table 4; *1961*, vol. 3.1, table 20; *1971*, vol. 3.2, table 2. *Census of Manitoba 1885–86*, table 11. *Census of the Prairie Provinces 1936*, vol. 2, table 7; *1946*, vol. 2, table 3.
[1] Professional female labour force: midwives and nurses, nuns, teachers.
[2] Midwives and nurses (counted in "domestic class" by the census), nuns, teachers.
[3] From 1911 to 1961 the occupations counted as "professional" by the census.
[4] 1971 figures not comparable.

Table 21
Women teachers, Manitoba, 1881–1971

| | 1881 | 1886 | 1911 | 1921 | 1931 | 1936 | 1941 | 1946 | 1951 | 1961 | 1971 |
|---|---|---|---|---|---|---|---|---|---|---|---|
| Male | 89 | 237 | 711 | 860 | 1,256 | 1,468 | 1,560 | 1,217 | 1,618 | 2,776 | 4,175 |
| Female | 58 | 227 | 2,125 | 3,465 | 4,288 | 4,020 | 3,688 | 3,666 | 3,985 | 5,998 | 8,075 |
| % female | 39 | 49 | 75 | 80 | 77 | 73 | 70 | 75 | 71 | 68 | 66 |

*Sources*: *Census of Canada 1880–81*, vol 2, table 14; *1911*, vol. 6, table 5; *1921*, vol. 4, table 2; *1931*, vol. 7, table 4; *1941*, vol. 7, table 4; *1951*, vol. 4, table 4; *1961*, vol. 3.1, table 20; *1971*, vol. 3.2, table 2. *Census of Manitoba 1885–86*, table 11. *Census of the Prairie Provinces 1936*, vol. 2, table 7; *1946*, vol. 2, table 3.

Table 22
Percentage of female teachers, Canada and provinces, 1881–1971

| | 1881 %F | 1911 %F | 1921 %F | 1931 %F | 1941 %F | 1951 %F | 1961 %F | 1971 %F |
|---|---|---|---|---|---|---|---|---|
| Newfoundland | | | | | | 67 | 63 | 65 |
| Nova Scotia | 61 | 85 | 91 | 87 | 82 | 83 | 82 | 72 |
| Prince Edward Is. | 46 | 68 | 81 | 76 | 73 | 82 | 83 | 78 |
| New Brunswick | 62 | 85 | 89 | 86 | 80 | 82 | 79 | 72 |
| Quebec | 87 | 89 | 84 | 82 | 80 | 77 | 77 | 67 |
| Ontario | 51 | 79 | 82 | 77 | 69 | 70 | 68 | 65 |
| Manitoba | 39 | 75 | 80 | 77 | 70 | 71 | 68 | 66 |
| Saskatchewan | | 64 | 75 | 71 | 66 | 68 | 65 | 67 |
| Alberta | | 66 | 73 | 71 | 64 | 66 | 69 | 67 |
| British Columbia | 56 | 71 | 75 | 71 | 62 | 63 | 60 | 64 |
| Canada, including Territories | 70 | 80 | 82 | 78 | 73 | 72 | 71 | 66 |

Sources: *Census of Canada 1880–81*, vol. 2, table 14; *1911*, vol. 6, tables 4 and 5; *1921*, vol. 4, table 2; *1931*, vol. 7, table 4; *1941*, vol. 7, table 4; *1951*, vol. 4, table 4; *1961*, vol. 3.1, table 20; *1971*, vol. 3.2, table 2.

Table 23
Distribution of Winnipeg teachers, male and female, 1943–1956

| | 1943 | | | 1946 | | | 1953 | | | 1956 | | |
|---|---|---|---|---|---|---|---|---|---|---|---|---|
| | M | F | % F | M | F | % F | M | F | % F | M | F | % F |
| Teachers | 172 | 711 | 80 | 220 | 756 | 77 | 329 | 893 | 73 | 379 | 1,010 | 73 |
| Principals[1] | 32 | 27 | 46 | 39 | 26 | 40 | 62 | 32 | 34 | 72 | 36 | 33 |

Sources: For 1943, *Winnipeg School Division Annual Report*, 1943, 9. For 1946, ibid., 1946, 10. For 1953, WTA, file 5, "Teachers' Collective Agreement," Memo. 9, 2 November 1953. For 1956, WTA, file 6, "Negotiations re 1957 Agreement," 25 October 1956.

[1] Principals and supervisors, 1943, 1946; "administrative positions," 1953, 1956.

Table 24
Distribution of Winnipeg teachers, male and female, 1943–1948

| | 1943 | | | 1944 | | | 1945 | | | 1946 | | | 1947 | | | 1948 | | |
|---|---|---|---|---|---|---|---|---|---|---|---|---|---|---|---|---|---|---|
| | M | F | %F | M | F | %F | M | F | %F | M | F | %F | M | F | %F | M | F | %F |
| ELEMENTARY | | | | | | | | | | | | | | | | | | |
| Principals and supervisors | 6 | 25 | 80 | 5 | 26 | 84 | 6 | 25 | 80 | 7 | 25 | 78 | 8 | 24 | 75 | 10 | 22 | 69 |
| Teachers | 2 | 437 | 99 | | 430 | 100 | 2 | 451 | 99 | 8 | 478 | 98 | 12 | 482 | 97 | 9 | 512 | 98 |
| JUNIOR HIGH | | | | | | | | | | | | | | | | | | |
| Principals and supervisors | 21 | 2 | 8 | 21 | 2 | 8 | 24 | 2 | 7 | 22 | 1 | 4 | 22 | 1 | 4 | 21 | 1 | 4 |
| Teachers, academic | 55 | 166 | 75 | 61 | 116 | 65 | 64 | 160 | 71 | 81 | 145 | 64 | 81 | 138 | 63 | 93 | 129 | 58 |
| Teachers, ind. arts & home ec. | 27 | 16 | 37 | 24 | 15 | 38 | 28 | 21 | 43 | 28 | 17 | 28 | 29 | 18 | 38 | 26 | 19 | 42 |
| SENIOR HIGH | | | | | | | | | | | | | | | | | | |
| Principals | 5 | | | 5 | | | 5 | | | 10 | | | 10 | | | 10 | | |
| Teachers, academic | 74 | 68 | 48 | 76 | 64 | 46 | 81 | 70 | 46 | 88 | 75 | 46 | 90 | 74 | 45 | 84 | 79 | 48 |
| Teachers, ind. arts & home ec. | 12 | 12 | 50 | 12 | 12 | 50 | 12 | 11 | 48 | 13 | 12 | 48 | 13 | 11 | 46 | 13 | 12 | 48 |
| Others | 2 | 12 | | 3 | 12 | | 2 | 28 | | 2 | 29 | | 6 | 28 | | 7 | 31 | |
| Total | 204 | 738 | 78 | 207 | 727 | 78 | 224 | 768 | 77 | 259 | 782 | 75 | 271 | 776 | 74 | 273 | 805 | 75 |

*Source:* Winnipeg School Division, annual reports, 1943–48.

Table 25
Average wages, professions, men and women, Canada and Manitoba, 1931–1971

| | 1931 Canada | | | 1931 Manitoba | | | 1941 Canada | | | 1941 Manitoba | | | 1951¹ Canada | | |
|---|---|---|---|---|---|---|---|---|---|---|---|---|---|---|---|
| | M $ | F $ | F % | M $ | F $ | F % | M $ | F $ | F % | M $ | F $ | F % | M $ | F $ | F % |
| Univ. profs.² | 2,564 | 1,721 | 67 | 3,211 | na | | 2,198 | 1,855 | 84 | 3,100 | 1,900 | 61 | 3,608 | 2,635 | 73 |
| Lawyers | 3,235 | 1,941 | 60 | 2,825 | na | | 2,833 | 1,510 | 53 | 2,350 | 1,733 | 74 | 3,987 | 2,471 | 62 |
| Physicians | 3,132 | 2,209 | 70 | 2,815 | na | | 2,813 | 1,272 | 45 | 2,563 | 1,576 | 61 | 4,268 | 1,756 | 41 |
| Nurses | na | 913 | | na | 889 | | 865 | 702 | 81 | 763 | 632 | 83 | 2,205 | 1,724 | 78 |
| Teachers | 1,575 | 917 | 58 | 1,483 | 1,042 | 70 | 1,416 | 793 | 56 | 1,173 | 856 | 73 | 2,667 | 1,664 | 62 |
| Labour force | 925 | 559 | 60 | | | | 993 | 490 | 49 | | | | 1,860 | 1,220 | 66 |

| | 1961 Canada | | | 1961 Manitoba | | | 1971 Canada | | | 1971 Manitoba | | |
|---|---|---|---|---|---|---|---|---|---|---|---|---|
| | M $ | F $ | F % | M $ | F $ | F % | M $ | F $ | F % | M $ | F $ | F % |
| Univ. profs.² | 7,113 | 5,039 | 71 | 8,759 | 6,388 | 73 | 15,720 | 11,402 | 72 | 15,258 | 11,791 | 65 |
| Lawyers | 7,359 | 4,362 | 59 | 6,399 | na | | 21,933 | 10,469 | 48 | 19,777 | na | |
| Physicians | 6,883 | 4,316 | 63 | 7,140 | 5,538 | 78 | 28,896 | 14,965 | 52 | 28,253 | 16,582 | 59 |
| Nurses | 3,459 | 2,752 | 79 | 3,727 | 2,816 | 75 | 6,677 | 6,351 | 95 | 6,561 | 5,880 | 90 |
| Teachers | 5,530 | 3,400 | 61 | 5,011 | 3,645 | 73 | 9,514 | 7,325 | 77 | 9,027 | 6,704 | 74 |
| Labour force | 3,170 | 1,993 | 63 | | | | 8,045 | 4,748 | 59 | | | |

*Sources:* Figures calculated from *Census of Canada 1931*, vol. 5, table 28; *1941*, vol. 6, table 6; *1961*, vol. 3.3, table 21; *1971*, vol. 3.6, table 18; and Noah M. Meltz, *Manpower in Canada 1931–1961*, 1969, tables A, 241, and C, 246.

¹ The wages given for 1951 are median rather than average wages.
² Includes school principals, 1931–61.

Table 26
Percentage of married, gainfully occupied women, selected occupations, Manitoba, 1931–1971

|  | 1931 % | 1936 % | 1941 % | 1946 % | 1951 % | 1961 % | 1971 % |
|---|---|---|---|---|---|---|---|
| Physicians | 22 | 14 | 27 | 46 | 44 | 50 | 65 |
| Teachers | 4 | 3 | 6 | 10 | 21 | 46 | 67 |
| Nurses | 4 | 2 | 4 | 11 | 29 | 52 | 64 |
| All professional occupations | 4 | 3 | 4 | 9 | 20 | 41 | |
| All occupations | 4 | 9 | 9 | 18 | 33 | 55 | 62 |

Sources: *Census of Canada 1931*, vol. 7, tables 53, 54; *1941*, vol. 7, table 5; *1951*, vol. 4, table 11; *1961*, vol. 3.1, table 17; *1971*, vol. 3.2, table 8. *Census of the Prairie Provinces 1936*, vol. 2, table 7; *1946*, vol. 2, table 3.

# Survey Respondents

## UNIVERSITY TEACHERS

Margaret Allen
Doris Baker
Janet Baldwin
Ruth Berry
Virginia Berry
Agnes Bishop
Eleanor Boyce
June Bradley
Vivian Bruce
Margaret Campion
Lottie Culham
Wendy Dahlgren
Emily Denny
Joan de Pena
Lois Emory
Elizabeth Feniak
Rosemarie Finlay
Judith Flynn
Margery Forgay
Audrey Fridfinnson
Helen Glass
Ruth Grahame
Shirley Grosser
Miriam Gutkin
Joan Harland
Margaret Hart
Miriam Hutton

Joan Irvine
Diane Jackman
Betty Johns
Elinor Kartzmark
Shirley Leach
Evelyn Loadman
Nora Losey
Imogen McIntyre
Mona McLeod
Enid Marantz
Sheila Maurer
Mrs W.L. Morton
Patricia Powell
Marjorie Robins
Doris Saunders
Elizabeth Shannon
Jennifer Shay
Elizabeth Smith
Marjorie Spence
Anna Storgaard
Joan Townsend
Odarka Trosky
Marion Vaisey-Genser
Mary Wees
Patricia Woolley
Esther Yamada

## PHYSICIANS

Gerda Allison
Margaret Anderson
Marguerite Archibald
Marjorie Bennett
Diane Biehl
Monique Dunlop
Margaret Fast
Donna Friesen
Lee Kohanek
Nancy Gemmell
Ruth Grahame
Georgina Hogg
Donalda Huggins
Audrey Llewelyn-Owens
Margaret Loewen
Dorothea Lowden
Jean McFarlane
Mary McKenty
Ethel McPhail
Enid McRuer

Elizabeth Malyska
Margaret Mann
Margaret Neave
M. Elizabeth Patriarche
Danuta Podkormoska
Eleanor Puttee
Irma Reich
Bernadine Roe
Sheila Rothstein
Gladys Salisbury
Brenda Devlin Schmidt
Cheryl Simmonds
Nancy Sirett
Marie Storrie
Rose Strachan
Ingrid Strautmanis
Agnes Thomson
Rivian Weiner
Betty Wood

## LAWYERS

Linda Anderson
Janet Baldwin
Yvonne Beaupré
Myrna Bowman
Annette Elliott
Ruth Feller
Rytsa Finkelstein
Catherine Forrest
Maxene Francis
Bonnie Helper
Svanhuit Josie
Marion Kelly

Ruth Krindle
Frances Labbus
Jeanne Macdonald
Antoinette Florence Matthews
Kay Pennock
Eva Pugh
Patricia Rithchie
Florence Margulies Rosenfeld
Jacqueline Simkin
Linda Vincent
Winifred Whitley
Elizabeth Yakmission

## NURSES

Karen Armour
Mariette Behling
Gertrude Bell

Elaine Bennett
Mary Brown
Noreen Cass

Margaret Chester
Patricia Chuckmala
Rae Coggan
Agnes Comack
Betty Cornwall
Anne Crossin
Joyce Doherty
F.L. Dougherty
Mary Duncan
Patricia Edward
Glenna Erickson
Diana Gemmel
Marion Grist
Joyce Hay
Shirley Hill
Hope Joyce
Lynella Kluchnik
Dawn McKeag
Esther McKenty
Ena Macklin
J. Macmorran

Margaret McTavish
Ellen Maxwell
Marion Mazinke
Margaret Mitchell
Ethel Moffatt
Diane Oakley
Lilja Olafson
Mabel Pratt
Isabelle Redhead
Cecile Ritchie
Patricia Scott
Joyce Sigurdson
Ann Simonsen
Jessie Stanbridge
Margaret Steele
Larame Steiman
Val Turnbull
Betty Ullberg
Lois Vincent
Katherine Weiermann
Janet Wyatt

## TEACHERS

Joyce Aitken
Virginia Andrew
Rose Baydock
Ruth Breckman
Aline Brown
Ethel Buchanan
Mary Bunting
Myrtle Conway
Janet Everall
Bernice Flood
Elsie Gauer
Shirley Gibb
Jean Green
Isobel Grierson
Jessie Guest
Bernice Hearn
Elva Humphries
Doris Hunt
Irene Huska

Valdine Johnson
Audrey Jones
Irma Kitson
Doris Kristjanson
Laurena Leskiw
Arvilla Lightly
Mary Macbride
Agnes MacDonald
Ruth McLean
Margaret McPherson
Alice Mark
Gloria Meadows
Phyllis Moore
Velma Motheral
Ann Nazeravich
Viola Pelletier
Mary Perfect
Verna Potoroka
Catherine Scott

Sybil Shack

Bea Sharpe

Joan Shume

Elsie Solar

Orma Sozansky

Margaret Wilkie

Jessie Wright

Mary Louise Zorniak

# Notes

ABBREVIATIONS

BPW Business and Professional Women

CFUW Canadian Federation of University Women

CPS College of Physicians and Surgeons of Manitoba

LSM Law Society of Manitoba

MTS Manitoba Teachers Society

NA National Archives of Canada

PAM Provincial Archives of Manitoba

UM University of Manitoba

UMA University of Manitoba Archives

UM, BOG University of Manitoba, Board of Governors

UM, FM, WM University of Manitoba, Faculty of Medicine, Women in Medicine File

WCLHA Western Canadian Legal History Archive

WGH Winnipeg General Hospital

WSB Winnipeg School Board

WSD Winnipeg School Division no. 1

WTA Winnipeg Teachers Association

CHAPTER ONE

1 Wollstonecraft, *Vindication of the Rights of Woman*, 147–9.

2 *Report of the Royal Commission on the Status of Women in Canada*, 154.

3 For an overview, see Prentice et al., *Canadian Women*, 218–63. In particular, see Armstrong and Armstrong, *Double Ghetto*; Lowe, *Women in the Administrative Revolution*; and Parr, *Gender of Breadwinners*. For women's paid work in Manitoba, see Barber, "The Servant Problem in Manitoba 1896–1930"; Kealey, "Women and Labour during World War I";

Mochoruk and Webber, "Women in the Winnipeg Garment Trade 1929–1945"; Lepp, Millar, and Roberts, "Women in the Winnipeg Garment Industry, 1950s–1970s"; and Jackel, "'First Days, Fighting Days.'" For women's unpaid work in Canada and particularly in Manitoba, see Strong-Boag, "Keeping House in God's Country" and "Pulling in Double Harness or Hauling a Double Load"; Luxton, *More than a Labour of Love*; Luxton, Rosenberg, and Arat-Koc, *Through the Kitchen Window*; Cohen, *Women's Work, Markets and Economic Development in 19th Century Ontario*; Cooper, "Farm Women: Some Contemporary Themes"; Kinnear, "Do You Want Your Daughter to Marry a Farmer?"; Sundberg, "Farm Women on the Canadian Prairie Frontier"; and Van de Vorst, "History of Farm Women's Work in Manitoba."

4  See Strong-Boag, *New Day Recalled*, 63–7; and the references attached to the following chapters. For France, a work on secondary schoolteachers "marks the first attempt to write a comprehensive history of French women in a middle-class profession"; Margadant, *Madame le Professeur*, 4.

5  See Friesen, *Canadian Prairies*, and Morton, *Manitoba*.

6  R. Cook, "Francis Marion Beynon and the Crisis of Christian Reformism."

7  Holcombe, *Victorian Ladies at Work*, 3–20.

8  Bebel, *Woman under Socialism*, 343.

9  Mill, *Subjection of Women*, 299.

10  Ibid., 300, 326.

11  George Eliot to Mrs Nassau Senior, 4 October 1869, in Letters of George Eliot, 5:58, quoted in Sutherland, "Movement for the Higher Education of Women," 91.

12  Bebel, *Woman under Socialism*, 158

13  Carl N. Degler, introduction to Gilman, *Women and Economics*, vi.

14  Gilman, *Women and Economics*, 149, 330, 117, 73.

15  Brittain, *Testament of Youth*, 41; First and Scott, *Olive Schreiner*, 276.

16  Schreiner, *Woman and Labour*, 275.

17  Shortt, "Physicians, Science and Status," 51.

18  Cott, *Grounding of Modern Feminism*, 216.

19  For example, Kimball, in *"True Professional Ideal" in America*, considers gender only briefly in connection with schoolteachers.

20  Freidson, "Theory of Professions," 35.

21  Kimball, *"True Professional Ideal" in America*, 3.

22  Parsons, "Professions," 536–47.

23  Perkins, *Rise of Professional Society*, 116–70 and passim.

24  Dingwall, "Introduction," 1–13, and Freidson, "Theory of Professions," 19–37.

25  Larson, *Rise of Professionalism*, x-xviii, 51, and passim.

26  McClelland, *German Experience*, 14.

27 Freidson, "Are Professions Necessary?" 10.

28 McClelland, *German Experience*, 7, 22–3, 233; Margadant, *Madame le Professeur*.

29 Etzioni, *Semi-Professions and their Organization*, v.

30 Witz, *Professions and Patriarchy*, 5, 39–69.

31 Norrie and Owram, *History of the Canadian Economy*, 491–8, 586–92.

32 Larson, *Rise of Professionalism*, 53; Freidson, "Are Professions Necessary?" 21.

33 Marshall, "Women in Male-Dominated Professions," 7–11; Goldin, *Understanding the Gender Gap*, 118.

34 Armstrong and Armstrong, *Double Ghetto*, 18–63.

35 See, for example Kealey, "Women and Labour during World War I," 76–80, 94–5; Sinclair, "Women, Work and Skill," 1–24; Amott and Matthaei, *Race, Gender and Work*, 11–28; Purvis, *Women's Education*, 1–10; and Vicinus, *Independent Women*, 2.

36 Boris, "Beyond Dichotomy," 163, 164; Reverby and Helly, "Converging on History," 1–17; see also Rhode, *Theoretical Perspectives*, 1–12, and Freedman, "Theoretical Perspectives Overview," 257–62.

37 Gollancz, "Introductory," 21.

38 Morgan and Taylorson, "Introduction: Class and Work," 2.

39 Ibid.

40 Fox-Genovese, *Feminism without Illusions*, 248.

41 See chapter 5.

42 Ward and Silverstone, "The Bimodal Career," 10–18; Purvis, *Hard Lessons*, 48–70.

43 See tables 5, 11, 16, 22, and 25 in appendix 1.

44 National Archives of Canada (hereafter cited as NA), Canadian Federation of University Women (hereafter cited as CFUW), Jessie Holmes Munro, "First ten women to graduate from the University of Manitoba," 1937.

45 She was Madame Moreau de Beauvrière. See Fraser, *History of the First Hundred Years of St. John's College*, 39.

46 Marion Rowell, Wesley, 1910–18, and Helen Ross, Manitoba, 1911–14. See Bedford, *University of Winnipeg*, 393–420.

47 Wilson, *History of Home Economics Education in Manitoba*.

48 University of Manitoba Faculty of Medicine, Women in Medicine file, Audrey Kerr to Carlotta Hacker Lemieux, 9 November 1973. First woman student admitted, in 1890, was Harriet Foxton Clarke.

49 Manitoba Dept of Culture, *Dr Amelia Yeomans*, 1–8.

50 Backhouse, *Petticoats and Prejudice*, 293–319; Gibson and Gibson, *Substantial Justice*; and *Manitoba Free Press*, 1 December 1911 and 26 November 1915.

51 Chaput, "The 'Misses Nolin' of Red River," 14–17.

52 Bonin, "The Grey Nuns and the Red River Settlement," 12–14.

53  Pinkham, "Selections," 1:21–3, 2:19–22, 3:11–17; Gregor and Wilson, *History of Education in Manitoba,* 41.

54  Gregor and Wilson, *History of Education in Manitoba,* 49.

55  Winnipeg Teachers Association, Fred D. Baragar, "Winnipeg Teachers' Organisations 1919–1957," n.d. [?1957], 1.

56  McPherson, "Skilled Service and Women's Work," 9.

57  Johns and Fines, *Winnipeg General Hospital and Health Sciences School of Nursing 1887–1987,* 47.

58  *Winnipeg Telegram,* 19 May 1904.

59  Lowe, *Women in the Administrative Revolution,* 1–9, 51.

60  Thomas, "Some Manitoba Women Who Did First Things," 13–25.

61  Sutherland, "Movement for the Higher Education of Women," 92.

62  Armstrong and Armstrong, *Theorizing Women's Work,* 135.

63  Ibid., 139.

64  Jayaratne and Stewart, "Quantitative and Qualitative Methods in the Social Sciences," 85–106.

65  See Geiger, "What's So Feminist about Women's Oral History?" 169–82.

66  Pugh, "My Statistics and Feminism: A True Story," 107.

67  See Anderson, "History of Women and the History of Statistics," 14–36.

68  For an appraisal of satisfactory but less than superlative evidence, see Parr, *Gender of Breadwinners,* 247–51.

69  Witz, *Professions and Patriarchy,* 192–210.

70  See for example Clark, *Working Life of Women in the Seventeenth Century*; Pinchbeck, *Women Workers and the Industrial Revolution*; and Abbott, *Women in Industry.* See also Tilly and Scott, *Women, Work and Family.*

CHAPTER TWO

1  Lerner, *Creation of Feminist Consciousness,* 192–3.

2  *Report of the Royal Commission on the Status of Women in Canada,* 93.

3  Morton, *One University,* 106.

4  University of Manitoba Archives (hereafter cited as UMA), *University of Manitoba Calendar,* 1961, 26–31; Gibson and Gibson, *Substantial Justice,* 152, 247–51, 302–4.

5  UMA, Lillian Allen Diary, 1921, 1:2, 14.

6  Maynard, *Raisins and Almonds,* 137.

7  UMA, *Calendar,* 1961, 28.

8  Fraser, *History of the First Hundred Years of St. John's College,* 39; Bedford, *University of Winnipeg,* 393–420.

9  UMA, Presidents' Papers 1907–74, W.J. Spence, "Historical Notes 1877–1917," 12. Information on University of Manitoba appointments is taken from annual calendars.

10  UMA, Lillian Allen Diary, 1924, 1:2, 25.

11 University of Manitoba, Board of Governors, (hereafter cited as UM, BOG), Minutes, 17 August and 9 November 1933, 9 August 1934.

12 Jones was unusual also in that she was married (to a professor of political economy from 1920 until he was dismissed for unspecified reasons in 1937); UM, BOG, 14 September 1937.

13 UMA, Presidents' Papers, Annual Reports, "Report of Dean of Women Students," 1923–24, 65.

14 UM, BOG, Minutes, 8 September 1933.

15 UM, BOG, Minutes, 5 April 1920, 111–12; 2 May 1921, 187–8; and 20 May 1926, 114–16.

16 Wilson, *History of Home Economics Education in Manitoba*, 54–5.

17 All faculties except medicine. The Faculty of Arts and Science was divided into two separate faculties in 1970. In this study, the faculties are retroactively defined by their post-1970 departmental organization.

18 Their contributions are cited in the references by name or by number, according to their preference. For a list of their names, see appendix 2.

19 The primary source for identification was the university calendars in the University of Manitoba Archives. These data were supplemented by material provided by the Staff Benefits Office. A list of surviving teachers was compiled, and addresses were found for 86 women. In response to an invitation to participate, 53 of them agreed to be surveyed (see appendix 2).

20 Although most (40) were appointed after 1955, the survey included respondents whose employment started in each decade, beginning with Doris Saunders in 1928.

21 Prentice and Theobald, "Historiography of Women Teachers," and Gelman, "Selected Bibliography." In addition to the works mentioned therein, see Backhouse, "Women Faculty at the University of Western Ontario"; Ford, *A Path Not Strewn with Roses*; Parr, *Still Running*; Prentice, "Bluestockings, Feminists or Women Workers?"; Stewart, *"It's Up to You"*; Solomon, *In the Company of Educated Women*; and Vickers and Adam, *But Can You Type?*

22 For example, Gillett and Sibbald, *A Fair Shake*, and Judson, *Breaking the Barrier*.

23 Aisenberg and Harrington, *Women of Academe*, x–xii, 20–40, 74.

24 Glazer and Slater, *Unequal Colleagues*, 211.

25 Prentice, "Bluestockings, Feminists or Women Workers?"; Prentice and Theobald, "Historiography of Women Teachers"; and the chapters in Prentice and Theobald, *Women Who Taught*. For other examples of scholarship that carefully examines the experience of women working at universities, see Backhouse, "Women Faculty at the University of Western Ontario"; Fingard, "College, Career and Community," and Solomon, *In the Company of Educated Women*.

26 Mary Wees.

27 For example, respondent 42, Lois Emory, respondent 30, and respondent 7, among many.

28 Respondent 32.

29 Respondent 5.

30 Respondent 41.

31 For example, respondents 13, 29, 19.

32 Respondent 3, Janet Baldwin, and Joan de Pena.

33 For example, Janet Baldwin and respondent 29.

34 Mona McLeod.

35 Marjorie Spence.

36 For example, respondent 35.

37 Esther Yamada; UMA, Lillian Allen Diary, 1926, 1:3, 2.

38 Respondent 2.

39 Wendy Dahlgren and Joan Townsend.

40 For example, respondent 5.

41 Wendy Dahlgren.

42 Respondent 17.

43 Joan Townsend, respondent 8, and respondent 5.

44 Respondents 1 and 21.

45 Moore, *Joe Doupe,* 57–62.

46 University of Manitoba Faculty of Law, Western Canadian Legal History Archive, "Legal Education in Manitoba," 4.

47 Doris Saunders and respondent 1.

48 Respondent 2 and Virginia Berry.

49 Wendy Dahlgren.

50 Respondent 10.

51 Respondent 5.

52 Esther Yamada.

53 Respondent 8.

54 Respondent 3.

55 Respondent 1.

56 Respondent 28.

57 Respondent 9.

58 Mary Wees.

59 Doris Saunders.

60 UMA, Presidents' Papers, Annual Reports, "Report of the Dean of Junior Women," 1943–44, 140.

61 Janet Baldwin.

62 Joan Townsend.

63 Esther Yamada.

64 UMA, Lillian Allen Diary, 1937, 1:5, 19.

65 Respondents 24 and 17.

66 Respondent 35.
67 Joan Harland.
68 Respondent 3.
69 UMA, Lillian Allen Diary, 1945, 1:6, 41.
70 Respondent 17.
71 Margery Forgay.
72 Respondent 15.
73 Ibid.
74 Respondent 24.
75 Respondent 9.
76 Wendy Dahlgren.
77 Respondent 21.
78 Respondent 8.
79 UMA, Lillian Allen Papers, "My Lament," 1:1.
80 University of Manitoba Faculty Association, Collective Agreement, 1975.
81 Respondent 17.
82 Esther Yamada.
83 Respondent 3.
84 Respondent 5.
85 Ruth Grahame.
86 Respondent 10.
87 Virginia Berry and respondent 24.
88 Janet Baldwin.
89 Esther Yamada.
90 Doris Saunders.
91 Shirley Leach.
92 Respondent 13.
93 Janet Baldwin.
94 Respondent 3.
95 Respondent 23.
96 Patricia Powell, Joan Townsend, respondent 25, and Shirley Leach.
97 Respondent 3.
98 Virginia Berry.
99 Respondent 21.
100 Margery Forgay.
101 Respondents 5, 2, and 25.
102 Respondent 20.
103 Respondent 5.
104 Respondent 25.
105 Mary Wees.
106 Respondent 1.
107 Respondent 23.
108 Doris Saunders, Elizabeth Feniak, and Audrey Fridfinnson.

109 Respondent 36.
110 UMA, School of Home Economics, "50th Anniversary 1910–1960," 28.
111 Mrs W.L. Morton.
112 Joan Harland, Audrey Fridfinnson, and Doris Saunders.
113 Marion Vaisey-Genser.
114 Respondent 25.
115 Respondent 21.
116 Respondent 5.
117 Joan Harland.
118 Margery Forgay.
119 Respondent 35.
120 Respondent 32.
121 Respondent 23.
122 Respondent 21.
123 Respondent 15.
124 Respondent 21.
125 Respondent 21.
126 Joan Townsend.
127 Emily Nett, Retirement speech, 16 April 1991.
128 Respondent 5.
129 Respondent 10.
130 Perkins, "Academic Profession in the United Kingdom," 13.

## CHAPTER THREE

1 Mitchinson, *Nature of Their Bodies*, 20, 14–30.
2 Provincial Archives of Manitoba, (hereafter cited as PAM), Ida Armstrong file, Dan E. Cameron to Ida Armstrong, 16 October 1942; Ida Armstrong, "Be Prepared," radio talk, 28 October 1942.
3 Mitchinson, *Nature of Their Bodies*, 14–30.
4 Howell, "Back to the Bedside," 185–94, and "Reform and the Monopolistic Impulse," 3–22; Mitchinson, "Canadian Medical History," 124–35; Rosenberg, "American Medicine in 1879," 21–34; Torrance, "Socio-Historical Overview," 6–32.
5 Mitchinson, *Nature of Their Bodies*, 14–30; Mitchinson and McGinnis, *Essays in the History of Canadian Medicine*, 13.
6 PAM, College of Physicians and Surgeons (hereafter cited as CPS), registration receipts; CPS, index cards.
7 University of Manitoba. Faculty of Medicine, Women in Medicine file (hereafter cited as UM, FM, WM), Natalia Pohorecki, "List of Female Graduates"; University of Manitoba Alumni Association, "Nominal List of Graduates."
8 Ida Armstrong, Elinor Black, and Evelyn Loadman.

9 Opinions expressed by the thirty-nine respondents came from women who qualified as early as 1935. Three respondents, who were prewar graduates, were not registered to work in Manitoba and worked elsewhere (Margaret Anderson and respondents 6 and 20). Five of the thirty-nine qualified elsewhere and migrated to the province. (Monique Dunlop, Sheila Rothstein, and respondents 17, 19, and 29.) Twenty-six were married (this figure includes subsequent widows and divorcées). Respondents indicated whether they wished to be acknowledged by name or anonymously. The latter are here acknowledged by a number. The former are acknowledged by their professional name, where known, or by a hyphenated maiden-married name when known to be married. The list of respondents can be found in appendix 2. Their qualifying dates are as follows: pre-1935 (3 respondents), 1936–40(5), 1941–45(5), 1946–50(7), 1951–55(5), 1956–60(4), 1961–65(4), and 1966–70(6).

10 Manitoba Department of Culture, *Dr Amelia Yeomans*, 1–8.

11 UM, FM, WM, Airdrie Bell Cameron, "Doctor Charlotte Whitehead Ross," 6–7; Barbara and Michael Angel, *Charlotte Whitehead Ross*, 33.

12 *Manitoba Medical Bulletin*, 76 (December 1927): 9.

13 Angel, *Charlotte Whitehead Ross*, 42, 44. See also Edge, *Iron Rose*.

14 Buck, *Doctor Rode Sidesaddle*, 28–31.

15 Mitchell, "Founding of Manitoba Medical College," 2.

16 UM, FM, WM, Audrey Kerr to Carlotta Hacker Lemieux, 9 November 1973.

17 de la Cour and Sheinin, "Ontario Medical College for Women 1883–1906," 206–14.

18 Hacker, *Indomitable Lady Doctors*, 140, 142, 146.

19 *Saturday Night*, 13 March 1920; PAM, Council of Women 1933.

20 Manitoba Department of Culture, *Dr Amelia Yeomans*, 5.

21 UM, FM, WM. Ellen Douglass, "Dr Charlotte Ross," 3 January 1940.

22 Mitchinson, *Nature of Their Bodies*, 10, 166.

23 Kinnear, "Do You Want Your Daughter to Marry a Farmer?" 150, 144. The wording in the survey was "ten miles or more."

24 Hryniuk, "Health Care in Rural East Galicia in the Late Nineteenth Century," 1–9, 317–22.

25 Enns, *Gretna*, 86, 26.

26 Loewen, "The Children, the Cows," 365.

27 PAM, CPS, Council Minutes, 6 April 1887.

28 Ibid., 6 September 1893, 7 October 1903.

29 Loewen, "The Children, the Cows," 24.

30 PAM, CPS, Council Minutes, 12 and 26 October 1932.

31 Registered in 1941 or before were: Gerda Allison, Agnes Archibald, Ida Armstrong, Velma Atkinson-Martin, Kathleen Borthwick-Leslie, Elinor Black, Marjorie Bennett, Sophie Bookhalter, Marie Cameron, Helen

Cameron, Ivy Falardeau, Elinor Fletcher-Kernohan, Esther Gorsey-Holenberg, Donalda Huggins, Sophie Granofsky, Leonora Hawirko, Molly Hendin-Markovits, Bella Kowalson, Eunice Leitch, Helen Marlatt-Wildman, Elizabeth Matheson, Frances McGill, Mary McKenty, Mary McKenzie-Bristow, Isobel McTavish, Sara Meltzer, Margaret Neave, Gladys Nitikman-Ellison, Dorothy Osovsky-Hollenberg, Margaret Patriarche, Leonora Peters, Dolores Pruedhomme-Bottomley, Dorothy Pound-Saxton, Sarah Pearl, Edith Ross, Emma Richter-Adamson, Elizabeth Steele, Mary Sokolofski, Harriet Smith, Ellen Taylor, Agnes Thomson, Aldis Thorlakson-Wengel, Alice Woodhead-Murray, Kathleen Wark-Walters, Ada Wilson-Wallace, Elaine Webb-Peacock; PAM, CPS, registration receipts.

Registered after 1941 were Virginia Johnston, Gerda Fremming-Allison, Florence McKim, Dorothea Wardrop-Lowden, Harriet Perry-Lederman, Alice Evelyn Loadman.

32  Ida Armstrong, Sophie Bookhalter, Ivy Falardeau, Esther Gorsey-Hollenberg, Sophie Granofsky, Molly Hendin-Markovits, Eunice Leitch, Elizabeth Matheson, Mary McKenty, M. Elizabeth Patriarche, Dolores Pruedhomme-Bottomley, Edith Ross, Harriet Smith, Elizabeth Steele, Aldis Thorlakson-Wengel, Ada Wilson-Wallace; PAM, CPS, registration receipts.

33  Elinor Black, Kathleen Borthwick-Leslie, Elinor Fletcher-Kernohan, Donalda Huggins, Bella Kowalson, Helen Marlatt-Wildman, Gladys Nitikman-Ellison, Dorothy Osovsky-Hollenberg, Sarah Pearl, Agnes Thomson, Elaine Webb-Peacock, Alice Woodhead-Murray; PAM, CPS, registration receipts.

34  Agnes Archibald, Velma Atkinson-Martin, Marjorie Bennett, Alice Evelyn Loadman, Frances McGill, Margaret Neave, Harriet Perry-Lederman, Ella Peters, Dorothy Pound-Saxton, Ellen Taylor, Dorothy Wardrop-Lowden, Kathleen Wark-Walters; PAM, CPS, registration receipts.

35  Mary Crawford, Ellen Douglass, Margaret Owens, Ethel Robertson, Isobel Ruthoen-Menzies, Leyda Sestrap; PAM, CPS, registration receipts.

36  Rose Butler, Charlotte Whitehead-Ross, Evelyn Witthof, Amelia Yeomans, Lillian Yeomans; PAM, CPS, registration receipts.

37  Jessie Belilias, Beverly Burns, Margretta Earls, Fanny Whittaker; PAM, CPS, registration receipts.

38  Margaret Anderson, Sigga Christianson-Houston, Doreen Corke, Diane Croll, Hilda Dawson-Behrens, Sara Dubo, Agnes Dodds, Elizabeth Findlay, Jessie Findlay, Harriet Foxton-Clarke, Helen Friedman-Brickman, Mary Garner, Alcina Hall-Kent, Dorothy Jefferson, Lois Kennedy, Hazel Krause, Mary Little-Browne, Helen Lousely-Cairncross, Lillian Malcove-Ormos, Myrtle McBean-Hoskins, Vera McDorman, Marjorie McIntyre, Lavinia McPhee, Claire Onhauser-Seale, Grace Pachal-Strachan,

Margaret Rioch-Anthonisen, Anne Skaletar-Leveton, Lois Stephens-Poole, Iva Stevens-Merritt, Verna Stevens-Young, Gladys Story-Cunningham, Dorothy Sugden-Hunter, Angelina Wiegerinck, Margaret Wilson-Goodwin; PAM, CPS, registration receipts.

39 Doreen Corke-Sheffield, Hilda Dawson-Behrens, Harriet Foxton-Clarke, Alcina Hall-Kent, Lois Kennedy, Lillian Malcove-Ormos, Myrtle McBean-Hoskins, Margaret Rioch-Anthonisen, Anne Skaletar-Leveton, Iva Stevens-Merritt, Verna Stevens-Young, Dorothy Sugden-Hunter; PAM, CPS, registration receipts.

40 Lois Kennedy.

41 Margaret Anderson, Sigga Christianson-Houston, Diane Croll, Agnes Dodds, Sara Dubo, Elizabeth Findlay-Anderson, Helen Friedman-Brickman, Mary Garner, Hazel Krause, Mary Little-Browne, Helen Lousely-Cairncross, Marjorie McIntyre, Claire Onhauser-Steele, Grace Pachal-Strachan, Lois Stephens-Poole, Angelina Wiegerinck, Margaret Wilson-Goodwin; PAM, CPS, registration receipts.

42 Margaret Anderson, Sigga Christianson-Houston, Elizabeth Findlay-Anderson, Helen Friedman-Brickman, Mary Garner, Mary Little-Browne, Helen Lousely-Cairncross, Claire Onhauser-Seale, Grace Pachal-Strachan, Lois Stephens-Poole, Margaret Wilson-Goodwin; PAM, CPS, registration receipts.

43 UM, FM, WM, Marion Ferguson, "List of Female Graduates from Medicine," 1942.

44 UM, FM, WM, Doreen Corke-Sheffield, Harriet Foxton-Clarke, Alcina Hall-Kent, Iva Stevens-Merritt, Verna Stevens-Young.

45 Strong-Boag, "Canada's Women Doctors," 120. See also Brouwer, *New Women for God*, and Hacker, *Indomitable Lady Doctors*, 93–128.

46 *Winnipeg Tribune*, 21 January 1937.

47 *British Columbia Medical Journal* 14, no. 12 (1972): 323.

48 See Smith, "Medical Missionaries," 199–204. See also Hacker, *Indomitable Lady Doctors*, ch. 6, "Healing for Christ".

49 UM, FM, WM, "Dr Jessica Findlay is Honored by King," *Winnipeg Free Press*, n.d. [late 1945].

50 Strong-Boag, "Canada's Women Doctors," 119, 120; Brouwer, *New Women for God*, 80–1, 194–6; Gagan, *Sensitive Independence*, 208–11.

51 *Winnipeg Free Press*, 12 July 1957.

52 Respondent 6.

53 Patriarche, "Vive la Différence!" 132, 866.

54 Margaret Anderson, Marjorie Bennett, Kathleen Borthwick-Leslie, Dorothea Lowden, Edith Ross, and respondent 15.

55 Dorothy Osovsky-Hollenberg and respondent 6.

56 Sara Meltzer.

57 Ella Peters.

58  Dorothy Osovsky-Hollenberg.

59  Harriet Perry-Lederman.

60  Sigga Christianson Houston, Esther Gorsey-Hollenberg, and Ada Wilson-Wallace.

61  Black, "Thinking Back," 144.

62  *Winnipeg Tribune,* 23 October 1971.

63  *Winnipeg Tribune,* 10 March 1943.

64  Ethel McPhail.

65  Pierson, "*They're Still Women After All,*" 120, 117.

66  NA, Federation of Medical Women of Canada, Minutes, Fifteenth Annual Meeting, Jasper, 1942.

67  Axelrod, *Making a Middle Class,* 75–6.

68  Barsky, "Numerus Clausus," 76.

69  *Winnipeg Free Press,* 16 March 1944.

70  Barsky, "Numerus Clausus," 78.

71  *Winnipeg Free Press,* 16 March 1944.

72  Ruth Grahame.

73  Respondent 24.

74  PAM, CPS, Council Minutes, 12 May 1944.

75  PAM, CPS, Brief to the University of Manitoba Board of Governors, 16 May 1944.

76  Barsky, "Numerus Clausus," 80–1.

77  *Winnipeg Free Press,* 20 March 1945.

78  Ruth Grahame.

79  Diane Biehl.

80  Margaret Fast.

81  Respondent 36.

82  Enid McRuer.

83  Margaret Nitychoruk considered this in her 1993 BSC (Med.) thesis on "Women in Medicine in Manitoba: Was Gender a Handicap?"

84  M. Elizabeth Patriarche.

85  Enid McRuer.

86  PAM, CPS, registration receipts.

87  Respondent 34.

88  Lorna Barnhouse, Elizabeth Lautsch, Ruth McDougall, Jessie McGeachy, Isobel Moon, Mary Parkin, Florence Scott, Marguerite Shea; PAM, CPS, registration receipts.

89  Katheen Elliott and Nona Wright. The remaining two were Marie Feng and Velda Weber; PAM, CPS, registration receipts.

90  Patricia Hutchison.

91  Janet Arnott, Margaret Beaumont, Elaine Binns, Isobel Buchanan, Pamela Cooper, Sheila Cross, Thelma Dafforn, Elizabeth Etherington, Brenda Fife, Beryl Gee, Vera Gillman, Dorothy Half, Marion Henderson, Audrey

Llewelyn-Owens, Jocelyn Mandelstam, Mary O'Dea, Jill Rosser, Mary Russell, Sheena Stuart, Helen Tennent, Pamela Willis; PAM, CPS, registration receipts.

92 Bernadette McGivern, Sheila Murphy, Ruth Reilly; PAM, CPS, registration receipts.

93 Elca Graf, Berta Krasine, Margaret Loewen, Katarina Marjanovich, Julia Wasilewska; PAM, CPS, registration receipts.

94 Margaret Abell, Clarice Baker, Allison Bell, Elaine Binns, Elizabeth Burge, Roma Cessford, Anna Donner, Jennifer Gegg, Joan Gilmour, Jean Harkness, Marie Kellock, June Lewis, Jean Marsh, Moira McLellan, Sheila Pattel, Annis Price, Mona Smith, Linda Underhill; PAM, CPS, registration receipts.

95 Edith Barnes, Bernadettte Cowan, Judith Doyle, Monique Dunlop, Alicia Kuffel, Anne Llewellyn, Jane Wong, Jean Wong, Virginia Wong; PAM, CPS, registration receipts.

96 Carmelita Cendana, Sue Chan, Mirla David, Maria Lee, Lydia Lucman, Josephine Lo, Lily Ly, Susanna Ong, Gwendolyn Rothman, Karen Shea, Erlinda Sy, Estela Violago, Roberta Wu; PAM, CPS, registration receipts.

97 Yung Liang, Jong Roh, Kim Tan; PAM, CPS, registration receipts.

98 Dorothy Bender, Margaret Crumpacker, Patricia Fitzmaurice, Theresa Howard, Mary Lou, Patricia Tsang, Jean Wong; PAM, CPS, registration receipts.

99 Marta Fiala, Stanislava Jurenka, Eleanora Kovacs, Anna Szetle; PAM, CPS, registration receipts.

100 Sue Chan.

101 Laila Sekla.

102 Respondent 29.

103 Respondent 17.

104 Monique Dunlop.

105 Ingrid Strautmanis.

106 Respondent 24.

107 Respondent 41.

108 Donna Friesen.

109 Respondent 16.

110 Margaret Anderson, Jean McFarlane, and respondents 22 and 34.

111 Georgina Hogg.

112 Enid McRuer.

113 Ruth Grahame.

114 Donna Friesen.

115 Jackson and Negrych, "Medicine: The Female Point of View," 15–16.

116 Enid McRuer.

117 Georgina Hogg.

118 Respondent 17.

119 Elinor Black, "Not So Long Ago," 55.

120 Respondent 24.

121 Respondent 18.

122 *Winnipeg Free Press*, 24 February 1956.

123 Thomson, "Women in Medicine," 31.

124 Ruth Grahame, Monique Dunlop, Donna Friesen, Nancy Gemmell, Respondent 18. See Naylor, *Private Practice, Public Payment.*

125 Marjorie Bennett, Diane Biehl, Georgina Hogg, Brenda Schmidt, Ingrid Strautmanis, and respondents 15, 16, 19, 20, 22, 32, and 36.

126 Respondents 4 and 24.

127 Agnes Thomson.

128 Eleanor Puttee.

129 Respondent 18.

130 Ethel McPhail and Nancy Sirett.

131 Marjorie Bennett, Eleanor Puttee, and respondents 15 and 36.

132 Diane Biehl, Georgina Hogg, Jean McFarlane, Ingrid Strautmanis, and respondent 19.

133 Respondents 16, 17, 29, and 42.

134 Marie Storrie. One other doctor did not answer this question.

135 Respondent 32.

136 Margaret Fast and Rose Strachan.

137 Sheila Rothstein.

138 Elizabeth Malyska and Ethel McPhail.

139 Donna Friesen.

140 Respondent 6.

141 Monique Dunlop.

142 Respondent 17.

143 Nancy Gemmell.

144 Respondent 27.

145 Respondent 17.

146 Margaret Anderson.

147 Marjorie Bennett.

148 Margaret Fast.

149 Elizabeth Malyska.

150 Patriarche, "Vive la Différence!" 641–3.

151 Respondent 31.

152 Jean McFarlane.

153 Enid McRuer.

154 Margaret Fast.

155 Respondent 36.

156 Respondent 27.

157 Donna Friesen.

158 Ingrid Strautmanis.

159 Respondent 31.

160 Georgina Hogg and Eleanor Puttee.

161 Donna Friesen and Diane Biehl.

162 American Academy of Pediatrics, *Report of the Task Force on Opportunities for Women in Pediatrics*, October 1982.

163 Loadman, "Women in the Pediatric Residency Program."

164 Marie Storrie.

165 Morantz-Sanchez, *Sympathy and Science*, 5.

166 Morantz-Sanchez, *Sympathy and Science*, 49; Cott, *Grounding of Modern Feminism*, 219.

167 Elston, "Medicine: Half Our Future Doctors?" 99, 106.

168 Ibid., 107. See also Ward, *Careers of Professional Women*, 31–3.

169 For a comparison of professional earned incomes, see table 25 in appendix 1.

### CHAPTER FOUR

1 Melrose Sissons, from a family of eight children, was admitted to the Bar in 1915. She practised for two years but retired after marriage to a lawyer, Earl Stuart Everall. She raised three children and was an active member of the United Church, the Women's Institute, and other community organizations in McCreary, Manitoba; Lester, "Sissons Called to the Bar," 5.

2 *Manitoba Free Press*, 20 May 1911.

3 Backhouse, *Petticoats and Prejudice*, 293–319.

4 Riddell, "Women as Practitioners of Law," 200–3.

5 *Manitoba Free Press*, 20 May 1911; Mossman,"'Invisible' Constraints on Lawyering," 567–79.

6 *Manitoba Free Press*, 1 December 1911.

7 Winnifred Wilton was born at Morden, Manitoba, daughter of Henry Wilton, who was a member of Wolseley's Red River Expedition in 1870. A year after admission to the Bar, she went to work in London, England, in the Estates division of the Canadian army. In 1919 she married Capt. A.S. Stearns Wilson, an American engineer at the United States embassy in Paris. In 1922 she was admitted to the New York Bar. See *Chitty's Law Journal* (1952): 73, and Law Society of Manitoba (hereafter cited as LSM), Winnifred Wilton file.

8 *Manitoba Free Press*, 26 November 1915.

9 Katharine Buckley (1945), Darlene Eliza Butler (1917), Elizabeth Carson (1915), Gertrude Donovan (1915), Grace Isabel Eakins (1937), Marie Francis Graves (1938), Mary Macdonald (1928), Isabella Jane McKinnon (1916), Edith Joyce McKinnon (1950), Mary Elvena McLean (1943),

Elizabeth Petryk (1956), Josephine Winkler (1923), Zora Zink (1959); University of Manitoba, Western Canadian Legal History Archive (hereafter cited as UM, WCLHA), LSM members' files.

10 Sara Abramanson-Harris (1920), Clara Allison Cameron (1920), Constance Cruickshank (1933), Annette Elliott (1970), Muriel Frith (1936), Anna Greer (1920), Mrs G. Harris (1954), Iva Jackson (1921), Sarah Metrick (1941), Genevieve Lipsett Skinner (1917), Patricia Smerchanski (1966), Lily Anna Wilson (1917), Elizabeth Yakmission (1959); UM, WCLHA, LSM members' files.

11 Sara Abrahamson-Harris; UM, WCLHA, LSM members' files.

12 Genevieve Skinner; ibid.

13 Lilly Wilson; ibid.

14 Elizabeth Yakmission; ibid.

15 Muriel Frith; ibid.

16 *Report of the Royal Commission on the Status of Women*, 387.

17 LSM, rolls, 1915, 1916, 1948.

18 LSM, rolls, annual reports 1921–71. See also UM, WCLHA, Gibson file, generated in preparation of Gibson and Gibson, *Substantial Justice*; ibid., Cameron Harvey file, generated in preparation of Harvey, "Women in Law in Canada," 10–37; and ibid., LSM members' files and scrapbooks.

19 Respondents indicated whether their comments should be acknowledged by name or anonymously. The latter are cited here by a number. For the list of respondents, see appendix 2.

20 Melrose Sissons.

21 Winnifred Wilton.

22 Alma McArthur.

23 Mary Wright.

24 Within two years: Yvonne Beaupré, Myrna Bowman, Jean Coleman, Caorline Cramer, Maxene Francis, Elizabeth Hagel, Maria Halcewycz, Bonnie Helper, Heather Henderson-Donnelly, Helen Hickling, Janet Hone, Isabel Maclean Hunt, Dorothy Hutchison, Svanhuit Josie, Marion Kelly, Ruth Krindle, Marjorie Kimmel, Frances Labbus, Katherine Lamont, Jorun Lindal, Edythe Macdonald, Jeanne Macdonald, Mildred McMurray, Betty Morrison, Kathleen Pennock, Eva Pugh, Patricia Ritchie, Florence Rosenfeld, Rosemary Simonite, Linda Vincent, Margaret Watterson, Mary Wawryko, and Winifred Yuill-Whitley. Twelve years or more: Linda Anderson, Helen Arpin, Helen Breen, Catherine Forrest, Irene Miller, and Lillian Schwarz. With an average gap of six years: Janet Baldwin, Ruth Feller, Rytsa Finkelstein, Elsie Kenzie, Florence Matthews, Nellie Sanders, Jacqueline Simkin. See LSM, rolls.

25 Unknown are Jean Coleman, Dorothy Hutchison, Elsie Kenzie, Katherine Lamont, Irene Miller, Betty Morrison, Lillian Schwarz, and Margaret Watterson.

26 Caroline Cramer, Elizabeth Hagel, Maria Halcewycz, Helen Hickling, Marjorie Kimmel, Frances Labbus, Jorun Lindal, Alma Graham McArthur, Rosemary Simonite, Melrose Sissons, Mary Wawryko, Mary Wright, Winifred Yuill-Whitley, and respondents 6, 14, 15, and 21.

27 Helen Arpin, Edythe Macdonald, and respondent 8.

28 Kathleen Pennock and respondent 17.

29 Winnifred Wilton, Isabel Maclean Hunt, Mildred McMurray, Nellie Sanders, Florence Rosenfeld, Florence Matthews, Heather Henderson, and respondents 9 and 10.

30 Florence Rosenfeld and respondent 9.

31 Linda Anderson and respondents 11, 13, and 20.

32 Janet Baldwin.

33 Helen Breen, Janet Hone, Jacqueline Simkin, and respondents 5, 12, and 24.

34 Heather Henderson, Edythe Macdonald, Florence Rosenfeld, Winnifred Wilton, and respondent 9.

35 Kathleen Pennock and Jacqueline Simkin.

36 Nellie McNichol Sanders was born 1906 in Ontario and graduated LLB from the University of Manitoba in 1932. She also became a registered social worker. She was in private practice and did legal work for the provincial Department of Welfare. After her husband's death in 1949, she was sole support for her two children and served as counsel for the Children's Aid Society of Winnipeg. In 1957 she was the first woman to be appointed to the bench and was a Juvenile and Family Court judge, a magistrate, and a provincial judge until her retirement in 1977. She was appointed QC in 1972. An Anglican, she served on diocesan and other community committees. She died in 1990. See *Winnipeg Tribune*, 4 February 1972, and *Winnipeg Free Press*, 8 August 1990.

Mary Wawryko was born 1912 in Saskatchewan, daughter of Ukrainian immigrant farmers. She supported herself in high school and university, and started law practice from an office in her home. She retired from practice after her marriage and raised three children, who were still small when she was widowed. Returning to work, she was appointed QC in 1965 and judge of the Winnipeg Juvenile and Family Court in 1968. In 1975 she was appointed judge responsible for the provincial judges' court of Winnipeg. Involved on the boards of many community organizations, she believed "community service is the rent we pay for the privilege of living upon this earth." She was first woman of Ukrainian descent to practise law in Canada. She died 1977. See *Winnipeg Free Press*, 18 and 21 April 1977.

37 Gibson and Gibson, *Substantial Justice*, 77, 128–9, 152.

38 University of Manitoba, Office of Institutional Analysis, "Numbers of Graduates by Faculty, 1891–1942."

39 Gibson and Gibson, *Substantial Justice*, 247–8.

40 Ibid., 249, 251, 295–302.
41 Clifford H.C. Edwards was an Englishman "with a cosmopolitan background" who had spent several years in Africa before coming to lecture in law at Manitoba in 1958. In 1964 he was appointed dean, and was responsible for introducing a three-year full-time program; Gibson and Gibson, *Substantial Justice*, 302–3.
42 Ibid., 302, 304.
43 Respondent 24.
44 Florence Rosenfeld.
45 Florence Matthews.
46 Elizabeth Yakmission.
47 Respondent 6.
48 Respondent 9.
49 Respondent 15.
50 Respondent 21.
51 Respondent 24.
52 Respondent 5.
53 Respondent 6.
54 G.P.R. Tallin was a Rhodes Scholar who had served in two world wars. He served as dean 1945–64. One of the most frequently repeated stories about him was that he would lie down at the front of a class and challenge students to stand on his stomach; Gibson and Gibson, *Substantial Justice*, 288.
55 Ibid.
56 Respondent 12.
57 Respondent 9.
58 Respondent 15.
59 Respondent 20.
60 Annette Elliott.
61 Jacqueline Simkin.
62 Frances Labbus.
63 Respondent 6.
64 Respondent 21.
65 Elizabeth Yakmission.
66 Annette Elliott.
67 Constance Cruickshank. See UM, WCLHA, Cameron Harvey file.
68 Respondent 13.
69 Lowe, *Administrative Revolution*, 73.
70 Respondent 20.
71 Respondent 12.
72 Respondent 24.
73 Caroline Cramer, Elizabeth Hagel, Helen Hickling, Jorun Lindal, Alma McArthur, Mary Wawryko, Mary Wright, Winifred Yuill-Whitley, and respondents 6 and 14.

74 Isabel Maclean Hunt and respondents 9 and 10.
75 Maria Halcewycz, Heather Henderson, Frances Labbus, Florence Matthews, Mildred McMurray, Florence Rosenfeld, Nellie Sanders, Melrose Sissons, Winnifred Wilton, and respondents 8, 15, and 21.
76 Respondent 10.
77 Jacqueline Simkin.
78 Respondent 24.
79 Frances Labbus.
80 Respondent 6.
81 Respondent 21.
82 Respondent 14.
83 Respondent 24.
84 Respondent 14.
85 Respondent 17.
86 Respondent 14.
87 Isabel Maclean Hunt, Nellie Sanders, and Mary Wawryko.
88 LSM, rolls.
89 Dorothy Hutchison, Katherine Lamont, Irene Miller, and Lillian Schwarz. Betty Morrison was single.
90 Helen Arpin, Helen Breen, Elizabeth Hagel, Heather Henderson, Helen Hickling, Janet Hone, Marjorie Kimmel, Rosemary Simonite, and Mary Wright.
91 As information was provided in most cases on a confidential basis, the data are presented here in summary form.
92 Elizabeth Yakmission.
93 Linda Anderson.
94 Respondent 12.
95 Respondent 24.
96 Respondent 6.
97 Respondent 15.
98 Respondent 8.
99 Respondent 9.
100 Florence Matthews.
101 Respondent 21.
102 Elizabeth Yakmission.
103 Linda Anderson.
104 Respondent 5.
105 Florence Matthews.
106 Respondent 20.
107 Respondent 6.
108 Respondent 17.
109 Respondent 14.
110 Respondent 13.
111 Frances Labbus.

112  Florence Matthews.

113  Respondent 14.

114  *Winnipeg Sun,* 13 November 1983.

115  Dorothy Hunt Campbell to author, 15 February 1990.

116  Florence Rosenfeld to author, 16 October 1990.

117  Ruth Feller to author, 13 November 1990.

118  *Winnipeg Free Press,* 4 November 1953.

119  Urquhart and Buckley, *Historical Statistics of Canada,* series A2–14.

120  Podmore and Spencer, "Women Lawyers in England," 342.

121  For material relating to women in Canada who trained in law before 1970, or near 1970, see Dranoff, "Women as Lawyers in Toronto," 177–90; Smith, Stephenson, and Quijano, "The Legal Profession and Women" 137–75; and Bankier, "Women and the Law School," 171–7.

122  Abel-Smith and Stevens, *Lawyers and the Courts,* 193, quoted in Smith, Stephenson, and Quijano, "The Legal Profession and Women," 143. See also Podmore and Spencer, "Women Lawyers in England," 339–42.

123  Smith, Stephenson, and Quijano, "The Legal Profession and Women," 143.

124  Janet Baldwin, Annette Elliott, Florence Matthews, Florence Rosenfeld, Jacqueline Simkin, Elizabeth Yakmission, and respondents 5, 6, 9, 11, 12, 14, 15, 17, 20, 21, and 24.

125  Linda Anderson, Frances Labbus, Kathleen Pennock, Winifred Yuill, and respondents 8, 10, and 13.

126  "17. Are you generally content with the opportunities that your legal training has presented to you? 18. Do you have any criticism or comment concerning the treatment of women lawyers generally in the legal profession? If so, kindly specify." See Harvey, "Women in Law in Canada," 32.

127  Ibid., 13.

128  For Canadian material, see Abella, "Women in the Legal Profession"; Bélanger, "Les femmes dans la profession juridique au Québec 1911–1985"; Dranoff, "Women as Lawyers in Toronto"; Rochette, "Les femmes dans la profession juridique au Québec"; Smith, Stephenson, and Quijano, "The Legal Profession and Women"; Harvey, "Women in Law in Canada"; Adam and Baer, "Social Mobility of Women and Men in the Ontario Legal Profession"; Adam and Lahey, "Professional Opportunities"; Mossman, "Portia's Progress"; Seidenberg, "The Bifurcated Woman." For American material, see White, "Women in the Law"; Epstein, *Women in Law*; Barnes, "Women and Entrance to the Legal Profession"; Chambers, "Accommodation and Satisfaction"; B. Cook, "Path to the Bench"; Drachman, "My Partner in Law and Life"; Hoff, *Law, Gender and Injustice*; Lazarou, "Fettered Portias"; Menkel-

Meadow, "Exploring a Research Agenda of the Feminization of the Legal Profession"; Rhode, *Justice and Gender*. See also the review of literature identified in Gibson, "What Price Discrimination for Women in the Legal Profession? A Survey of Studies, 1967–1982," paper prepared for M.J. Mossman Women and the Law Seminar 1982, on file in the Faculty of Law, University of Manitoba; and Sheehy and Boyd, *Canadian Feminist Perspectives on Law: An Annotated Bibliography of Interdisciplinary Writings*.

129 Mossman, "'Invisible' Constraints on Lawyering and Leadership," 585–8.

130 Menkel-Meadow, "The Comparative Sociology of Women Lawyers," 24; Epstein, "Women and Elites," 3–15; Kanter, *Men and Women of the Corporation*.

131 Mossman, "Invisible Constraints," 592.

132 Kanter, "Reflections on Women and the Legal Profession," 10, 14, 16.

133 Barnett, "Women Practicing Law," 218.

134 Rhode, "Perspectives on Professional Women," 1186, 1187. See also Williams, "Deconstructing Gender," 822, 828, 829–32; Abella, "Women in the Legal Profession"; Chambers, "Accommodation and Satisfaction," 257–8; Fossum, "Reflection on Portia," 1389–93; and Podmore and Spencer, "Women Lawyers in England," 344–5.

CHAPTER FIVE

1 University teacher respondent 53.

2 Baly, *Florence Nightingale and the Nursing Legacy*, 143–9 and passim.

3 Kergin, "Nursing as a Profession," 46–63; McIntyre, "Towards a Redefinition of Status"; Cohen and Dagenais, "Le métier d'infirmière," 155–77; Reverby, *Ordered to Care*.

4 McPherson, "Skilled Service and Women's Work," 56.

5 Coburn, "I See and Am Silent," 460.

6 Keddy et al., "Nurses' Work," 38. See also Melosh, "More than 'The Physician's Hand.'"

7 James, "Writing and Rewriting Nursing History," 568–84.

8 Daigle, "Devenir infirmière," 80.

9 Katz, "Nurses," 54–81.

10 McClelland, *The German Experience of Professionalisation*; B.R. Clark, *Academic Profession*.

11 Mill, *Subjection of Women*, 321.

12 Gibbon and Matthewson, *Three Centuries of Canadian Nursing*, 137–40; Carr, "Light on the Prairie," 26–7.

13 Shortt, "The Canadian Hospital in the 19th Century," 3–14.

14 Johns and Fines, *Winnipeg General, School of Nursing*, 1, 5.

15 Gibbon and Matthewson, *Three Centuries of Canadian Nursing*, 189.

16 Johns and Fines, *Winnipeg General, School of Nursing*, 12.

17 Ibid., 12–15.

18 Ibid., 21–31.

19 Ibid., 10.

20 Birtles, "Mary Ellen Birtles," 5–6.

21 Roland, "Early Years of Antiseptic Surgery in Canada"; McPherson, "Skilled Service," 250.

22 Johns and Fines, *Winnipeg General, School of Nursing*, 24–6.

23 *Winnipeg Telegram*, 14 and 18 June 1902.

24 *Manitoba Free Press*, 24 June 1902.

25 *Winnipeg Telegram*, 26 June 1902; *Town Topics*, 28 June 1902.

26 Johns and Fines, *Winnipeg General, School of Nursing*, 34.

27 Ibid. 43.

28 Carr, "Light on the Prairie," 26–9.

29 *Report on Hospitals*, 17–19.

30 Johns and Fines, *Winnipeg General, School of Nursing*, 44.

31 Street, *Watchfires on the Mountains*, 41.

32 Ibid., 45.

33 Fines, "History of the Manitoba Association of Registered Nurses," 15.

34 Ibid., 16.

35 Street, *Watchfires on the Mountains*, 59.

36 Fines, "History of the Manitoba Association of Registered Nurses," 18.

37 Johns and Fines, *Winnipeg General, School of Nursing*, 47.

38 McPherson, "Skilled Service," 355; Street, *Watchfires on the Mountains*, 62.

39 *Report on Hospitals*, 356.

40 Artibise, *Winnipeg*, 223–4, 351–2.

41 McPherson, "Skilled Service," 119.

42 Weir, *Nursing Education*, 88.

43 Ibid., 89.

44 McPherson, "Skilled Service," 122–5. See also Melosh, "More than 'The Physician's Hand,'" 483–6.

45 Respondent 8. The Alumnae Association of the Winnipeg General Hospital School of Nursing kept extensive records of all the women who graduated as registered nurses from the school. For most years before 1970, there were twice-yearly intakes of new students, who then normally trained for three years. Each intake had a class representative. I asked each class representative for all years up to 1967 to participate in the study or to suggest a delegate. Forty-five participated directly. In this way, nurses whose beginning training year ranged from 1926 to 1967 agreed to participate in a survey by mail questionnaire. Three from Roman Catholic hospitals also participated. Respondents chose whether they wished to be acknowledged by name or anonymously. The latter are acknowledged by number. The list of respondents is given in appendix 2.

46  Lilja Olafson.
47  Respondent 5.
48  McPherson, "Skilled Service," 125.
49  Respondent 3; McPherson, "Skilled Service," 153.
50  Weir, *Nursing Education*, 95, 103, 124.
51  Ibid., 124.
52  Hart "Voices from the Past," 16–18.
53  Provincial Archives of Manitoba, Red Cross, Annual Report, 1925, 21, 22, 23; Hadashville Women's Institute, *Packsack of Seven Decades*, 57–8.
54  Private collection, Ruth Evans Papers, Hilda St Germaine to Ivy Broadfoot, 21 May 1953.
55  Ibid., Ruth Evans, "Red Cross Outposts in Manitoba," paper presented to Manitoba Nurse History Interest Group, June 1988, 2, 3.
56  Ibid., Ruth Evans, "A Chapter of History," News and Views, Canadian Red Cross Society, Manitoba Division 18, 4, December 1987.
57  Ibid., "Phyllis Martin, Red Cross Nurse on the Bay Line" [c. 1959], 1–36.
58  Ibid., Evans, "Red Cross Outposts," 3–4.
59  Katherine Weiermann.
60  Weir, *Nursing Education*, 101.
61  Ibid., 107.
62  Ibid., 115–17.
63  McIntyre, "Towards a Redefinition of Status," 19.
64  Ibid., 34–5, 65, 71–4.
65  Ibid., 45, 46, 61–2.
66  Ibid., 25, 96.
67  Ibid., 50.
68  Ibid., 49, 64.
69  Respondent 14.
70  Respondent 13.
71  Ena Macklin.
72  Taylor, *Health Insurance and Canadian Public Policy*, 161–238.
73  Bellaby and Oribabor, "History of the Present," 171–2.
74  Weir, *Nursing Education*, 391–2.
75  Growe, *Who Cares?* 157.
76  Table 26, appendix 1.
77  Respondent 21.
78  Marion Mazinke.
79  Respondent 35.
80  Esther McKenty.
81  Respondent 40.
82  Respondent 41.
83  Betty Ullberg.
84  Respondent 41.

85 Joyce Sigurdson.

86 Respondent 47.

87 Anne Crossin.

88 Respondent 48.

89 Respondent 40.

90 Respondent 43.

91 Respondent 21.

92 Margaret Chester.

93 Respondent 20.

94 Respondent 16.

95 Respondent 40.

96 Marion Mazinke.

97 Respondent 13.

98 Respondent 19.

99 Anne Crossin.

100 Respondent 41.

101 Betty Ullberg.

102 Respondent 48.

103 Respondent 47.

104 Esther McKenty.

105 Hart, "Voices from the Past," 59.

106 Respondent 11.

107 Respondent 25.

108 Respondent 28.

109 J. MacMorran.

110 Betty Ullberg.

111 Lilja Olafson.

112 Betty Cornwall.

113 Respondent 8.

114 Respondent 13.

115 J. Macmorran.

116 Respondent 38.

117 Joyce Sigurdson.

118 Respondent 21.

119 Esther McKenty.

120 Ibid.

121 Respondent 29.

122 Respondent 25.

123 Respondent 41.

124 Respondent 13.

125 Joyce Hay.

126 Responent 16.

127 Respondent 38.

128 Respondent 11.
129 For example, Margaret Chester and respondents 5 and 42.
130 Respondent 13.
131 Respondent 41.
132 Respondent 38.
133 Marion Mazinke, Katherine Weiermann, and respondents 3, 19, 29, 41, and 47.
134 Respondent 45.
135 Anne Crossin.
136 Reverby, "The Search for the Hospital Yardstick," 219.
137 Respondent 13.

### CHAPTER SIX

1 Apple, *Teachers and Texts,* 35.
2 Chafe, *An Apple for the Teacher,* 94–6.
3 See, for example, Oram, "Sex Antagonism" and Kessler-Harris, *A Woman's Wage.* In Ontario, exceptionally, women comprised half the number of secondary teachers by 1930; Gelman, "'Feminization' of the High Schools?" 139.
4 Winnipeg School Division no. 1, Committee Minutes Book (hereafter cited as WSD, CMB), Minutes, vol. 12, 8 May 1930, A-488–9.
5 A similar separatist organization had been founded in Toronto in 1885; Smaller, "A Room of One's Own", 111.
6 Prentice, "The Feminization of Teaching"; Danylewycz and Prentice, "Teachers, Gender and Bureaucratizing School Systems in Nineteenth-Century Montreal and Toronto"; Prentice and Theobald, "Historiography of Women Teachers," 10–12. For an American comparison, see Richardson and Hatcher, "Feminization of Public School Teaching 1870–1920," and Rury, "Who Became Teachers?"
7 Marshall, "Women in Male-Dominated Professions," 8.
8 For the distribution of women teachers at the secondary level for an earlier period in Toronto and Ontario, when the female percentage was lower than in wartime Winnipeg, see Gelman, "'Feminization' of the High Schools?"
9 For descriptions of early teacher training in Manitoba, see Gregor and Wilson, *Education in Manitoba,* and Peters, "Historical Survey of Some Major Aspects of Pre-Service Teacher Education in Manitoba."
10 Hébert, "Proud of Yesterday," 14.
11 Gregor and Wilson, *Education in Manitoba,* 2:54; *Report of the Royal Commission on Education,* 101–4.
12 *Manitoba Teacher,* 1959; Gregor and Wilson, *Education in Manitoba* 2:97–8.
13 "Manitoba Teachers Better Qualified," *Manitoba Teacher,* February 1975.

14 Nuffield, *With the West in Her Eyes*, 94, 102.

15 McClung, *Clearing in the West*, 247.

16 Teachers belonging to retired teachers' associations were surveyed with a questionnaire by mail and in interview. Seventy were requested to participate; of these, six requests were returned by Canada Post, nine declined to be involved, nine made no reply, and forty-six made responses. Respondents indicated whether they wished to be acknowledged by name or anonymously. The latter are here acknowledged by a number. For the list of respondents, see appendix 2.

17 Myrtle Conway.

18 Respondent 7.

19 Ruth Breckman.

20 Agnes MacDonald.

21 *Report of the Royal Commission on Education*, 78, 81–2.

22 Gregor and Wilson, *Education in Manitoba*, 2:81.

23 W.C. Lorimer, interview, 5 May 1992.

24 Respondent 7.

25 Ruth McLean.

26 Shirley Gibb.

27 Phyllis Moore. For a similar situation in Toronto, see Reynolds, "Too Limiting a Liberation," 157.

28 Agnes MacDonald.

29 Asper, "Factors Affecting the Entry of Women Teachers into Administrative Positions of the Manitoba Public School System," 148. For Ontario, see Reynolds, "Naming the Experience."

30 Shack, *Women in Canadian Education*, 51, and *Two-Thirds Minority*, 37–42.

31 Shack, "One Woman's View of Women Teaching in Manitoba."

32 Vidal, "History of the Manitoba Teachers Society," 3, 7.

33 Ibid., 4.

34 Chafe, *Chalk, Sweat and Cheers*, 3, 4.

35 *Manitoba Teacher*, April 1927, 5.

36 Ibid., April 1929, 2.

37 Provincial Archives of Manitoba, Manitoba Teachers Society, Tenure Report, Executive Minutes, 7 July 1926.

38 *Winnipeg Tribune*, 10 March 1943. See Kinnear, "Mostly for the Male Members," 1–20.

39 Kessler-Harris, *A Woman's Wage*, 67–80; Arbus, "Grateful to Be Working," 169–90.

40 *Manitoba Teacher*, May 1940, 12–14.

41 Ibid., December 1931, 16.

42 Chafe, *Chalk, Sweat and Cheers*, 76–9.

43 Winnipeg School Division no. 1 (hereafter cited as WSD), Scrapbook, "Education in Winnipeg School Division No. 1 as seen in the Daily Newspapers 1930–1980," vol. 1, 15.

44 Ibid.
45 Winnipeg Teachers Association (hereafter cited as WTA), "The Winnipeg Board of Trade," 3 February 1933.
46 Ibid; WTA, file 1, Women's Local, "Analysis of the Proposed Schedule," December 1932.
47 WTA, file 2, Vera Patrick, 1935.
48 Ibid., Mr A.F. Brown to Miss I. Robson, January 1937.
49 Ibid., "Statement of the Views of the Men Teachers," January 1937.
50 Ibid., "Statement of the Women Teachers," January 1937.
51 *Winnipeg Tribune,* 10 March 1943.
52 Winnipeg School Board (hereafter cited as WSB), Minutes, vol. 20, 18 January 1944, A-1667.
53 WTA, file 2, "Brief submitted by the Winnipeg Men's Local," December 1943.
54 Ibid., "Statement of the Views of the Women's Local," n.d. [late 1943].
55 WSB, CMB, Minutes, vol. 20, 29 February 1944, A-1680, and 16 March 1944, A-1765.
56 WTA, Contract, 13 June 1946.
57 Vidal, "Manitoba Teachers' Society," 103.
58 Chafe, *Chalk Sweat and Cheers,* 11.
59 *Census of Canada 1931,* vol. 7, table 54.
60 WSD, CMB, Minutes, vol. 12, 8 May 1930, A-488–9, and 5 June 1930, A-498–9.
61 Ibid., vol. 12, 4 September 1930, A-514, and 28 October 1930, A-526.
62 Ibid., vol. 12, 14 July 1930, A-506.
63 Ibid., vol. 17, 4 July 1940, A-1349.
64 Ibid., vol. 19, 18 March 1943, F-959.
65 Ibid., vol. 19, 9 May 1943, F-967, and vol. 20, 16 November 1944, A-1900–1.
66 *Winnipeg Free Press,* 11 March 1943.
67 *Winnipeg Tribune,* 10 March 1943.
68 WSD, CMB, vol. 20, 20 January 1946, A-1889, and 14 February 1946, A-1900–1.
69 Reynolds, "Too Limiting a Liberation," 160.
70 Table 26, appendix 1.
71 *Winnipeg Tribune,* 27 March 1943.
72 WTA, file 4, Women's Local to Winnipeg District Association, 31 March 1946.
73 Clifford, "Man/Woman/Teacher," 314.
74 WTA, file 5, Women's Local to membership, 4 February 1952; Women's Local to Provincial Council, Manitoba Teachers' Society, April 1953.
75 Vidal, "Manitoba Teachers' Society," 115.
76 WTA, file 5, Women's Local to Winnipeg District Association, 24 February 1953; Men's Local to Winnipeg District Association, 27 February 1953.

77 WTA, file 5, School Board to MTS, 24 September 1953; Winnipeg District Association, 19 October 1953.

78 WTA, file 6, Winnipeg District Association memorandum by the Conference Committee, October 1957.

79 Chafe, *Chalk Sweat and Cheers*, 3–4; Gregor and Wilson, *Education in Manitoba*, 2:88.

80 W.C. Lorimer, interview, 5 May 1992.

81 Prentice et al., *Canadian Women*, 331–3. For earlier equal-pay campaigns of teachers in Ontario, see Smaller, "A Room of One's Own," 105–21.

82 Kojder, "The Saskatoon Women Teachers' Association"; Prentice, "Themes in the Early History of the Women Teachers' Association of Toronto"; Walker, *Story of the Women Teachers' Association of Toronto*; Gaskell, "Problems and Professionalism of Women Elementary Public School Teachers in Ontario 1944–1954"; Reynolds, "Ontario Schoolteachers 1911–1971."

83 Prentice, "Multiple Realities," 135.

84 Verna Potoroka.

85 Respondent 37.

86 Agnes MacDonald.

87 Respondent 30.

88 Phyllis Moore.

89 Shack, "One Woman's View."

90 Myrtle Conway.

91 Ethel Buchanan.

92 Respondent 7.

93 Respondent 35.

94 Laurena Leskiw.

95 Respondent 36.

96 Respondent 45.

97 Respondent 42.

98 Virginia Andrew.

99 Apple, *Teachers and Texts*, 66.

100 Catherine Scott.

101 S. Carter, "Incentives and Rewards to Teaching," 55.

102 Verna Potoroka.

103 Ruth McLean.

104 Doris Hunt.

105 Respondent 28.

106 Shirley Gibb.

107 Respondent 7.

108 Respondent 14.

109 Respondent 41.

110 Joyce Aitken.

111 Ruth Breckman.

112  Respondent 45.
113  Respondent 16.
114  Myrtle Conway.
115  Respondent 13.
116  Respondent 17.
117  Agnes MacDonald
118  Phyllis Moore.
119  Respondent 30.
120  Asper, "Entry of Women Teachers," 6.
121  Ibid., 149.
122  Respondent 16.
123  Respondent 12.
124  Respondent 27.
125  Respondent 38.
126  Phyllis Moore.
127  Alice Mark.
128  Laurena Leskiw.
129  Mary Macbride.
130  Shirley Gibb.
131  Ethel Buchanan.
132  Respondent 21.
133  Interview with Irene Grant, 19 November 1990.
134  Respondents 19 and 35.
135  Jessie Guest and respondent 36.
136  Ruth Breckman.
137  Laurena Leskiw.
138  Doris Hunt, "Presentation of Agnes MacDonald," Retired Women
     Teachers' Association, 1 May 1986.
139  Agnes MacDonald.
140  Respondent 37.
141  Joyce Aitken.
142  Respondent 13.
143  Respondent 12.
144  Respopndent 7.
145  Doris Hunt.
146  Mary Macbride.
147  Respondent 28.
148  Phyllis Moore.
149  Irma Kitson.
150  Respondent 35.
151  Respondent 27.
152  Laurena Leskiw.
153  Sybil Shack.

154 Respondent 42.

155 WTA, Conference Committee Minutes, October–November 1953.

156 For example, *Manitoba Teacher*, May–June 1953, November–December 1957, and January–February 1958.

157 *Manitoba Teacher*, September–October 1952.

158 Woods, *Education in Manitoba*, 1:24.

159 Gregor and Wilson, *Education in Manitoba*, 2:6.

160 Danylewycz and Prentice, "Revising the History of Teachers," 135.

161 For example, *Manitoba Teacher*, May–June 1961 and 1962, September–October 1962.

162 Apple, *Teachers and Texts*, 48, 54–78.

163 Agnes MacDonald.

164 Asper, "Entry of Women Teachers," 5–6.

165 Oram, "Sex Antagonism," 288.

CHAPTER SEVEN

1 University Teacher respondents 2 and 13.

2 University of Manitoba Archives, "Report of the Presidential Committee to Recommend Terms of Reference for an Appointment related to Concerns of Women on Campus," 24 June 1974, 1.

3 Julie Vanderwoort to author, 15 January 1990. See also Vandervoort, *Tell the Driver*.

4 Ruth Grahame.

5 University Teacher respondent 34.

6 Dr Mindel Sheps, *Winnipeg Free Press*, 16 January 1973.

7 *Winnipeg Free Press*, 24 November 1959.

8 Isabel Maclean Hunt (1953) and Mary Wawryko (1965). Nellie Sanders was appointed QC in 1971.

9 Nellie Sanders (1957) and Mary Wawryko (1968).

10 Asper, "Factors Affecting the Entry of Women Teachers into Administrative Positions of the Manitoba Public School System," 5.

11 NA, Confederation of University Women (hereafter CFUW), Minutes, 26 August 1919, 4–6.

12 PAM, University Women's Club, Minutes, 28 October 1920.

13 NA, CFUW, Minutes of Executive, 1 April 1932; also speech to McGill Alumnae Society (1934), Montreal *Gazette*, 20 May 1934.

14 Kinnear, *Margaret McWilliams*, 144–7.

15 *Report of the Subcommittee on the Post-War Problems of Women*, 9–10.

16 PAM, Business and Professional Women's Club, National Conventions, Employment Conditions, 300.20.1.

17 Ibid., Canadian Federation of Business and Professional Women's Clubs, seventeenth biennial convention, Winnipeg, reports, 1958–60, 67.

See also Strong-Boag, *New Day Recalled*, 42, 50; and Prentice et al., *Canadian Women: A History*, 221, 367–378.

18 Stricker, "Cookbooks and Law Books," 1–19.

19 University Teacher respondent 21.

20 See chapter 4.

21 Law respondent 12.

22 Ward and Silverstone, "The Bimodal Career," 13.

23 WSD, CMB, vol. 20, 24 January 1946, A-1889, and 14 February 1946, A-1900–1.

24 Gollancz, "Introductory," 24.

25 Shanley, *Feminism, Marriage and the Law in Victorian England*, 5–10, Armstrong and Armstrong, *Double Ghetto*, 32–41.

26 "Women in Management," *Economist*, 28 March 1992, 17–18; "Sexism in Engineering Decried," *Globe and Mail*, 8 April 1992.

27 Apter, *Professional Progress*, 253.

28 Oddson, *Employment of Women in Manitoba*, app. B, table 18b.

29 Milkman, "New Research in Women's Labor History," 381.

30 Glazer and Slater, *Unequal Colleagues*, 14.

31 Gordon, *Gender and Higher Education in the Progressive Era*, 4; Finkelstein, "Conveying Messages to Women," 680–99; Margadant, *Madame le Professeur*, 3–13.

32 Nancy Gemmell.

33 Marie Storrie.

34 Doris Saunders.

35 Law respondent 6.

36 Bégin, "Royal Commission on the Status of Women in Canada," 21; Lerner, *Creation of Feminist Consciousness*, 281–2.

37 Margadant, *Madame le Professeur*, 9.

38 Brittain, "What Talkers Men Are!" 116.

39 Nemiroff, "That Which Divides Us; That Which Unites Us," 272, 280–5.

40 Ursel, *Private Lives, Public Policy*, 11.

# Bibliography

PRIMARY SOURCES

*Manuscript Collections*

LAW SOCIETY OF MANITOBA
Rolls
Annual Reports, 1921–71

NATIONAL ARCHIVES OF CANADA
Canadian Federation of University Women
Federation of Medical Women of Canada

PRIVATE COLLECTION
Ruth Evans

PROVINCIAL ARCHIVES OF MANITOBA
Ida Armstrong
Business and Professional Women's Club
College of Physicians and Surgeons of Manitoba
Local Council of Women
Manitoba Teachers Society
Red Cross
University Women's Club

UNIVERSITY OF MANITOBA ARCHIVES
Annual Reports
Board of Governors
Calendars, 1910–71

Lillian Allen Papers
Presidents' Papers 1907–74
School of Home Economics Fiftieth Anniversary, 1910–1960

UNIVERSITY OF MANITOBA FACULTY ASSOCIATION
Collective Agreement, 1975

UNIVERSITY OF MANITOBA FACULTY OF LAW
Western Canadian Legal History Archive

UNIVERSITY OF MANITOBA FACULTY OF MEDICINE
Women in Medicine file

WINNIPEG GENERAL HOSPITAL SCHOOL OF NURSING ALUMNAE
ASSOCIATION
*Alumnae Journal*
Membership Lists

WINNIPEG SCHOOL DIVISION
Annual Reports
Committee Minutes
Minutes
Scrapbooks

WINNIPEG TEACHERS ASSOCIATION
Minutes

### Census Publications

Census of Canada, 1881–1971
Census of Manitoba, 1885–86
Census of the Prairie Provinces 1936, 1946

### Newspapers and Journals

*Manitoba Medical Bulletin*
*Manitoba/Winnipeg Free Press*
*Manitoba Teacher*
*Saturday Night*
*University of Manitoba Medical Journal/Manitoba Medicine*
*Winnipeg Telegram*
*Winnipeg Tribune*
*Winnipeg Sun*

SECONDARY SOURCES

Abbott, Edith. *Women in Industry: A Study in American Economic History.* 1909. Reprint, New York: Arno, 1969.

Abella, Rosalie Silberman. "Women in the Legal Profession." Paper prepared for Continuing Legal Education, Law Society of Upper Canada, 1986.

Abel-Smith, Brian, and Robert Stevens. *Lawyers and the Courts: A Sociological Study of the English Legal System 1750–1965.* London: Heinemann, 1967.

Adam, Barry D., and Douglas E. Baer. "The Social Mobility of Women and Men in the Ontario Legal Profession." *Canadian Review of Sociology and Anthropology* 21 (1984): 21–46.

Adam, Barry D., and Kathleen A. Lahey. "Professional Opportunities: A Survey of the Ontario Legal Profession." *Canadian Bar Review* 59 (1981): 674–86.

Aisenberg, Nadya, and Mona Harrington. *Women of Academe: Outsiders in the Sacred Grove.* Amherst: University of Massachusetts Press, 1988.

American Academy of Pediatrics. *Report of the Taskforce on Opportunities for Women in Pediatrics.* Elk Grove, Ill.: American Academy of Pediatrics, 1982.

Amott, Teresa L., and Julie A. Matthaei. *Race, Gender and Work: A Multicultural Economic History of Women in the United States.* Boston: South End Press, 1991.

Anderson, Margo. "The History of Women and the History of Statistics." *Journal of Women's History* 4 (Spring 1992): 14–36.

Angel, Barbara, and Michael Angel. *Charlotte Whitehead Ross.* Winnipeg: Peguis Publishers, 1982.

Apple, Michael. *Teachers and Texts: A Political Economy of Class and Gender Relations in Education.* New York: Routledge and Kegan Paul, 1986.

Apter, Terri. *Professional Progress: Why Women Still Don't Have Wives.* London: Macmillan, 1993.

Arbus, Judith. "Grateful to Be Working: Women Teachers during the Great Depression." In *Feminism and Education,* ed. Forman et al., 169–90. Toronto: Centre for Women's Studies in Education, OISE, 1990.

Armstrong, Pat, and Hugh Armstrong. *The Double Ghetto: Canadian Women and Their Segregated Work.* Rev. ed. Toronto: McClelland and Stewart, 1984.

– *Theorizing Women's Work.* Toronto: Garamond Press, 1990.

Artibise, Alan F.J. *Winnipeg: A Social History of Urban Growth 1874–1914.* Montreal and Kingston: McGill-Queen's University Press, 1975.

Asper, Linda. "Factors Affecting the Entry of Women Teachers into Administrative Positions of the Manitoba Public School System." MED thesis, University of Manitoba, 1974.

Axelrod, Paul. *Making a Middle Class: Student Life in English Canada during the Thirties.* Montreal and Kingston: McGill-Queen's University Press, 1990.

Axelrod, Paul, and John G. Reid, eds. *Youth, University, and Canadian Society: Essays in the Social History of Higher Education.* Montreal and Kingston: McGill-Queen's University Press, 1989.

Backhouse, Constance. *Petticoats and Prejudice: Women and Law in Nineteenth-Century Canada.* Toronto: Women's Press, for the Osgoode Society, 1991.
– "Women Faculty at the University of Western Ontario: Reflections on the Employment Equity Award." *Canadian Journal of Women and the Law* 4 (1990): 36–65.
Backhouse, Constance, and David H. Flaherty, eds. *Challenging Times: The Women's Movement in Canada and the United States.* Montreal and Kingston: McGill-Queen's University Press, 1992.
Baines, Carol, Patricia Evans, and Sheila Neysmith, eds. *Women's Caring: Feminist Perspectives on Social Welfare.* Toronto: McClelland and Stewart, 1991.
Baly, Monica. *Florence Nightingale and the Nursing Legacy.* London: Croom Helm, 1986.
Bankier, Jennifer K. "Women and the Law School: Problems and Potential." *Chitty's Law Journal* 22 (1974): 171–7.
Barber, Marilyn. "The Servant Problem in Manitoba 1896–1930." In *First Days, Fighting Days*, ed. Mary Kinnear, 100–19. Regina: Canadian Plains Research Centre, 1987.
Barnes, Janette. "Women and Entrance to the Legal Profession." *Journal of Legal Education* 23 (1971): 276–308.
Barnett, Martha. "Women Practicing Law: Changes in Attitudes, Changes in Platitudes." *Florida Law Review* 42 (1990): 209–28.
Baron, Ava, ed. *Work Engendered: Toward a New History of American Labor.* Ithaca: Cornell University Press, 1991.
Barsky, Percy. "How 'Numerus Clausus' Was Ended in the Manitoba Medical School." *Canadian Jewish Historical Society Journal* 1 (1977): 75–81.
Bebel, August. *Woman under Socialism*, trans. D. de Leon. New York: Source Book Press, 1904.
Bedford, A.G. *The University of Winnipeg: A History of the Founding Colleges.* Toronto: University of Toronto Press, 1976.
Bégin, Monique. "The Royal Commission on the Status of Women in Canada: Twenty Years Later." In *Challenging Times*, ed. Constance Backhouse and David H. Flaherty, 21–38. Montreal and Kingston: McGill-Queen's University Press, 1992.
Bélanger, Sylvie. "Les femmes dans la profession juridique au Québec, 1911–1985." Paper presented to the Canadian Historical Association, Kingston, 1991.
Bellaby, Paul, and Patrick Oribabor. "'The History of the Present': Contradiction and Struggle in Nursing." In *Rewriting Nursing History*, ed. Celia Davies, 147–74. London: Croom Helm, 1980.
Bellan, Ruben. *Winnipeg First Century: An Economic History.* Winnipeg: Queenston, 1978.
*Beneath the Veneer: Report of the Task Force on Barriers to Women in the Public Service.* Ottawa: Canadian Government Publishing Centre, 1990

Berry, Paul, and Alan Bishop. *Testament of a Generation: The Journalism of Vera Brittain and Winifred Holtby.* London: Virago Press, 1985.

Birtles, William. "Mary Ellen Birtles: A Tribute to Pioneer Nurses of Manitoba." *Nurscene,* May 1989, 5–6.

Black, Elinor. "Not So Long Ago." *University of Manitoba Medical Journal* 45, no. 2 (1975): 54–6.

– "Thinking Back." *Canadian Medical Association Journal* 105, no. 24 (1971): 143–4.

Blitz, Rudolph. "Women in the Professions, 1870–1970." *Monthly Labor Review,* May 1974, 34–40.

Bonin, Marie. "The Grey Nuns and the Red River Settlement." *Manitoba History* 11 (Spring 1986): 12–14.

Boris, Eileen. "Beyond Dichotomy: Recent Books in North American Women's Labor History." *Journal of Women's History* 4, no. 3 (1993): 162–79.

Brittain, Vera. *Testament of Youth.* 1933. Reprint, London: Virago Press, 1978.

– "What Talkers Men Are!" In *Testament of a Generation: The Journalism of Vera Brittain and Winifred Holtby,* ed. Paul Berry and Alan Bishop, 114–16. London: Virago Press, 1985.

Brouwer, Ruth Compton. *New Women for God: Canadian Presbyterian Women and India Missions, 1876–1914.* Toronto: University of Toronto Press, 1990.

Brumberg, Joan Jacobs, and Nancy Tomes. "Women in the Professions: A Research Agenda for American Historians." *Reviews in American History,* June 1982, 275–96.

Bruno-Jofré, Rosa del C., ed. *Issues in the History of Education in Manitoba: From the Construction of the Common School to the Politics of Voices.* Lewiston/ Queenston/Lampeter: Edwin Mellen Press, 1993.

Buck, Ruth Matheson. *The Doctor Rode Sidesaddle.* Toronto: McClelland and Stewart, 1974.

Canada. Department of Labour. *Occupational Trends in Canada 1891–1931.* Bulletin M4. Ottawa: Queen's Printer, 1931

– *Occupational Trends in Canada 1931–61.* Report 11. Ottawa: Queen's Printer 1963.

Carr, Ian. "Light on the Prairie: The Early Days of St. Boniface General Hospital." *Manitoba Medicine* 61, no. 1 (1991): 26–7.

Carter, Michael J., and Susan Carter. "Women's Recent Progress in the Professions, or, Women Get a Ticket to Ride after the Gravy Train Has Left the Station." *Feminist Studies* 7, no. 3 (1981): 477–504.

Carter, Susan B. "Academic Women Revisited: An Empirical Study of Changing Patterns in Women's Employment as College and University Faculty, 1890–1963." *Journal of Social History* 14, no. 4 (1981): 675–99.

– "Incentives and Rewards to Teaching." In *American Teachers,* ed. Donald Warren, 49–62. New York: Macmillan, 1989.

Chafe, J.W. *An Apple for the Teacher: A Centennial History of the Winnipeg School Division.* Winnipeg: Winnipeg School Division 1, 1967.

– *Chalk, Sweat and Cheers: A History of the Manitoba Teachers Society 1919–1969.* Winnipeg: Manitoba Teachers Society, 1969.

Chambers, David L. "Accommodation and Satisfaction: Women and Men Lawyers and the Balance of Work and Family." *Law and Social Inquiry* 14 (1989): 251–87.

Chaput, Donald. "The 'Misses Nolin' of Red River." *Beaver*, Winter 1975, 14–17.

Clark, Alice. *The Working Life of Women in the Seventeenth Century.* London: Routledge, 1919.

Clark, Burton R., ed. *The Academic Profession: National Disciplinary and Institutional Settings.* Berkeley: University of California Press, 1987.

Clifford, Geraldine Joncich. "Eve: Redeemed by Education and Teaching School." *History of Education Quarterly* 21, no. 4 (1981): 479–91.

– "Man/Woman/Teacher: Gender, Family and Career in American Educational History." In *American Teachers*, ed. Donald Warren, 293–343. New York: Macmillan, 1989.

– "Women's Liberation and Women's Professions: Reconsidering the Past, Present and Future." In *Women and Higher Education*, ed. John M. Faragher and Florence Howe, 165–82. New York: Norton, 1988.

Coburn, Jodi. "'I See and Am Silent': A Short History of Nursing in Ontario, 1850–1930." In *Health and Canadian Society: Sociological Perspectives*, 2d edition, ed. David Coburn, 441–62. Toronto: Fitzhenry & Whiteside, 1987.

Cockburn, Cynthia. *In the Way of Women: Men's Resistance to Sex Equality in Organisations.* London: Mamillan, 1991.

Cohen, Marjorie Griffin. *Women's Work, Markets and Economic Development in 19th Century Ontario.* Toronto: University of Toronto Press, 1988.

Cohen, Yolande, and Michele Dagenais. "Le métier d'infirmière: Savoirs féminins et reconnaissance professionelle." *Revue d'histoire de l'Amérique* 41, no. 2 (1987): 155–77.

Cook, Beverley Blair. "The Path to the Bench: Ambitions and Attitudes of Women in the Law." *Trial* 19 (August 1983): 49–56.

Cook, Ramsay. "Francis Marion Beynon and the Crisis of Christian Reformism." In *The West and the Nation*, ed. Carl Berger and Ramsay Cook, 187–208. Toronto: McClelland and Stewart, 1976.

Cooper, Barbara J. "Farm Women: Some Contemporary Themes." *Labour/Le Travail* 24 (1989): 165–80.

Cott, Nancy. *The Grounding of Modern Feminism.* New Haven: Yale University Press, 1987.

*Countdown: Canadian Nursing Statistics.* Ottawa: Canadian Nurses' Association, 1967, 1971.

Daigle, Johanne. "Devenir infirmière: Les modalités d'expression d'une culture soignante au XXe siècle." *Recherches féministes* 4, no. 1 (1991): 67–86.

Danylewycz, Marta, and Alison Prentice. "Revising the History Teachers: A Canadian Perspective." *Interchange* 17, no. 2 (Summer 1986): 135–46.

– "Teachers, Gender and Bureaucraticizing School Systems in Nineteenth-Century Montreal and Toronto." *History of Education Quarterly* 24 (Spring 1984): 75–100.

Dawson, C.A., and Eva R. Yonge. *Pioneering in the Prairie Provinces.* Vol. 8, *The Social Side of the Settlement Process.* Toronto: Macmillan, 1940.

De la Cour, Lykke, and Rose Sheinin. "The Ontario Medical College for Women 1883–1906: Lessons from Gender-Separatism in Medical Education." In *Re-Thinking Canada: The Promise of Women's History*, 2d edition, ed. Veronica Strong-Boag and Anita Clare Fellman, 206–14. Toronto: Copp Clark Pitman, 1991.

Dingwall, Robert. Introduction to *The Sociology of the Professions*, ed. Dingwall and Philip Lewis, 1–13. New York: St Martin's Press, 1983.

Dingwall, Robert, and Philip Lewis, eds. *The Sociology of the Professions: Lawyers, Doctors and Others.* New York: St Martin's Press, 1983.

Drachman, Virginia D. "'My Partner in Law and Life': Marriage in the Lives of Women Lawyers in late 19th and Early 20th Century America." *Law and Social Inquiry* 14, no. 2 (1989): 221–50.

Dranoff, Linda Silver. "Women as Lawyers in Toronto." *Osgoode Hall Law Journal* 10 (1972): 177–90.

Edge, Fred. *The Iron Rose: The Extraordinary Life of Charlotte Ross* M.D. Winnipeg: University of Manitoba Press, 1992.

Elston, Mary Ann. "Medicine: Half Our Future Doctors?" In *Careers of Professional Women*, ed. Rosalie Silverstone and Andrey Ward, 99–139. London: Croom Helm, 1980.

Enns, F.G. *Gretna: Window on the Northwest.* Altona: Friesen, 1987.

Epstein, Cynthia Fuchs. "Encountering the Male Establishment: Sex-Status Limits on Women's Careers in the Professions." *American Journal of Sociology* 75 (July 1969–May 1970): 965–82.

– "Women and Elites: A Cross-National Perspective." In *Access to Power: Cross-National Studies of Women and Elites*, ed. Cynthia Epstein and R.L. Coser, 3–15. London: Allen and Unwin, 1981.

– *Women in Law.* New York: Basic Books, 1982.

Etzioni, Amitai. *The Semi-Professions and Their Organization.* New York: Free Press, 1969.

Faragher, John M., and Florence Howe, eds. *Women and Higher Education in American History.* New York: Norton, 1988.

Fines, Beatrice. "History of the Manitoba Association of Registered Nurses." Typewritten paper, May 1978.

Fingard, Judith. "College, Career and Community: Dalhousie Co-eds, 1881–1921." In *Youth, University, and Canadian Society*, ed. Paul Axelrod and John G. Reid, 26–50. Montreal and Kingston: McGill-Queen's University Press, 1989.

Finkelstein, Barbara. "Conveying Messages to Women: Higher Education and the Teaching Profession in Historical Perspective." *American Behavioural Scientist* 32, no. 6 (1989): 680–99.

First, Ruth, and Ann Scott. *Olive Schreiner: A Biography.* London: Andre Deutsch, 1980.

Fonow, Mary Margaret, and Judith A. Cook, eds. *Beyond Methodology: Feminist Scholarship as Lived Research.* Bloomington: Indiana University Press, 1991.

Ford, Anne Rochon. *A Path Not Strewn with Roses: One Hundred Years of Women at the University of Toronto 1884–1894.* Toronto: University of Toronto Press, 1985.

Forman, Frieda, et al., eds. *Feminism and Education: A Canadian Perspective.* Toronto: Centre for Women's Studies in Education, OISE, 1990.

Fossum, Donna. "A Reflection on Portia." *American Bar Association Journal* 69 (October 1983): 1389–93.

Fox-Genovese, Elizabeth. *Feminism without Illusions: A Critique of Individualism.* Chapel Hill: University of North Carolina Press, 1991.

Fraser, William J. *A History of the First Hundred Years of St. John's College Winnipeg 1866–1966.* Winnipeg: Wallingford Press, 1966.

Freedman, Estelle B. "Theoretical Perspectives on Sexual Difference: An Overview." In *Theoretical Perspectives on Sexual Difference*, ed. Deborah Rhode, 257–62. New Haven: Yale University Press, 1990.

Freidson, Eliot. "Are Professions Necessary?" In *The Authority of Experts: Studies in History and Theory*, ed. Thomas Haskell, 3–27. Bloomington: Indiana University Press, 1984.

– "The Theory of Professions: State of the Art." In *Sociology of the Professions*, ed. Robert Dingwall and Philip Lewis, 19–37. New York: St Martin's Press, 1983.

Friesen, Gerald. *The Canadian Prairies: A History.* Toronto: University of Toronto Press, 1984.

Fudge, Judy, and Patricia McDermott. *Just Wages: A Feminist Assessment of Pay Equity.* Toronto: University of Toronto Press, 1991.

Gagan, Rosemary R. *A Sensitive Independence: Canadian Methodist Women Missionaries in Canada and the Oreint, 1881–1925.* Montreal and Kingston: McGill-Queen's University Press, 1992.

Gamarnikow, Eva, et al. *Gender, Class and Work.* London: Gower, 1985.

Gaskell, Jane. "Conceptions of Skill and the Work of Women: Some Historical and Political Issues." In *The Politics of Diversity: Feminism, Marxism and Nationalism*, ed. Roberta Hamilton and Michele Barrett, 361–80. London: Verso, 1986.

Gaskell, Sandra. "The Problems and Professionalism of Women Elementary Public School Teachers in Ontario 1944–1954." DED thesis, University of Toronto, 1989.

Geiger, Susan. "What's So Feminist about Women's Oral History?" *Journal of Women's History* 2, no. 1 (1990): 169–82.

Gelman, Susan. "The 'Feminization' of the High Schools? Women Secondary School Teachers in Toronto 1871–1930." *Historical Studies in Education* 2, no. 1 (1990): 119–48.

– "Selected Bibliography." In *Women Who Taught*, ed. Alison Prentice and Marjorie Theobald, 285–301. Toronto: University Press, 1991.

Gibson, Dale, and Lee Gibson. *Substantial Justice: Law and Lawyers in Manitoba 1670–1970.* Winnipeg: Peguis Publishers, 1972.

Gibson, John Murray, and Mary S. Matthewson. *Three Centuries of Canadian Nursing.* Toronto: Macmillan, 1947.

Gillett, Margaret, and Kay Sibbald, eds. *A Fair Shake: Autobiographical Essays by McGill Women.* Montreal: Eden Press, 1984.

Gilman, Charlotte Perkins. *Women and Economics*, with introduction by Carl N. Degler. New York: Harper Torchbooks, 1966.

Glazer, Penina Migdal, and Miriam Slater. *Unequal Colleagues: The Entrance of Women into the Professions 1891–1940.* New Brunswick, N.J.: Rutgers University Press, 1987.

Goldin, Claudia. *Understanding the Gender Gap: An Economic History of American Women.* New York: Oxford University Press, 1990.

Gollancz, Victor. "Introductory: A Restatement." In *The Making of Women*, ed. Gollancz, 11–35. London: Allen and Unwin, 1917.

– ed. *The Making of Women: Oxford Essays in Feminism.* London: Allen and Unwin, 1917.

Gordon, Lynn D. *Gender and Higher Education in the Progressive Era.* New Haven: Yale University Press, 1990.

Gregor, Alexander, and Keith Wilson. *History of Education in Manitoba.* Winnipeg: University of Manitoba, 1983.

Growe, Sarah Jane. *Who Cares? The Crisis in Canadian Nursing.* Toronto: McClelland and Stewart, 1991.

Hacker, Carlotta. *The Indomitable Lady Doctors.* Toronto: Clarke Irwin, 1974.

Hadashville Women's Institute. *A Packsack of Seven Decades.* Hadashville, Man.: Hadashville WI, 1970.

Hart, Margaret. "Voices from the Past." In 75th Anniversary *Nurses' Alumnae Journal 1979*, 16–18. Winnipeg: Alumnae Association of the Winnipeg General Hospital and Health Sciences Centre School of Nursing, 1979.

Harvey, Cameron. "Women in Law in Canada." *Manitoba Law Journal* 4, no. 1 (1970): 9–38.

Hatcher, Brenda Wooden. "The Feminization of Public School Teaching 1870–1920." *Work and Occupations* 10, no. 1 (1983): 81–99.

Heap, Ruby, and Alison Prentice, eds. *Gender and Education in Ontario: An Historical Reader.* Toronto: Canadian Scholars' Press, 1991.

Hébert, Monique. "Les grandes gardiennes de la langue et de la foi: L'histoire des franco-manitobaines 1916–1947." PHD thesis, University of Manitoba, 1994.

– "Proud of Yesterday ... and Here to Stay." Paper presented to the Women and History Association of Manitoba, April 1993.

Helly, Dorothy O., and Susan M. Reverby, eds. *Gendered Domains: Rethinking Public and Private in Women's History*. Ithaca: Cornell University Press, 1992.

*Historical Compendium of Education Statistics*. Ottawa: Queen's Printer, 1978

Hoff, Joan. *Law Gender and Injustice: A Legal History of U.S. Women*. New York: New York University Press, 1991.

Hoffman, Nancy. *Woman's "True" Profession: Voices from the History of Teaching*. Old Westbury: Feminist Press, 1981.

Holcombe, Lee. *Victorian Ladies at Work*. Hamden: Archon, 1973.

Houston, C. Stuart. "A Pioneer Woman Doctor, Sigga Christianson Houston." *Manitoba Medicine* 63 (June 1993): 55–8.

Howell, Colin D. "Back to the Bedside: Recent Work on the History of Medicine in Canada." *Acadiensis* 17, no. 2 (1988): 185–94.

– "Reform and the Monopolistic Impulse: The Professionalization of Medicine in the Maritimes." *Acadiensis* 11, no. 1 (1981): 3–22.

Hryniuk, Stella. "Health Care in Rural East Galicia in the Late Nineteenth Century: The Role of Women." In *Economic Development in the Hapsburg Monarchy and in the Successor States*, ed. J. Komlos, 2:1–9, 317–22. Boulder: East European Monographs, 1990.

Iacovetta, Franca, and Mariana Valverde. *Gender Conflicts: New Essays in Women's History*. Toronto: University of Toronto Press, 1992.

Jackel, Susan. "'First Days, Fighting Days': Prairie Presswomen and Suffrage Activism 1906–1916." In *First Days, Fighting Days*, ed. Mary Kinnear, 53–75. Regina: Canadian Plains Research Centre, 1987.

Jackson, Pat, and Sylvia Negrych. "Medicine: The Female Point of View." *University of Manitoba Medical Journal* 3, no. 2 (1961): 15–16.

James, Janet Wilson. "Writing and Rewriting Nursing History: A Review Essay." *Bulletin of the History of Medicine* 58 (1984): 568–84.

Jayaratne, Toby Epstein, and Abigail J. Stewart. "Quantitative and Qualitative Methods in the Social Sciences: Current Feminist Issues and Practical Strategies." In *Beyond Methodology*, ed. Mary M. Fonow and Judith A. Cook, 85–106. Bloomington: Indiana University Press, 1991.

Johns, Ethel, and Beatrice Fines. *The Winnipeg General Hospital and Health Sciences School of Nursing 1887–1987*. Winnipeg: Alumnae Association of the Winnipeg General Hospital and Health Sciences Centre School of Nursing, 1990.

Judson, Margaret. *Breaking the Barrier: A Professional Autobiography by a Woman Educator and Historian before the Women's Movement*. New Brunswick, N.J.: Rutgers University Press, 1984.

Kanter, Rosabeth Moss. *Men and Women of the Corporation*. New York: Basic Books, 1977.

– "Reflections on Women and the Legal Profession: A Sociological Perspective." *Harvard Women's Law Journal* 1, no. 10 (1978): 1–18.

Katz, Fred E. "Nurses." In *The Semi-Professions and Their Organization*, ed. Amitai Etzioni, 54–81. New York: Free Press, 1969.

Kealey, Linda. "Women and Labour during World War I: Women Workers and the Minimum Wage in Manitoba." In *First Days, Fighting Days*, ed. Mary Kinnear, 76–99. Regina: Canadian Plains Research Centre, 1987.

Keddy, Barbara, et al. "Nurses' Work: Scientific or 'Womanly Ministering'?" *Resources for Feminist Research* 16, no. 4 (1987): 38.

Kempeneers, Marianne, and Marie-Hélène Saint-Pierre. "Discontinuité professionnelle et charges familiales: Regards sur les données canadiennes." *Cahiers québécois de démographie* 18, no. 1 (1989): 63–85.

Kergin, Dorothy, "Nursing as a Profession." In *Nursing Education in a Changing Society*, ed. Mary Q. Innis, 46–63. Toronto: University of Toronto Press, 1970.

Kessler-Harris, Alice. *A Woman's Wage: Historical Meanings and Social Consequences.* Lexington: University of Kentucky Press, 1990.

– *Out to Work: A History of Wage-Earning Women in the United States.* New York: Oxford University Press, 1982.

Kimball, Bruce A. *The "True Professional Ideal" in America: A History.* Cambridge: Blackwell, 1992.

Kinnear, Mary. "Disappointment in Discourse: Women University Professors at the University of Manitoba before 1970." *Historical Studies in Education* 4, no. 2 (1992): 269–87.

– "Do You Want Your Daughter to Marry a Farmer?': Women's Work on the Farm, 1922." *Canadian Papers in Rural History* 6 (1988): 137–53.

– "Female Medical Students of the 1940s: How Difference Made a Difference." *Manitoba Medicine* 63, no. 4 (1993): 135–6.

– *Margaret McWilliams: An Interwar Feminist.* Montreal and Kingston: McGill-Queen's University Press, 1991.

– "'Mostly for the Male Members': Teaching in Winnipeg, 1933–1966." *Historical Studies in Education* 6, no. 1 (1994): 1–20.

– "'That There Woman Lawyer': Women Lawyers in Manitoba 1915–1970." *Canadian Journal of Women and the Law* 5, no. 2 (1992): 411–41.

– ed. *First Days, Fighting Days: Women in Manitoba History.* Regina: Canadian Plains Research Centre, 1987.

Klegon, Douglas. "The Sociology of Professions: An Emerging Perspective." *Sociology of Work and Occupations* 5 no. 3 (1978): 259–83.

Kojder, Apolomja Maria. "The Saskatoon Women Teachers' Association: A Demand for Recognition." In *Shaping the Schools of the Canadian West*, ed. David C. Jones et al., 177–91. Calgary: Detselig, 1979.

Larson, Margali Sarfatti. *The Rise of Professionalism.* Berkeley: University of California Press, 1977.

Lazarou, Kathleen. "'Fettered Portias': Obstacles Facing Nineteenth-Century Women Lawyers." *Women Lawyers' Journal* 69, no. 1 (1978): 21–30.

Leavitt, Judith, ed. *Women and Health in America: Historical Readings.* Madison: University of Wisconsin Press, 1984.

Lee, Judy. "Women in Academia: A Growing Minority." *Perspectives*, Statistics Canada 75–001E, Spring 1993, 24–30.

Lepp, Annalee, David Millar, and Barbara Roberts. "Women in the Winnipeg Garment Industry 1950s–1970s." In *First Days, Fighting Days*, ed. Mary Kinnear, 149–72. Regina: Canadian Plains Research Centre, 1987.

Lerner, Gerda. *The Creation of Feminist Consciousness: From the Middle Ages to Eighteen-seventy*. New York: Oxford University Press, 1993.

Lester, Tanya. "Sissons Called to the Bar." *Herizons*, November 1984, 5.

Loadman, Evelyn. "Women in the Pediatric Residency Program." Address, Department of Pediatric, University of Manitoba, 9 June 1983.

Loewen, Royden. "'The Children, the Cows, My Dear Man and My Sister': The Transplanted Lives of Mennonite Farm Women 1874–1900." *Canadian Historical Review* 73 (1992): 244–73.

Lowe, Graham S. *Women in the Administrative Revolution*. Toronto: University of Toronto Press, 1987.

Luxton, Meg. *More than a Labour of Love: Three Generations of Women's Work in the Home*. Toronto: Women's Press, 1980.

Luxton, Meg, Harriet Rosenberg, and Sedef Arat-Koc, eds. *Through the Kitchen Window*. 2d ed. Toronto: Garamond, 1990.

McClelland, Charles. *The German Experience of Professionalisation*. Cambridge: Cambridge University Press, 1991.

McClung, Nellie. *Clearing in the West*. Toronto: Thomas Allen, 1935.

McIntyre, Linda B. "Towards a Redefinition of Status: Professionalism in Canadian Nursing 1939–1945." MA thesis, University of Western Ontario, 1984.

McPherson, Kathryn Mae. "Skilled Service and Women's Work: Canadian Nursing 1920–1939." PHD thesis, Simon Fraser University, 1989.

Manitoba Department of Culture, Heritage and Recreation. *Dr Amelia Yeomans*. Winnipeg: Manitoba Department of Culture, Heritage and Recreation, 1985.

Manitoba Department of Education. *Annual Reports*.

Margadant, Jo Burr. *Madame le Professeur: Women Educators in the Third Republic*. Princeton: Princeton University Press, 1990.

Marshall, Katherine. "Women in Male-Dominated Professions." *Canadian Social Trends*, Winter 1987, 7–11.

Maynard, Fredelle Bruser. *Raisins and Almonds*. Toronto: Doubleday, 1972.

Melosh, Barbara. "More than 'The Physician's Hand': Skill and Authority in Twentieth-Century Nursing." In *Women and Health in America*, ed. Judith Leavitt, 483–6. Madison: University of Wisconsin Press, 1984.

– "'Not Merely a Profession': Nurses and Resistance to Professionalization." *American Behavioural Scientist* 32, no. 6 (1989): 668–79.

– *"The Physician's Hand": Work, Culture and Conflict in American Nursing*. Philadelphia: Temple University Press, 1982.

Meltz, Noah M. *Manpower in Canada 1931–1961: Historical Statistics of the Canadian Labour Force*. Ottawa: Research Branch, Program Development Service, Department of Manpower and Immigration, 1969.

Menkel-Meadow, Carrie. "The Comparative Sociology of Women Lawyers: The 'Feminization' of the Legal Profession." *Osgoode Hall Law Journal* 24 (1987): 897–918.

– "Exploring a Research Agenda of the Feminization of the Legal Profession: Theories of Gender and Social Change." *Law and Social Inquiry* 14, no. 2 (1989): 289–318.

Milkman, Ruth. "New Research in Women's Labor History." *Signs* 18 (Winter 1993): 376–88.

Mill, John Stuart. "The Subjection of Women." In *Collected Works*, vol. 21, ed. John Stuart M. Robson. Toronto: University of Toronto Press, 1984.

Mitchell, Ross. "The Founding of Manitoba Medical College." *Manitoba Medical Association Bulletin* 67 (March 1927): 1–4.

Mitchinson, Wendy. "Canadian Medical History: Diagnosis and Prognosis." *Acadiensis* 12, no. 1 (1982): 124–35.

– *The Nature of Their Bodies: Women and Their Doctors in Victorian Canada.* Toronto: University of Toronto Press, 1991.

Mitchinson, Wendy, and Janice Dickin McGinnis, eds. *Essays in the History of Canadian Medicine*. Toronto: McClelland and Stewart, 1988.

Mochoruk, James D., and Donna Webber. "Women in the Winnipeg Garment Trade 1929–1945." In *First Days, Fighting Days*, ed. Mary Kinnear, 134–48. Regina: Canadian Plains Research Centre, 1987.

Moore, Terence. *Joe Doupe: Bedside Physiologist.* Toronto: Dundurn Press, 1989.

Morantz-Sanchez, Regina. *Sympathy and Science: Women Physicians in American Medicine*. New York: Oxford University Press, 1985.

Morgan, David H.J., and Daphne E. Taylorson. "Introduction: Class and Work – Bringing Women Back In." In *Gender, Class and Work*, ed. Eva Gamarnikow et al., 1–10. London: Gower, 1985.

Morton, W.L. *Manitoba: A History*. 2d ed. Toronto: University of Toronto Press, 1967.

– *One University: A History of the University of Manitoba*. Toronto: McClelland and Stewart, 1957.

Mossman, Mary Jane. "'Invisible' Constraints on Lawyering and Leadership: The Case of Women Lawyers." *Ottawa Law Review* 20 (1988): 567–600.

– "'Portia"s Progress: Women as Lawyers. Reflections on Past and Future." *Windsor Yearbook of Access to Justice* 8 (1988): 252–66.

Naylor, C. David. "Canada's First Doctors' Strike: Medical Relief in Winnipeg, 1932–4." *Canadian Historical Review* 77, no. 2 (1986): 151–80.

– *Private Practice, Public Payment: Canadian Medicine and the Politics of Health Insurance 1911–1966*. Montreal and Kingston: McGill-Queen's University Press, 1986.

Nemiroff, Greta Hofmann. "That Which Divides Us: That Which Unites Us." In *Challenging Times*, ed. Constance Backhouse and David H. Flaherty, 271–88. Montreal and Kingston: McGill-Queen's University Press, 1992.

Norrie, Kenneth, and Douglas Owram. *A History of the Canadian Economy*. Toronto: Harcourt Brace Jovanovich, 1991.

Nuffield, E.W. *With the West in Her Eyes: Nellie Hislop's Story*. Winnipeg: Hyperion Press, 1987.

Oddson, Asta. *Employment of Women in Manitoba*. Winnipeg: Economic Survey Board, Province of Manitoba, 1939.

Offen, Karen, Ruth Roach Pierson, and Jane Rendall, eds. *Writing Women's History: International Perspectives*. Bloomington: Indiana University Press, 1991.

Oram, Alison. "Sex Antagonism in the Teaching Profession: Equal Pay and the Marriage Bar, 1910–1939." In *Gender and the Politics of Schooling*, ed. Madeleine Arnot and Gaby Weiner, 276–89. London: Unwin Hyman and the Open University, 1990.

Palmieri, Patricia A. "Here Was Fellowship: A Social Portrait of Academic Women at Wellesley College, 1895–1920." *History of Education Quarterly* 23 (1983): 195–214.

Parr, Joy. *The Gender of Breadwinners*. Toronto: University of Toronto Press, 1990.

– ed. *Still Running*. Kingston: Queen's University Alumnae Association, 1987.

Parrish, John B. "Women in Professional Training." *Monthly Labor Review*, May 1974, 41–58.

Parsons, Talcott. "Professions." In *International Encyclopedia of the Social Sciences*, vol. 12, ed. D. Sills. New York: Macmillan, 1968.

Patriarche, M. Elizabeth. "Medical Women: Vive la Différence!" *British Columbia Medical Journal* 27, no. 10 (1985): 641–3.

Peitchinis, Stephen G. *Women at Work: Discrimination and Response*. Toronto: McClelland and Stewart, 1989.

Perkins, Harold. "The Academic Profession in the United Kingdom." In *The Academic Profession*, ed. Burton R. Clark, 13–59. Berkeley: University of California Press, 1987.

– *The Rise of Professional Society: England since 1880*. London: Routledge, 1990.

Peters, William. "A Historical Survey of Some Major Aspects of Pre-service Teacher Education in Manitoba." MED thesis, University of Manitoba, 1963.

Pierson, Ruth Roach. *"They're Still Women After All": The Second World War and Canadian Womanhood*. Toronto: McClelland and Stewart, 1986.

Pinchbeck, Ivy. *Women Workers and the Industrial Revolution*. 1930. Reprint, London: Cass, 1977.

Pinkham, Mrs W.C. "Selections from the Unpublished Recollections of Mrs W.C. Pinkham." *Manitoba Pageant*, Winter 1974, 21–3; Spring 1974, 19–22; Autumn 1974, 11–17.

Podmore, David, and Anne Spencer. "Women Lawyers in England: The Experience of Inequality." *Work and Occupations* 9 (1982): 337–61.

Prentice, Alison. "Bluestockings, Feminists or Women Workers? A Preliminary Look at Women's Early Employment at the University of Toronto." *Journal of the Canadian Historical Association* 2, no. 2 (1991): 231–62.

– "The Feminization of Teaching." In *The Neglected Majority: Essays in Canadian Women's History*, ed. Susan Mann Trofimenkoff and Alison Prentice, 49–65. Toronto: McClelland and Stewart, 1977.

– "Multiple Realities: The History of Women Teachers in Canada." In *Feminism and Education*, ed. Frieda Forman et al., 125–44. Toronto: Centre for Women's Studies in Education, OISE, 1990.

– "Themes in the Early History of the Women Teachers' Association of Toronto." In *Women's Paid and Unpaid Work*, ed. Paula Bourne, 97–121. Toronto: New Hogtown Press, 1985.

Prentice, Alison, and Marjorie Theobald. "The Historiography of Women Teachers: A Retrospect." In *Women Who Taught*, ed. Prentice and Theobald, 3–33. Toronto: University of Toronto Press, 1991.

– eds. *Women Who Taught: Perspectives on the History of Women and Teaching*. Toronto: University of Toronto Press, 1991.

Prentice, Alison, et al. *Canadian Women: A History*. Toronto: Harcourt Brace Jovanovich, 1988.

Pugh, Anne. "My Statistics and Feminism: A True Story." In *Feminist Praxis*, ed. Liz Stanley, 103–12. London: Routledge, 1990.

Purvis, June. *Hard Lessons: The Lives and Education of Working-Class Women in Nineteenth-Century England*. Minneapolis: University of Minnesota Press, 1989.

– *A History of Women's Education in England*. Milton Keynes: Open University Press, 1991.

Redclift, Nanneke, and M. Thea Sinclair, eds. *Working Women: International Perspectives on Labour and Gender Ideology*. London: Routledge, 1991.

Reinharz, Shulamit. *Feminist Methods in Social Research*. New York: Oxford University Press, 1992.

*Report of the Royal Commission on the Status of Women in Canada*. Ottawa: Information Canada, 1970.

*Report of the Subcommittee on the Post-War Problems of Women*. Ottawa: Queen's Printer, 1944.

*Report on Hospitals and Nurses' Training Schools in Manitoba* (Gray Report). Winnipeg: Queen's Printer, 1929.

Reskin, Barbara A., and Patricia A. Roos. *Job Queues, Gender Queues: Explaining Women's Inroads into Male Occupations*. Philadelphia: Temple University Press, 1990.

Reverby, Susan. *Ordered to Care: The Dilemma of American Nursing 1850–1945*. Cambridge: Cambridge University Press, 1987.

- "The Search for the Hospital Yardstick: Nursing and the Rationalization of Hospital Work." In *Health Care in America*, ed. Reverby and David Rosner, 206–25. Philadelphia: Temple University Press, 1979.

Reverby, Susan, and Dorothy Helly. "Converging on History." In *Gendered Domains: Rethinking Public and Private in Women's History*, ed. Helly and Reverby, 1–24. Ithaca: Cornell University Press, 1992.

Reynolds, Cecilia. "Naming the Experience: Women, Men and Their Changing Work Lives as Teachers and Principals." PHD thesis, University of Toronto, 1987.

- "Ontario Schoolteachers 1911–1971: A Portrait of Demographic Change." MA thesis, University of Toronto, 1983.

- "Too Limiting a Liberation: Discourse and Actuality in the Case of Married Women Teachers." In *Feminism and Education*, ed. Frieda Forman et al., 145–68. Toronto: Centre for Women's Studies in Education, OISE, 1990.

Rhode, Deborah. *Justice and Gender*. Cambridge: Harvard University Press, 1989.

- "Perspectives on Professional Women." *Stanford Law Review* 40 (1988): 1163–207.

- ed. *Theoretical Perspectives on Sexual Difference*. New Haven: Yale University Press, 1990.

Richardson, John G., and Brenda Wooden Hatcher. "The Feminization of Public School Teaching 1870–1920." *Work and Occupations* 10, no. 1 (1983): 81–99.

Riddell, "Women as Practitioners of Law." *Journal of Comparative Legislation* 18 (1918): 200–3.

Riegler, Natalie N. "The Work and Networks of Jean I. Gunn, Superintendent of Nurses, Toronto General Hospital 1913–1941: A Presentation of Some Issues in Nursing during Her Lifetime 1882–1941." PHD thesis, University of Toronto, 1992.

Rochette, Maud. "Les femmes dans la profession juridique au Québec: De l'accès a l'intégration, un passage couteux." MA thesis, Laval, 1988.

Roland, Charles G. "The Early Years of Antispetic Surgery in Canada." In *Medicine in Canadian Society*, ed. S.E.D. Shortt, 237–54. Montreal and Kingston: McGill-Queen's University Press, 1981.

Rosenberg, Charles E. "American Medicine in 1879." In *"Send Us a Lady Physician": Women Doctors in America 1835–1920*, ed. Ruth J. Abrams, 21–34. New York: Norton, 1985.

Rury, John L. "Who Became Teachers? The Social Characteristics of Teachers in American History." In *American Teachers*, ed. Donald Warren, 9–47. New York: Macmillan, 1989.

Saks, Mike. "Removing the Blinkers? A Critique of Recent Contributions to the Sociology of the Professions." *Sociological Review* 31, no. 1 (1983): 1–21.

Schreiner, Olive. *Woman and Labour*, with preface by Jane Graves. London: Virago, 1978.

Seidenberg, Faith A. "The Bifurcated Woman: Problems of Women Lawyers in the Courtroom." *Canadian Journal of Women and the Law* 1 (1985): 219–25.

Shack, Sybil. "One Woman's View of Women Teaching in Manitoba." University of Manitoba, Address, 4 December 1991.

– *The Two-Thirds Minority*. Toronto: Guidance Centre, University of Toronto, 1973.

– *Women in Canadian Education*. Toronto: Gage Educational Publishing, 1975.

Shanley, Mary Lyndon. *Feminism, Marriage and the Law in Victorian England 1850–1895*. Princeton: Princeton University Press, 1989.

Sheehy, Elizabeth, and Susan B. Boyd. *Canadian Feminist Perspectives on Law: An Annotated Bibliography of Interdisciplinary Writings*. Toronto: Resources for Feminist Research, OISE, 1989.

Shortt, S.E.D. "Antiquarians and Amateurs: Reflections on the Writing of Medical History in Canada." In *Medicine in Canadian Society*, ed. Shortt, 1–17.

– "The Canadian Hospital in the Nineteenth Century: An Historiographic Lament." *Journal of Canadian Studies* 18, no. 4 (1983): 3–14.

– "Physicians, Science and Status: Issues in the Professionalization of Anglo-American Medicine in the Nineteenth Century." *Medical History* 27 (1983): 51–68.

– ed. *Medicine in Canadian Society: Historical Perspectives*. Montreal and Kingston: McGill-Queen's University Press, 1981.

Sicherman, Barbara. "College and Careers: Historical Perspectives on the Lives and Work Patterns of Women College Graduates." In *Women and Higher Education*, ed. John M. Faragher and Florence Howe, 130–64. New York: Norton, 1988.

Silverstone, Rosalie, and Audrey Ward, eds. *Careers of Professional Women*. London: Croom Helm, 1980.

Sinclair, Thea. "Women, Work and Skill." In *Working Women*, ed. Nanneke Redclift and Sinclair, 1–24. London: Routledge, 1991.

Smaller, Harry. "'A Room of One's Own': The Early Years of the Toronto Women's Teachers' Association." In *Gender and Education*, ed. Ruby Heap and Alison Prentice, 105–26. Toronto: Canadian Scholars' Press, 1991.

Smith, Ellen J. "Medical Missionaries: 'Ourselves Your Servants for Jesus' Sake.'" In *"Send Us a Lady Physician": Women Doctors in America 1835–1920*, ed. Ruth J. Abrams, 199–204. New York: Norton, 1985.

Smith, Lynn, Marylee Stephenson, and Gina Quijano. "The Legal Profession and Women: Finding Articles in British Columbia." *University of British Columbia Law Review* 8 (1973): 137–75.

Sokoloff, Natalie. *Black Women and White Women in the Professions: Occupational Segregation by Race and Gender, 1960–1980*. New York: Routledge, 1992.

Solomon, Barbara Miller. *In the Company of Educated Women: A History of Women and Higher Education in America*. New Haven: Yale University Press, 1985.

Stanley, Liz, ed. *Feminist Praxis: Research, Theory and Epistemology in Feminist Sociology*. London: Routledge, 1990.

Stewart, Lee. *"It's Up To You": Women at UBC in the Early Years.* Vancouver: University of British Columbia Press, 1990.

Street, Margaret. *Watchfires on the Mountains: The Life and Writings of Ethel Johns.* Toronto: University of Toronto Press, 1973.

Stricker, Frank. "Cookbooks and Law Books: The Hidden History of Career Women in Twentieth Century America." *Journal of Social History* 10, no. 1 (1976): 1–19.

Strong-Boag, Veronica. "Canada's Women Doctors: Feminism Constrained." In *A Not Unreasonable Claim: Women and Reform in Canada, 1880s–1920s,* ed. Linda Kealey, 109–29. Toronto: Women's Educational Press, 1979.

– "Keeping House in God's Country: Canadian Women at Work in the Home." In *On the Job: Controlling the Labour Process in Canada,* ed. Craig Heron and Robert Storey, 124–51. Montreal and Kingston: McGill-Queen's University Press, 1986.

– *The New Day Recalled: Lives of Girls and Women in English Canada 1919–1939.* Toronto: Copp Clark Pitman, 1988.

– "Pulling in Double Harness or Hauling a Double Load: Women, Work and Feminism on the Canadian Prairie." *Journal of Canadian Studies* 21, no. 3 (1986): 32–52.

Sundberg, Sara Brooks. "Farm Women on the Canadian Prairie Frontier." In *Rethinking Canada: The Promise of Women's History,* ed. Veronica Strong-Boag and Anita Fellman, 95–106. Toronto: Copp Clark Pitman, 1986.

Sutherland, Gillian, "The Movement for the Higher Education of Women: Its Social and Intellectual Context in England c.1840–80." In *Politics and Social Change in Modern Britain: Essays Presented to A.F. Thompson,* ed. P.J. Waller, 91–116. Brighton: Harvester Press, 1987.

Taylor, Malcolm G. *Health Insurance and Canadian Public Policy.* 2d ed. Kingston and Montreal: McGill-Queen's University Press, 1987.

Thomas, Lillian Beynon. "Some Manitoba Women Who Did First Things." *Transactions of the Historical and Scientific Society of Manitoba* 3, no. 4 (1947–48): 13–25.

Thomson, Kay. "Women in Medicine." *University of Manitoba Medical Journal* 42, no. 1 (1970): 31–2.

Tilly, Louise, and Joan Scott. *Women, Work and Family.* New York: Holt, Rinehart & Winston, 1978.

Torrance, George M. "Socio-Historical Overview: The Development of the Canadian Health System." In *Health and Canadian Society,* ed. David Coburn, 6–32. Toronto: Fitzhenry & Whiteside, 1987.

Urquhart, M.C., and K.A.H. Buckley. *Historical Statistics of Canada,* 2d ed. Ottawa: Statistics Canada, 1983.

Ursel, Jane. *Private Lives, Public Policy: One Hundred Years of State Intervention in the Family.* Toronto: Women's Press, 1992.

Vandervoort, Julie. *Tell the Driver: A Biography of Elinor Black M.D..* Winnipeg: University of Manitoba Press, 1992.

Van der Vorst, Charlotte. "A History of Farm Women's Work in Manitoba." MA thesis, University of Manitoba, 1988.

Vicinus, Martha. *Independent Women: Work and Community for Single Women 1850–1920*. Chicago: University of Chicago Press, 1985.

Vickers, Jill McCalla, and June Adam. *But Can You Type? Canadian Universities and the Status of Women*. Toronto: Clarke Irwin, in association with the Canadian Association of University Teachers, 1977.

Vidal, Haraldur Victor. "The History of the Manitoba Teachers Society." MED thesis, University of Manitoba, 1958.

Walker, Eva K. *The Story of the Women Teachers' Association of Toronto 1931–1963*. Toronto: Copp Clark, 1963.

Ward, Audrey, and Rosalie Silverstone. "The Bimodal Career." In *Careers of Professional Women*, ed. Silverstone and Ward, 10–18. London: Croom Helm, 1980.

Warren, Donald, ed. *American Teachers: Histories of a Profession at Work*. New York: Macmillan, 1989.

Weir, G.M. *Survey of Nursing Education in Canada*. Toronto: University of Toronto Press, 1932.

White, James J. "Women in the Law." *Michigan Law Review* 65 (1967): 1051–122.

Williams, Joan C. "Deconstructing Gender." *Michigan Law Review* 87 (1989): 797–895.

Wilson, Johanna Gudrun. *A History of Home Economics Education in Manitoba*. Winnipeg: Manitoba Home Economics Association, 1969.

Witz, Anne. *Professions and Patriarchy*. London: Routledge, 1992.

Wollstonecraft, Mary. *A Vindication of the Rights of Woman*, ed. Carol H. Postan. New York: Norton, 1975.

Woods, D.S. *Education in Manitoba*. Winnipeg: Economic Survey Board, Province of Manitoba, 1938.

# Index

Allen, Lillian 32
Amos, Flora Ross 33
Antisepsis 103, 107
Apprenticeship 30, 53, 82–7, 89, 162
Armstrong, Ida 53
Asper, Linda 131
Avukah Zionist Society 64–5

Bachelor of Nursing 114–15, 118
Ballu, Céline 33
Bar admission 6, 21, 26, 79, 83, 87, 162
Bebel, August 4, 5
Bell, Dean Lennox 69
Birtles, Mary Ellen 103
Bissett, Maude 32
Black, Elinor 61, 68–9, 153
Bulman, Eileen 33, 35
Business and Professional Women's Club 48, 157–8

Canadian Women's Army Corps 63
Census 7, 18–20, 23, 24, 54, 80
Chaplin, Lucy 33
Charlatans 58–9
Cherniack Sheps, Mindel 62, 138, 139–41
Chilly climate 50–1
Christianity 56, 57, 73

Clergy 7, 9, 10, 12, 16, 20, 30
College of Physicians and Surgeons 20, 21, 25, 53–77 passim
Community health 61, 70, 107–11
Crawford, Mary 56, 61, 106

de Beauvrière, Mme Moreau 32
Dental hygiene 37, 47
de Pisan, Christine 30
Discrimination 3, 42, 43, 46, 50–1, 68, 75–7, 84–5, 92, 95–7
Divorcées 46, 90, 117
Domestic service 15, 19, 22
Douglass, Ellen 57
Dudley, Margaret 33
Duval, Lorraine 32

Education 4, 5, 6, 7, 8, 10, 11, 12, 20, 30–52 passim, 123–51 passim
Edwards, Dean C.H.C. 84, 85
Eliot, George 4, 5
Epstein, Cynthia 96
Equality 5, 6, 30, 46, 47
Equal pay for equal work 16, 135–9, 142
Equal pay for work of equal value 16
Ethnicity 5, 6, 63–6, 84

Evans, Ruth 109–10

Faculty Wives' Association 47
Family 15, 16, 17, 37, 38, 49, 66, 70, 71–2, 81, 85, 86–8, 89–93, 115–17, 132, 146. *See also* Marriage
Family wage 16, 17, 133–9
Federation of Medical Women of Canada 63, 75
Findlay, Jessie 60
Foxton, Harriet 56
Freidson, Eliot 9, 11
French, Mabel 78–9

Gender 9, 35, 39, 40, 41, 42, 47, 72–7, 89, 95–7, 98, 123, 124, 133, 135–48, 151, 154
Gilman, Charlotte Perkins 4, 5, 6
Gollancz, Victor 15, 161
Graham, Alma 79
Great Depression 19, 37, 59, 62, 87, 92, 108, 111, 124, 135, 143, 150
Green, T.H. 10
Grey Nuns 21, 105

Haynaud, Mlle 33
Hislop, Nellie 129
Homeopaths 53

Hospitals 53–77 passim,
    98–128 passim, 154

Imperialism 60–1
India 60–1, 73
Internship 64–6, 69, 162

Jefferson, Dorothy 60
Johns, Ethel 103–6
Jones, Anna 33

Kaczmarski, Anna 58
Kanter, Rosabeth Moss 96

Labour force 3, 4, 14–16,
    18–20, 38, 162–3. See
    also Segregated labour
    force
Larson, Margali 11
Law Society of Manitoba 6,
    21, 26, 31, 78–97
    passim
Lister, Joseph 103
Loadman, Evelyn 74, 75

McClung, Nellie 129
Macdonnell, Ursula 33–4
Macfarlane Royal
    Commission 128, 130,
    150
Machray, Archbishop 20
Maclean Hunt, Isabel 79,
    92–3
McMurray, Mildred 154
McPhee, Lavinia 57
McTavish, Isabel 60
Manitoba Agricultural
    College 20, 31
Manitoba Association of
    Graduate Nurses 105,
    106
Manitoba Association of
    Registered Nurses 118
Manitoba College 20, 25,
    31, 32, 78
Manitoba Law School 31
Manitoba Medical College
    20, 31, 32, 56
Manitoba Teachers
    Federation/Society 21,
    28, 39, 124, 132–5, 142,
    145, 147, 149, 150

Marriage 15, 16, 17, 18, 22,
    37–8, 45, 48, 60, 85,
    86, 87, 89–93, 124, 130,
    138–41, 146, 156–63.
    See also Family
Martin, Clara Brett 78–9
Mathers, Dean A.T. 63–5,
    68
Matheson, Archbishop 22
Matheson, Elizabeth Scott
    55, 61
Medical College for
    Women, Vellore 60–1,
    73
Medical Rehabilitation 37
Menkel-Meadow, Carrie 96
Mennonites 58–9, 73, 128
Midwives 7, 19, 58
Mill, John Stuart 4, 5, 100
Misener, Geneva 156, 161
Missionaries 57, 60–1, 73
Mossman, Mary Jane 96
Motherhood 35, 47,
    48–50, 52, 71–2, 76,
    89–93, 97, 115–17, 145,
    159–61. See also Family

Newton, Ada 105
Nightingale, Florence 98
Nolin, Angélique 21
Nolin, Marguerite 21
Normal school 21, 127,
    130, 150
Nuns 7, 19, 20, 128

Old boys' club 44, 51, 76,
    84, 162
Ontario Medical College
    for Women 56, 57
Oral history 3, 4, 23–9
Outsiders in the Sacred Grove
    36, 52

Parsons, Talcott 10, 30
Patterson, Adah 102
Perkins, Harold 10
"Persons" 78–9, 106
Political Equality League
    57
Pope, Emma 33
Portia club 92–3
Prentice, Alison 36

Private-duty nursing 108,
    111, 113, 116, 154
Professions: access to 3, 5,
    6, 8, 12, 20–2, 64–5,
    63–6; autonomy of 11,
    12, 14, 46, 99–101,
    150; career progress in
    10, 11, 17, 18, 45, 52,
    75; certification test 7,
    10, 11, 21, 104–7, 128;
    code of ethics 11, 12;
    definition 4, 6–14, 30,
    75, 98–101, 149–51;
    entry into 35, 36–8, 73,
    98–9, 102, 120–1,
    143–4, 162–3; gender
    in 9, 12, 16, 17–18;
    models 17–18, 48–50,
    75, 89–93, 152–3,
    159–67; monopoly 11,
    12, 53, 54; numbers
    18–20, 32–5, 59–60,
    65, 66–7, 70, 71, 81–2,
    93–5, 108–9, 115,
    125–7, 158–60; pay 11,
    12, 13, 15, 17, 34,
    44–6, 63, 70, 87, 89,
    108–9, 111, 113,
    116–17, 123–4, 134–9,
    148, 150–1, 155; pio-
    neers 20–2, 32–4, 54–9,
    78–80, 103–6; regula-
    tion 7, 11, 12, 21, 153–5;
    service to the public 7,
    10, 11, 12; status 8, 9, 11,
    148; training 36–8, 53,
    59–62, 67–9, 82–7, 93,
    111, 113, 119–21,
    127–32

Quotas 64–6

Red Cross 109–10, 154
Research 41–4, 62
Rhode, Deborah 97
Roberts, Jessie 33, 35
Roblin, Premier Duff 141
Ross, Charlotte Whitehead
    55, 57
Ross, Helen 32
Rowell, Marion 32
Royal Commission on the

Status of Women 3,
30–1, 80

St Germaine, Hilda 109
St Boniface College 20, 24,
31
St Boniface Hospital 27,
104, 106
St John's College 20, 24,
25, 31, 32, 42, 48
Sanders, Nellie 82
Saunders, Doris 33, 42,
45
School medical inspectors
56, 61
School trustees 62, 134,
138, 142
Schreiner, Olive 4, 6, 29
Scudder, Ida 60, 73
Segregated labour force 4,
9, 14–16, 143. *See also*
Labour force
Semi-professions 12
Shack, Sybil 132
Single-sex schools 37
Sissons, Melrose 21, 78
Stewart, Isabel Maitland
103, 105
Suffrage 3, 4, 55, 57

Taché, Archbishop 20

Tallin, Dean G.P.R. 86, 92,
94
Temperance 55, 57
Theobald, Marjorie 36
Thomas, Lillian Beynon 22
Thomsonians 53
Tokenism 96
Trade school 39, 43–4
Trade unions 8, 114,
117–8, 121

*Unequal Colleagues* 36, 52,
163–5
United College 25, 31, 32
United Farm Women of
Manitoba 58
United Kingdom 18, 59,
67, 76, 94–5, 114
United States 6, 11, 13–14,
18, 41, 42, 43, 53, 59,
67, 76, 94, 108, 144,
164
University of Manitoba 6,
20, 25, 26, 30–52, 54,
59
University of Winnipeg 25
University Women's Club
48, 57, 156–8

Wawryko, Mary 82
Weir, G.M. 111, 114

Wesley College 20, 25, 31,
32
Widows 46, 51, 90
Wilton, Winnifred 21, 79
Winnipeg General Hospital
21, 22, 27, 101–12
passim
Winnipeg Teachers
Association 123
Winnipeg Women
Teachers 123, 124, 132,
135–42, 150, 154, 165,
166
Wollstonecraft, Mary 3, 5
Woman's Medical College,
Toronto 56
Women healers 57–9, 101
Women Lawyers'
Association 93
Women's Medical College,
Kingston 55
World War I 20, 25, 107
World War II 18, 19, 35, 36,
37, 39, 40, 48, 54,
63–6, 111, 113, 134,
145, 159
Wright, Mary Grant 80

Yeomans, Amelia 21, 54–5,
56, 57
Yeomans, Lillian 21, 54–5